The
BELOVED
DISCIPLE

The
BELOVED
DISCIPLE

FOLLOWING JOHN TO THE HEART OF JESUS

BETH MOORE

with DALE MCCLESKEY

BROADMAN
&HOLMAN
PUBLISHERS

NASHVILLE, TENNESSEE

0-8054-2753-8

Published by Broadman & Holman Publishers
Nashville, Tennessee

Dewey Decimal Number: 225.92
Subject Heading: JOHN, APOSTLE \ BIBLE. N.T. JOHN—
STUDY \ DISCIPLESHIP TRAINING—WOMEN

Unless otherwise stated all Scripture citations are from the NIV, the Holy Bible, New International Version, copyright © 1973, 1978, 1984 by International Bible Society; other versions cited are NASB, the New American Standard Bible, © the Lockman Foundation, 1960, 1962, 1963, 1968, 1971, 1972, 1973, 1975, 1977; used by permission; NKJV, New King James Version, copyright © 1979, 1980, 1982, Thomas Nelson, Inc., Publishers; AMP, The Amplified Bible, Old Testament copyright © 1962, 1964 by Zondervan Publishing House, used by permission, and the New Testament © The Lockman Foundation 1954, 1958, 1987, used by permission; CEV, the Contemporary English Version, © American Bible Society 1991, 1992; used by permission; *The Message,* the New Testament in Contemporary English, © 1993 by Eugene H. Peterson, published by NavPress, Colorado Springs, Colo.; The Interlinear Bible; and KJV, the King James Version.

3 4 5 6 7 8 9 10   07 06 05 04 03

Dedication

To my new son, Curt—
If I could have looked the world over for a life partner for my firstborn,
I would have chosen you. No need. God already had.
My dear Curt, as I wrote this study, I often thought how very much you
favor the apostle John. You are a true man of vision, driven to the *Logos*
by godly affection. You are the essence of a deeply beloved disciple.
I love you.

Contents

CONTENTS

Introduction

The Beloved Disciple explores one of the most intriguing relationships in history, between Jesus and His youngest apostle, and it traces the life of that young follower. John would certainly qualify as one of the most fascinating characters in Scripture. He anonymously penned the Gospel that most people consider their favorite. He identified himself only as the "disciple whom Jesus loved." He took the other Gospel accounts of Jesus the Messiah and wrote as if to say, "You've heard what Jesus did, now let me show you who He really was." Thus John shows us the cosmic Christ who created the world, died to redeem it, and lives to reclaim it.

The apostle John's life includes unbelievable moments of courage and greatness. Of the twelve, only John stayed near for the crucifixion, and he became the recipient of the capstone of Scripture: the Revelation. John walked in the inner circle with Jesus to places like the Mount of Transfiguration and the resurrection chamber of Jairus' daughter (Luke 8:51), yet between those mountaintops John experienced many long years when others stood in the limelight. From this disciple we gain an intimate and personal perspective of both Jesus and of a beloved follower.

So come along with me for a wonderful journey with the apostle John. Together we'll scale the heights and plumb the depths. My prayer is that in the process we'll come to identify personally with this long-lived follower of Christ. In the end, I hope you'll make the discovery that he did so long ago—the discovery that affection counts for more than ambition. That loving and being loved by Jesus matters more than all that the world can obtain or contain.

I hope you love your journey because I love you.

Part 1

FRESH WINDS OVER GALILEE

I love new beginnings. Don't you? I am honored to embark on this new beginning with someone like you. Let's count on God to take us places with Him we've never been and accomplish a work we didn't know He could. As James and John cast their nets on the sun-kissed waters of the Galilee, they had no idea the Son of God was casting His net for them. Soon they'd find themselves caught by His call and compelled by His love. Let's allow the same divine affection to catch us as we, too, are called to be disciples of Jesus Christ.

Chapter 1

SINCE THAT TIME

The Law and the Prophets were proclaimed until John. Since that time,
the good news of the kingdom of God is being preached. (Luke 16:16)

The year was A.D. 28, give or take a few. For a chosen people who hadn't heard a word from God in four centuries, life was pretty good. The Jews had covered their insecurities with a blanket of sameness. The absence of a fresh encounter with God had them clutching to what they had left—the Law. Interesting, isn't it? The Hebrew people climbed to the summit of their legalism during the silent years between Malachi and Matthew. That's what really religious people do when they don't have much of a relationship with God.

In those days sons followed in their father's footsteps. Girls had no need of formal education. After all, they would simply grow up and do exactly as their mothers had done. The devoted uttered the same prayer in the morning that had fallen from their lips the last time the sun came up. Tomorrow would repeat the process.

Courtesy of a Herod who desperately needed their favor, the Jewish people finally had their temple, and, boy, was it a beaut. For the most part, they had things just the way they wanted them.

The Hebrew people wanted to know what they could expect out of life, so they formed themselves an expectation and enforced it with a vengeance. They arranged life the way they wanted it, threw it over their heads like a security blanket, and hid from change.

I can relate. I've done the same thing a few times.

If anyone questioned the status quo, the committed acted like the blanket had always been right there. No doubt many ascribed to the same prevailing attitude described by 2 Peter 3:4 many years later: "Ever since our fathers died, everything goes on as it has since the beginning of creation."

But they were wrong. Since the beginning of creation, things have never simply gone on. A plan of inconceivable perfection has been under careful execution. Always. Even in the silent years of Israel's history, God was never inactive.

We have no idea how busy God's hands are even when His mouth seems closed. Where God is concerned, silence never equals slumber. For those of us looking for an overall grasp of what the God of the universe is doing with planet Earth, few titles of Christ are more significant than those issued from His own mouth in Revelation 22:13. He is "the Alpha and the Omega, the First and the Last, the Beginning and the End."

I cannot describe how impressed I am with the manifold perfections and consistencies of Scripture. The book that unfolds with the words "in the beginning" draws to a conclusion with the One who declares Himself both that very Beginning and the End. Life on this planet had a precisely executed beginning, and it will have a certain end. He who planned them both to perfection did not leave everything in between to go on as it would . . . or as it always had.

God in heaven has a will for this Earth. Before He ever uttered, "Let there be light," every day of His kingdom calendar from beginning to end was filled with events. Man can refuse to cooperate, but he cannot keep God from executing the critical events on His schedule. And thankfully, no amount of tradition can stop God when He has a mind to change things.

Just about the time the establishment got things the way they wanted and swore they had always been, someone had the gall to stick his head out from under the security blanket. Sooner or later he'd lose his head for doing it, but in the meantime he'd shake a few things up. Don't miss the implication of a very deliberate God keeping a precise schedule on a kingdom calendar. Luke 3:1–2 says, "In the fifteenth year of the reign of Tiberius Caesar . . . during the high priesthood of Annas and Caiaphas" something very critical happened. The word of God came to a man named John.

Somehow John got labeled "the Baptist," but "the preacher" would fit better. He came declaring, "You brood of vipers! Who warned you to flee from the coming wrath? Produce fruit in keeping with repentance. And do not begin to say to yourselves, 'We have Abraham as our father.' For I tell you that out of these stones God can raise up children for Abraham. The ax is already at the root of the trees, and every tree that does not produce good fruit will be cut down and thrown into the fire" (Luke 3:7–9).

I began this chapter with a quote out of Christ's own mouth: "The Law and the Prophets were proclaimed until John. Since that time, the good news of the kingdom of God is being preached" (Luke 16:16). Jesus referred to the life of John as a pivot point of change on the kingdom calendar. After four hundred years of silence, suddenly the Word of God came.

After such a long wait to see God reveal Himself afresh to mortal creatures, I wonder if all of heaven hushed to hear it. Of course, those on earth didn't have to hush. The Baptizer talked nice and loud. Loud enough, in fact, that according to Matthew's version, Pharisees and Sadducees from Jerusalem went all the way to the fringe of the security blanket on the banks of the Jordan to see what all the commotion was about (Matt. 3:5, 7). Theirs were among the few heads that stayed dry that day. They held their security blankets over their heads to keep from getting doused in change.

Always one to swim against the current, John the Baptist's message traveled the Jordan upstream into the waters of a handful of fisherman in a village called Bethsaida. Drawn like fish to bait, several of them trekked to hear him and hung on every word he said. In fact, John 1:35 refers to them as disciples of John the Baptist.

Don't let the term *disciples* seem heretical to you. The label seems almost sacred to many of us in evangelical Christianity, but keep in mind the only thing that made the twelve disciples of Christ sacred was the One they followed. *Disciple* simply indicates a pupil and follower of someone's teaching.

Thankfully, John the Baptist turned out to be a man worth following precisely because they followed him straight to Jesus.

The religious leaders challenged the baptizer: "What do you say about yourself?" Who was he? Was he Elijah? Was he the Christ? Some other prophet? The preacher clearly declared, "I am the voice of one calling in the desert, 'Make straight the way for the Lord' . . . I baptize with water . . . but among you stands one you do not know. He is the one who comes after me, the thongs of whose sandals I am not worthy to untie" (John 1:22–23, 26–27). John the Baptist defined himself in two ways:

1. He was not the Christ.

2. He was the one sent to prepare for the Christ.

The question the religious leaders asked isn't a bad one for us to ask ourselves as we launch this boat together. So, what about you? What do you say about yourself? What we don't say in words, we ultimately say in deeds. Daily we say all sorts of things about ourselves. Sometimes what we say about ourselves is not necessarily accurate, but it's what we believe.

Trust me. I know about this one. I lived much of my life with a highly inaccurate estimation of who I wasn't and who I was. As a young person, I swung dizzily between feelings of "I am a victim and I'm not as good as anybody else" to "I'm no one's victim and I'm going to be better than everyone else." As I stare at that brief testimony, I sigh at the recollection of it all. Believing and living a lie was so exhausting. What finally got me off of the swing? Learning to see myself in relationship to Jesus Christ.

Don't get the idea that I've arrived or that whatever I've learned so far hasn't been a process. I still struggled with my identity even as I got a little healthier. Still do at times. During my first years of ministry, I tried so hard to be just like my mentor and to do everything just as she did it.

Have you discovered that trying to be someone else is exhausting?

Because of Jesus, John knew who he was and who he wasn't. Who wasn't he? The Christ. Much of his public was plenty willing to hail him as the Messiah had he let them. He didn't.

So who was John the Baptist according to his own definition? "I am the voice of the one calling in the desert, 'Make straight the way of the Lord.'" I find what he said about himself very refreshing. He understood the greatness of Christ and how unworthy he was in comparison, but he didn't give himself the value of an inchworm under a rock. His life had value through its connection to the Messiah. John the Baptist introduced a concept that another John will carry on for us throughout our travel together. Among many other things, we're going to learn how to define ourselves by our relationship to Jesus Christ. We'll arrive at an important place of maturity when we're able to accurately assess and articulate who we are . . . and who we are not.

As we try to compare ourselves to John the Baptist, we might be tempted to think, "Well, one thing is certain. No one's going to get me confused with Christ." On the contrary, some people will try to make anyone with a semblance of spiritual maturity and identity their personal saviors.

Have you ever had anyone try to make a savior of sorts out of you? Our most convenient response might be shifting all responsibility to the poor, confused person. After all, can we help it if someone mistakes us for more than we are? John the Baptist's example might suggest that we can and must "help it" whenever possible. Like him, when circumstances and relationships call for appropriate reassessment, we don't want to fail to confess, but to confess freely, things such as

- "I'm so sorry if I've led you to believe otherwise, but I am not your salvation. I have no power to deliver you."
- "I can't be our entire family's rock. If you're all standing on me for stability, we're all about to have a sinking spell."
- "Not only do I not have all the answers; I'm still trying to figure out the questions."

So do we just let everyone down? No, we ask them to let *us* down— right off that man-made pedestal of toothpicks. Our role in the lives of those God authentically sends our way for help is not altogether unlike John the Baptist's. We become a voice in their desert helping them prepare a way for the Lord.

I can't wait to see why God has invited me along on this journey. I have no preconceived notions. No idea where this study is going. An unknown adventure lies ahead of me as surely as it does for you. I've rarely been more excited about starting a study because I simply have no idea what awaits us.

I dearly love an adventure! I can't wait to see all the stops we'll make and all the keepsakes we'll pick up along the way. But when all is said and done, I have a feeling we will learn much about identity. Whose? Christ's and two of His very important disciples. One we'll meet in our next chapter. The other you can meet in the nearest mirror.

As we conclude this first chapter, let's form a baseline of our present perceived identity so we'll be able to draw comparisons as we get much further down the road on this journey. Please be completely honest. Just between God and you, who have you discovered that you aren't? And who have you discovered that you are?

I'm so glad you've joined me. Let's have a blast in the Word of God. We'll begin with a look at one of the most important elements in Jewish life . . . family.

Chapter 2

THE IDENTITY OF FAMILY

Going on from there, he saw two other brothers, James son of
Zebedee and his brother John. (Matthew 4:21)

*F*amily. Only God Himself could be more important. To the devout Jew, the familial could not be detached from the spiritual. God Himself wove the two together from the beginning when He created Eve as the complement to Adam (Gen. 2:21–22)—a spiritual act if you'll ever find one. Then, in Genesis 4:1, God added the first child to the mix.

Family life became synonymous with family problems almost from the start, but God never abandoned the concept. Indeed, family was a very good idea and became a powerful medium through which God has worked throughout history. The meshing of the familial and spiritual was emphasized so strongly in the Old Testament that space permits me only a few of many references: Exodus 12:25–27 says, "When you enter the land that the LORD will give you as he promised, observe this ceremony. And when your children ask you, 'What does this ceremony mean to you?' then tell them, 'It is the Passover sacrifice to the LORD, who passed over the houses of the Israelites in Egypt and spared our homes when he struck down the Egyptians.'"

Joshua 4:5–7 says, "Go over before the ark of the LORD your God into the middle of the Jordan. Each of you is to take up a stone on his shoulder, according to the number of the tribes of the Israelites, to serve as a sign among you. In the future, when your children ask you, 'What do these stones mean?' tell them that the flow of the Jordan was cut off before the ark of the covenant of the LORD."

Hebrew parents and children talked. The Lord did not say, "*if* your children ask you," but, "*when* your children ask you." Fathers were even more involved in the education of their children than were mothers. In a typical ancient Jewish home, communication was virtually constant; to remove the spiritual significance from their conversation would have served to nearly silence them.

You are probably Gentile by heritage, just as I am. Any time we study the life of someone steeped in an entirely different culture, we have to be very intentional about seeing them in their world rather than ours. We can make countless applications to our world but only after we have viewed the historical figure such as John in his or her own. Not only was ancient Orthodox Judaism an entirely different culture than ours, God made sure it compared to none. He did not want His nation to be like any others. I'll let God talk for Himself from Deuteronomy 14:1–2: "You are the children of the LORD your God . . . for you are a people holy to the LORD your God. Out of all the peoples on the face of the earth, the LORD has chosen you to be his treasured possession."

The people we will study together were Jews at a time when Judaism had perhaps never been more Jewish. By this expression I mean that although they were under Roman rule, they enjoyed significant freedom to live out their culture. They were firmly established in their land and had their temple. Every sect of religious life was functioning at full throttle: the Pharisees, the Sadducees, and the teachers of the law, to name only a few.

Life in the Galilean villages of Capernaum and Bethsaida must have seemed light-years away from the hub of religious life amid Herod's temple in Jerusalem, but one thing varied little from Hebrew to Hebrew: YHWH* was life. Provider, Sustainer, Sovereign Creator of all things. To them, to have little thought of God was to have little thought at all.

Our John the apostle came from the rural land to the north. If the more sophisticated Jew in the Holy City thought the simple settlers on the Sea of Galilee envied him, he was surely mistaken. Neither was without the

---

*YHWH is the divine name of God, never pronounced by the Jews; in English it is often referred to as Yahweh or Jehovah.

inevitable troubles that make living part of life. Each had his preferences. Each had a point of view. One awakened to the brilliance of the sun dancing off the gleaming walls of the temple. The other saw the sun strolling on the surface of the lake. A fisherman would have been hard to convince that the glory of God dwelled more powerfully in a building made of stone than in a bright pink and purple sunset over the Sea of Galilee. I know this for a fact. I live with a fisherman.

Two pairs of sons grew up not far from each other on the northern tip of the Sea of Galilee. Four pairs of feet earned their calluses on the pebbles of a familiar shore. From the time their sons were knee-high to them, Zebedee and Jonah were responsible not only for making sure their rambunctious offspring didn't drown but for harnessing their insatiable curiosity with their trades. The fathers were the walking day-care centers for their sons, and their sons' mothers would be expecting them home in one piece before dusk or after a long night of fishing.

Peter, Andrew, James, and John. They were trees planted by streams of water being raised to bring forth their own fruit in season (Ps. 1:3). If those fathers had only known what would become of their sons, I wonder if they would have raised them any differently. Come to think of it, I doubt it. They were simple men with one simple goal: to teach their sons all they knew.

Our task is to piece together what our protagonist's life might have been like in childhood and youth before a Lamb came and turned it upside down. We first meet John on the pages of the New Testament in Matthew 4:21. There we read that the fishing boat contained "James son of Zebedee and his brother John."

Scholars are almost unanimous in their assumption that John was the younger brother of James. In the earlier references, he is listed after his brother, James, which was often an indication of birth order in Scripture and other ancient Eastern literature.

In their world, if any name existed more common than James (a hellenized form of *Iakob* or Jacob), it was John. Since the family used the Hebrew language, they actually called him Jehohanan. It may sound a little fancier, but the name was as common as could be. I don't get the feeling James and John were the kinds of boys about whom the neighbors mused,

"I can't wait to see what they'll turn out to be. Mark my word. They'll be something special!" Those who watched them grow up assumed the sons of Zebedee would be fisherman. Just like their father.

If we're right and James was the older brother, he held the coveted position in the family birth order. Special rights and privileges belonged to him as well as a birthright that assured him a double portion of his father's estate. The firstborn was a leader in the family, commanding a certain amount of respect for a position he did nothing to earn. John? He was just the little brother.

Most of us have experienced the ambiguity of being known by little more than our relationship to someone else. I love being Keith Moore's wife, Amanda and Melissa's mother, and Curt's mother-in-law, but that's probably because I've lived enough of life to figure out who I am. I can remember feeling lost in a whole line of siblings growing up. I have fond memories of my mother calling me every name in our big family but mine. I often grinned while she scrambled for the right one and then, exasperated, finally would say, "If I'm looking at you, I'm talking to you!" I'd giggle, "Yes, ma'am!" and run off while she was still doing her best to remember what my name was.

What about you? Can you identify? Have you been identified by your relationship to others?

Some things about parenting must be universal. Surely Zebedee looked straight at Jehohanan and accidentally called him Iakob at times. If so, would young John have been the type to let it go unnoticed, or might he have said, "Abba! I am Jehohanan!" These are thoughts I love to explore imaginatively when studying a character.

Either way John was no doubt accustomed to being Zebedee's other son and James's little brother. However common his name, the meaning was extraordinary: "God has been gracious."[1] Growing up on the shore of Jesus' favorite sea, John had no idea at this point just how gracious God had been. He would soon get a glimpse.

John may have been an ordinary name for an ordinary boy; but based on maternal persuasions through the ages, we can be fairly certain he was extraordinary to his mother. We will discover later in our journey that she considered nothing too good for her sons. Who was this woman anyway, this wife of Zebedee and mother of James and John?

Let's look ahead just a moment for the sake of her identification. By comparing Matthew 27:55–56 and Mark 15:40, we learn that her name was probably Salome. Most scholars I have researched believe John's mother is positively identified by name in the latter verse. Some scholars go as far as saying that Salome was actually Jesus' mother Mary's sister, based on a comparison of John 19:25: "Near the cross of Jesus stood his mother, his mother's sister, Mary the wife of Clopas, and Mary Magdalene."

As you can see, we have no way of knowing if John identified three different women or four. Mary the wife of Clopas could have been the one identified as Jesus' maternal aunt, but two daughters in one family with the name Mary seems a little peculiar. On the other hand, to draw an airtight conclusion that Salome was Mary's sister from comparing lists like these is probably risky. Although I don't doubt the families may have known each other and even been somehow related, I tend to agree with R. Alan Culpepper, who wrote, "Surely, if John had been Jesus' first cousin, this relationship would have been recognized more prominently in the early Christian traditions about the apostle."[2]

As you and I will learn in the coming chapters, a fair amount of tradition was recorded by the early church fathers about John, but we find little mention of him being Jesus' maternal cousin. I am certainly no expert, but from what I have gleaned from those who are, I will write from the basis that familiarity probably existed between the two families; however, I'm not convinced of blood relationship. Thankfully, at the cross, all those who wished to have relationship with Jesus Christ became blood relatives.

I have made very few sacrifices to do what God has called me to do. Without a doubt, Christ is the one who made the significant sacrifices. One occasional sacrifice brings me small waves of heartache from time to time. I don't get many opportunities to cultivate new relationships of great personal depth. I am a people person. I can sit in a shopping mall happy as a clam to become a student of people who walk past me! When I drive by a house in the country, I always want to know what the people inside are like. I love people! But seasonally my calling pulls me away from studying and exploring the uniqueness of individuals with any depth.

I have just realized as if hit with a sudden burst of revelation that in-depth Bible study focused primarily on the life of one figure is an utterly creative way God has given me to do two things I love most. In this hide-away office where I must be alone with God to write, I'm about to get to know a "new" person very well. You are too!

Chapter 3

FOR THEY WERE
FISHERMAN

Without delay he called them, and they left their father Zebedee in the boat
with the hired men and followed him. (Mark 1:20)

*P*assover was just around the corner.* Soon the hillcrest of Eremos in
northern Galilee would be covered in red anemones and blue iris. Spring
had finally arrived but not a moment too soon for a band of fisherman who
spent their days on the water.

Winter temperatures ranging anywhere from fifty to sixty-five degrees
Fahrenheit during the daytime may not seem so cold to landlubbers, but
fisherman have a different point of view. Sometimes their wet, sandaled
feet felt like blocks of ice, and their fingers were so frigid they would temporarily lose their dexterity. During the winter season they spent their few
hours at home trying to get the chill off their bones. Just about the time
they thawed, the boat had to be pushed from shore back into the water.
They were fortunate to get any sunshine at all.

The Sea of Galilee is a freshwater lake called by three other names in
Scripture: the Sea of Chinnereth, which is the Hebrew word for "harp-
shaped" and describes the general outline of the lake;[1] the Lake of
Gennesaret, named for a fertile plain nearby; and the Sea of Tiberias, associated with the capital of Herod Antipas.

---

*This time frame is strictly a deduction I have made from comparing time references in
John 1:43, John 2:1, and John 2:12–13. I could certainly be mistaken if time lapses
existed that weren't noted in these portions of Scripture.

At the time Andrew, Peter, James, and John were casting their nets on those waters, a vigorous fishing industry was booming all over the lake. Many villages populated the shores of this body of water. Not only was it the food basket of the region; the sight was breathtaking. It still is. The surrounding hills cup the lake like water in the palm of a large hand. I've seen with my own eyes how the early spring sunrise hangs lazily in the clinging winter mist. Since the first time I saw the Sea of Galilee, I understood why Christ seemed to favor the villages near its shore over the metropolis of Jerusalem.

Bethsaida lies at the northern tip where the Jordan River feeds the lake. The name *Bethsaida* means "house of fishing,"[2] and it lived up to its name. The Sea of Galilee boasts eighteen species of fish,[3] so fishing could be profitable almost anywhere. Near Bethsaida the warm springs at the foot of the Eremos hill bubbled into the lake, attracting the fish looking for a blanket in winter. The fish that have since been labeled "Peter's fish" are tropical and often swarm the warmer temperatures where the springs flow into the lake, giving our fisherman a decided advantage over many of their competitors.

We know for a fact that Andrew and Peter were from Bethsaida, and we can safely assume Zebedee also raised his sons in the village since they were all partners. As we will soon discover, at some point Andrew and Peter moved to nearby Capernaum where Peter lived with his wife and mother-in-law (Mark 1:21, 29). We don't know for certain which of the two villages housed James and John at this point in their lives, but we do know they all continued to work together.

Obviously Zebedee was the one who owned the fishing enterprise. We read in Mark 1:20 that James and John "left their father Zebedee in the boat with the hired men." While I don't want to intimate that Zebedee was wealthy (since few villagers were), we'd probably be mistaken to think him poor. The reference to the hired servants tells us that he owned his own business and was profitable enough to have servants in addition to two healthy and able sons. Both boats might easily have been in his ownership. Peter and Andrew could have fished from one (which was considered "theirs," Luke 5:3) while a little farther away (Mark 1:19) James and John fished from another.

God wisely equipped us with four Gospels because we learn far more from hearing several accounts of anything especially noteworthy. The facts one writer included may not have been noted by another because each point of view was tinted by the individual's perspective and priorities. While writing *Jesus the One and Only*, I learned I could almost always expect Luke to be a little more specific than the other Gospel writers, which made perfect sense to me. He was a doctor, and a good doctor pays attention to details. You'll find this principle to hold true in the passage at hand.

In his fifth chapter Luke recorded the call of Peter, Andrew, James, and John. Simon Peter told Jesus that they had fished all night. Obviously our little band of fisherman worked the graveyard shift at times. I can only think of one thing worse than fishing in the cold. That would be not catching anything. It happens to the best of fisherman. When it happens to my husband Keith, I always ask him the typical sanguine woman question: But did you have fun with your friends anyway? My personality is given to the philosophy that the question is not so much whether you succeeded or failed but if you have fun in the process. I wish I had a picture of Keith's face when I ask him that question. I'd put it in the margin for your amusement.

I can go no further without musing over Christ's divinely uncanny ability to waltz right into a life and turn it upside down, inside out, and every which way but loose. Just think how many times those fishermen had prepared and cast their nets together. Picture how many years they had practiced a routine. They weren't fishing for the pure enjoyment of it as my husband does. Fishing was their job. I don't doubt they loved it as most men would, but don't think for a moment it wasn't work.

Peter answered Jesus, "Master, we've worked hard all night and haven't caught anything." They worked hard. Day in. Day out. Then one day Jesus walked up and everything changed.

Oh, beloved, isn't that exactly like Him? Jesus walks right up, catches us in the act of being—again today—exactly who we were yesterday, and offers to turn our routine into adventure. Hallelujah! Have you allowed Christ to do that for you? If you're bored with life and stuck in a rut of routine, you may have believed in Christ, but you may not yet have agreed to follow Him. Christ is a lot of things, but boring? Not on your life! Life with Him is a great adventure.

You don't necessarily have to leave behind what you do if He proves your present course to be His will, but I assure you He will have you leave the boredom and routine of it behind. When Jesus Christ takes over our lives, things get exciting! Consider where you are in this present season of your life. Keep in mind that even our "spiritual" or religious practices can become very routine. Also keep in mind that living in what we'll call the Great Adventure doesn't mean you don't have challenges or even times of suffering, but it means that you can "see" and take part in the breathtaking work of Christ in your life.

Notice that Simon called Jesus "Master." We can assume that these fishermen had familiarity with Jesus. John's Gospel clarifies by telling of an earlier encounter. Two disciples were with John the Baptizer (John 1:35). Verse 40 identifies one as Andrew. As a rule John did not identify himself in his writings. Many scholars believe that John the disciple was the other. We know for certain that Peter met Christ at this earlier time because John 1:42 tells us Andrew brought him to meet Jesus.

The words "Jesus looked at him and said . . ." put chills up my spine. According to *Strong's Concordance* the Greek word for "looked" means "to look on, i.e. to observe fixedly, or (absolutely) to discern clearly."[4] I think Christ looked Peter straight in the eyes with a penetrating look that could have drilled a hole through him and said, "'You are Simon son of John. You will be called Cephas' (which, when translated, is Peter)."

To our knowledge Peter and the other fishermen didn't receive their call from Jesus until after the encounter recorded in John 1. Without a doubt, at the time of the Luke 5 event, Peter, Andrew, James, and John knew Christ at least by reputation based on John the Baptist's faithful ministry, and at least several of them knew Him by a prior encounter. When Jesus approached them at their boats, they were primed and readied by God—even if through a short period of time—to leave everything behind and follow Christ anywhere.

I'd like to suggest that just as James and John were preparing their nets, they themselves had been prepared. The word *preparing* in Mark 1:19 can also mean "repairing." The exact same word is used in Galatians 6:1 for restoring a fallen brother. Oh, how thankful I am that the same God who *prepares* also *repairs* and *restores*. At this season of your life, what do you sense you need most: preparation for a fresh work of God? repair from a tear? restoration from a "fall"?

Joshua 3:5 contains a wonderful challenge: "Consecrate yourselves, for tomorrow the LORD will do amazing things among you." God can perform a miracle in any one of us at any time, but amazing things happen when you and I are willing to get prepared for a mighty work of God. Included in that mighty work will most assuredly be what we need most—whether a fresh work, a repair, or a full-scale restoration.

As we get to know John and see events through his eyes, I trust God will be preparing us also. Let's allow God to consecrate us and lay the groundwork for something spectacular. I pray that by the time we reach the last half of this study, God will be amazing and astonishing to us. Right this moment, let Jesus look you straight in the eyes and tell you that He knows who you are and who He wants to make you.

We'll see that John followed Jesus on some amazing paths. Are you willing to follow Him? That's the only way you and I will ever discover the One who calls us and the one we were born to be. Child, a great adventure awaits you.

Chapter 4

OLD TIES AND NEW TIES

After this he went down to Capernaum with his mother and brothers and
his disciples. There they stayed for a few days. (John 2:12)

*J*esus walked up to the four fishermen at the shore. How do you picture Christ's expression and demeanor as He called them to follow Him? How do you think Peter and Andrew felt about Jesus also stopping by the second boat and calling James and John? Keep in mind the partnership they shared in business. Do you think the sight of Peter and Andrew accompanying Christ had any kind of impact on the response of James and John?

Mark 1:20 tells us, "Without delay he called them [James and John], and they left their father Zebedee in the boat with the hired men and followed him." How do you think Zebedee reacted? Just so you're exploring all the options, keep in mind that Zebedee probably had some familiarity with Jesus. At the same time, don't forget he was a strong Jewish father with his own plans for his sons. What do you think?

I'm so glad God chose to include the name of James and John's father in Scripture. He wasn't just any man. He wasn't just any father. He was Zebedee. He had a name. He had feelings. He had plans. He was probably close enough to each of his sons' births to hear Salome, his young, inexperienced wife, cry out in pain. He probably wept when he was told he had a son. And then another. No doubt, he praised God for such grace. Daughters were loved, but every man needed a son to carry on the family line, after all.

Two fine sons. That's what Zebedee had. He named them himself. They played in his shadow until they were old enough to work; and if

I know anything about teenage boys, they still played plenty behind his back even when they were supposed to be working. Just about the time Zebedee grew exasperated with them, he'd look in their faces and see himself.

At the time when Christ called James and John, I have a feeling they had never been more pleasure or more support. Life is curious. Just about the time you get to reap some of the fruit of your parenting labors, the young, flourishing tree gets transplanted elsewhere.

Keith and I are in the season of life I'm describing. Our daughters have never been more delightful, never been any easier to care for, and never had more to offer in terms of company and stimulating conversation. The summers of their college years have been great fun, and we never secretly wanted to push them back to school or down an aisle. They are simply very little trouble right now. I wonder if Zebedee felt the same way about his young adult sons.

Just when Zeb was reaping a harvest of parental rewards, James and John jumped ship. All he had to show for it was a slimy fishing net. What would happen to the business? What about Zebedee and Sons? No matter how Zebedee felt, I have a pretty good feeling God had great compassion on him. After all, He knew how Zebedee felt when John had to be called away from his father's side in order to fulfill his destiny.

Chances are pretty good Zebedee thought their sudden departure was a phase and they'd get over it. Glory to God, they never did. Once we let Jesus Christ really get to us, we never get over Him. "Come, follow me," Jesus said, "and I will make you fishers of men."

I love the fact that Jesus talks in words and images His listeners can understand. When He said, "I will make you fishers of men," He obviously used terminology Andrew, Peter, James, and John could understand. He didn't use the same terminology with Philip, Nathanael, or Matthew, but I am convinced one part of the sentence applies to every single person Jesus Christ calls. "Come, follow me and *I will make you.* . . ." Decades later when God had used these men to change the face of "religion" forever, they still could not boast in themselves. Christ made them the men and the influences they were.

I can't express what these thoughts mean to me. I was such a broken and scattered mess. So emotionally unhealthy. So insecure and full of fear. I am not falsely modest when I tell you that when Christ called me, He had pitifully little to work with. I was a wreck . . . and stayed that way for longer than I'd like to admit. I have such a long way to go, but this I can say: I followed Christ, and anything that I am or have of value is completely from Him. Do you already have a similar testimony? Perhaps you are still in the broken, scattered state I described. If so, can you accept by faith what He can do if you follow Him?

So how does Christ make a man or a woman? We will explore many ways, but the most immediate way He began building His new followers into the people He wanted them to be was by spending intense time with them and showing them how He worked.

Piecing the Gospels together in a precise chronological order is a task far too challenging for me. I'm relieved to know that it is also a little too challenging for other Bible commentators. What we do know is that Christ and His small and yet incomplete band of followers attended a wedding in Cana together very soon after their union. In fact, John 2:1 says on the third day a wedding took place in Cana in Galilee, but we can't be entirely sure what he meant. It sounds like the third day after John began to follow Jesus.

We are going to explore the wedding more fully when we study the uniqueness of John's Gospel, but for now I'd like you to view the verse immediately following the celebration. John 2:12 says, "After this he went down to Capernaum with his mother and brothers and his disciples. There they stayed for a few days."

Christ's family and His disciples obviously enjoyed at least a brief season of peace and harmony. I didn't give that idea any thought until researching for this study. The schism in Christ's family didn't develop until a little while later (John 7:3–5). Eventually we will behold the reconciliation brought by the power of the resurrection. For now, however, picture Christ surrounded by both His family and His new disciples.

I am fairly convinced that we don't really know people until we stay with them for a few days. Can I hear an amen? Although I'm grinning,

I have almost always been more blessed than less. Not long ago Amanda and I got stranded in Tennessee after a conference due to a serious flood in Houston. When I learned the airport was closed, I frantically called Travis, my dear friend and worship leader, and asked if he had room for two more in his van back to Nashville. Without making a single preparation for us, his young family of four graciously received us into their home for two nights. Although we were already very close friends, we bonded for life. The treasure of having part of my ministry family and part of my natural family in fellowship together was priceless.

The disciples were new on the scene. They probably didn't have quite the comfort level interacting with Christ's family for those several days that I enjoyed with my worship leader's family. Still, they got to see Christ interact with His own family—an opportunity that I think was critical. Soon they would see Him perform all manner of miracles. They already had witnessed the changing of water to wine, but the sights they would soon see would nearly take their breath away. You see, people are much harder to change than water.

As they watched this man named Jesus, this carpenter's son, and they fellowshipped with Him then witnessed His work, what do you think they saw? Consistency? Versatility? Unwavering passion? Or a lamb as often as a lion? The center of all attention? Or a teacher that became a student of all those around Him? We know they saw absolute authenticity, but how do you imagine they saw it portrayed?

Don't think for a minute that thinking about such matters is a waste of time. The more we grasp the flesh-and-blood reality of these encounters and try to imagine the intimate details the disciples witnessed in Christ the better! What we're studying isn't religious fiction or simple Christian tradition. Christ walked into people's lives and transformed them. You and I want nothing less. We read in Isaiah 53:2 that Jesus had no beauty or majesty to attract them to Him, nothing in His appearance that they should desire Him, yet there was something about Him that caused grown men to walk away from established lives and keep following Him to the death. What do you suppose some of those things were?

25

Let's take a look at several Scriptures that applied to Christ at this time of His ministry. Notice how each of the following references describes Jesus in ways that would have attracted people to Him.

- "Jesus grew in wisdom and stature, and in favor with God and men" (Luke 2:52).
- "Jesus returned to Galilee in the power of the Spirit, and news about him spread through the whole countryside. He taught in their synagogues, and everyone praised him" (Luke 4:14–15).
- "They were amazed at his teaching, because his message had authority" (Luke 4:32).
- "A man with leprosy came to him and begged him on his knees, 'If you are willing, you can make me clean.' . . . 'I am willing,' he said. 'Be clean!' Immediately the leprosy left him and he was cured" (Mark 1:40–42).

Do you see, beloved? Christ was everything of any real value. He still is. People knew He was unique even before they knew He was God. He would have left the heads of the folks spinning. He can't be limited to a single personality type based on biased traits. He was the rarity. An honest-to-goodness whole person . . . embodied by the fullness of the Godhead (Col.2:9).

Jesus had favor. Power. Authority. Compassion. He was the perfect man. He had hands strong enough to turn over merchants' tables yet tender enough to touch the leper's rotting flesh and make him whole. Those who appreciated His uniqueness were drawn to it. Those who were threatened by it either ran or wanted Him destroyed.

As we conclude this lesson, allow me to ask you a question I sense the Holy Spirit prompting. Are you by any chance threatened by Jesus and His desire for you to follow Him with complete abandon? Don't answer quickly. Meditate on the question and see if the Holy Spirit surfaces anything. Are you afraid of anything? Are you unwilling to give up the things He might require? Think about it.

If you are willing to cast away all your fears, hindrances, and unanswered questions and follow Him, I can promise that you're going to see His glory.

Chapter 5

A HARD ACT TO FOLLOW

Jesus replied, "Let us go somewhere else—to the nearby villages—so I can preach there also. That is why I have come." (Mark 1:38)

*T*he disciples saw Christ perform eye-opening miracles almost from the start. Although we are saving further comments on the wedding at Cana for later, we know that it was the location of Christ's first miracle and that John's reference to the time frame of the wedding was "the third day" (John 2:1). The next occurrence in sequence was Christ's trip to Capernaum with His mother, brothers, and disciples (John 2:12). The events we will study next probably happened during the same stay in Capernaum, so imagine them falling next in sequence.

Jesus had just called Andrew, Peter, James, and John. Mark tells us they went to Capernaum (Mark 1:21). Picture these four fishermen mingling in the crowd gathered that Sabbath in the synagogue. I have an idea Christ's new disciples didn't just watch Jesus as He preached. I have a feeling they watched the reaction of others who were listening to Him as well. Mind you, at least Peter and Andrew lived in Capernaum at that time (v. 29). A town this size had only one Jewish synagogue, so they worshiped with virtually the same people week after week. They knew them personally. Some were relatives. Others were neighbors or business associates. Imagine the kinds of reactions the disciples saw on these familiar faces as Jesus preached.

Talk about an interesting service! If an "amazing" message were not enough excitement, just then a man in their synagogue who was possessed by an evil spirit cried out, "What do you want with us, Jesus of Nazareth?"

Suddenly their heads turned toward the opponent, almost like spectators in a tennis match.

I wonder if the crowd knew this man had an evil spirit before this moment or if they had been oblivious for years to the nature of his problems. Had they known, I'm not sure they would have allowed him in the synagogue, so my feeling is that the man may have kept it covered to some extent. Goodness knows Satan loves a good disguise. Somehow, however, when the authority of Christ was released in that place, the demons lost their cover. Jesus has a way of bringing the devil right out of some people, doesn't He?

The mere presence of Jesus caused the man—or should we say the demon?—to cry out, "What do you want with us, Jesus of Nazareth? Have you come to destroy us? I know who you are—the Holy One of God!" (v. 24).

Jesus commanded the demons to come out of the man. Christ also added something more. He commanded the spirit to be quiet.

Picture John witnessing these events. Many scholars believe he was the youngest of the disciples. One strong basis for this deduction is his positioning and apparent role at the Passover meal just before Jesus' crucifixion. We'll examine those events later, but for now keep in mind that the youngest at the Passover meal usually sat nearest the father or father figure so he could ask the traditional questions. I will refrain from building any doctrines on this deduction since I could be off base, but I am personally convinced enough that John was the youngest that I'll adopt this philosophy. If he was, can you imagine his face in particular while Jesus encountered—then cast out—these demons?

I think he probably experienced an entire concoction of emotions. Young men dearly love competitions, so he must have savored seeing his new team "win," even if only one Player was involved in the match. I have to think the encounter also scared him half to death. One thing that might have offset his fear was that he had to be indescribably impressed with his new mentor. He wasn't the only one. Mark 1:21 tells us the crowds were amazed by Christ's teachings, but Mark 1:27 intensifies the adjectives by saying they were "so amazed" by His demonstration of authority over the demons.

We do love a show, don't we? When I think how patient Christ has been with our human preference for divine fireworks, I am more amazed than ever. Christ knows us intimately. He knows how to get our attention, but He also desires that we grow up and seek His presence and glory more than the display of His might. John and the other disciples would see many miracles, but Jesus was after something more. He was out to build maturity into this group.

I have a feeling by the time the fishermen reached Capernaum with Jesus, something more tagged along—the news of their leaving Zebedee holding the net. I don't doubt for a minute that these young men whose reputations were on the line reveled in the grand reaction people in the community had to their new Leader. What could be more exciting than being associated with the most powerful and popular new man on the scene? But the day was far from over. Peter's mother-in-law was sick, but the doctor was on his way.

Think of events such as Jesus' birth, baptism, crucifixion, and resurrection as primary events that can indeed be placed in time sequence. Then consider the specific incidents from Jesus' life as secondary events. We won't often be able to put the secondary events of the four Gospels into an unquestionable chronological order. Each of the Gospel writers selected the events and stories for specific reasons. Matthew wrote to show that Jesus is the Jewish Messiah. Mark wrote to tell the Romans about what Jesus did. Luke wrote to show that Jesus came to be the Savior for all peoples, and John wrote to show the meaning of Jesus' ministry. The Spirit led them to write to convey the message, not to tell us the order of events.

Based on identical time sequencing in Mark and Luke and with nothing in Matthew or John to refute it, however, I believe we can rightly assume that the first healing of the sick ever witnessed by the disciples was in Simon Peter's home.

Before we talk about the healing, however, let's consider a bit about the order of events in the Gospels. Surely an early turning point came in the hearts and minds of the disciples when healing hit home. I know it did for me. Seeing Him work in a church service is one thing. Witnessing His healing in the life of your own family is another. That's when a person begins to get it through her head that Jesus doesn't just love church. He loves people.

By comparing Mark 1:21 and 29, we see it was the Sabbath day. Jesus had delivered the demon-possessed man in the synagogue. "As soon as they left the synagogue, they went with James and John to the home of Simon and Andrew" (v. 29). Christ raised the ire of the Pharisees on more than a few occasions over picking this particular day of the week for healings. It seems as if He were making a point. Later we're going to see that in many ways this was the perfect day of the week for healing.

I didn't realize until researching for this lesson that even His first healing was on the Sabbath. Obviously, Christ saw the purpose of the day far differently than many of His contemporaries. Apparently Simon Peter's mother-in-law was healed just in time to rise from the bed and get ready for company. As soon as the sun set, the whole town gathered at her door. They brought Jesus the sick and demon possessed for healing.

Have you ever seen someone receive an instantaneous physical healing like those described in this text? I've known plenty of people God healed physically, but I haven't had many chances to watch the manifestation of an instant healing take place before my very eyes. Can you imagine what these sights were like for the disciples? Think about the last time you encountered someone who was suffering terribly. What kinds of feelings did you have in response to their suffering?

Few of us choose to confront the suffering around us because we feel so helpless. Imagine the contrast between the agony of seeing human suffering and the ecstasy of seeing them healed. What would such an experience have been like for Mother Teresa, for instance, as she daily died to her own desire for personal comfort and confronted the unimaginable suffering in Calcutta? Then to see many healed? Somehow my mind can hardly even fathom the range of emotions. Picture being one of Christ's disciples. John was a human being just like you. How do you suppose these kinds of sights affected him?

John had observed hundreds of Sabbaths in his life. Imagine that he awakened that morning with a fresh wave of, "I can hardly believe what I've done! I wonder what my mom and dad are thinking right now." He must have been excited and unsure, and his soul was filled with the reality that something new was looming on the horizon.

Perhaps Lamentations 3:22–23 swirled through his mind as he recited his morning prayers of thanksgiving for God's provisions: "It is of the LORD's mercies that we are not consumed, because his compassions fail not. They are new every morning: great is thy faithfulness" (KJV). He prepared to go to the synagogue for services just as he had done all his life, only this time he got a bit more than he bargained for. The scroll was unraveled, and the Scripture for the day's service was read. Then Jesus took the role of rabbi, sat down, and preached the curly locks nearly off their heads.

Just then a man possessed by demons started shouting, and John saw Jesus get stern, perhaps for the first time. In an astounding show of power, Jesus cast out the demons, causing the man to shake violently. John thought as long as he lived, he would never forget the sound of those demons shrieking. He and the other disciples walked together to Simon Peter's house, whispering all the way about what they'd seen. Simon Peter's mother-in-law was sick with a fever, so Jesus took her by the hand, helped her up, and the fever left her so instantaneously she began to serve them.

"Don't tax yourself! You need to sit down and give yourself time to recover," the family insisted.

"You don't understand. I feel fine! I don't even feel weak. Let me serve you."

Then they begin to hear sounds at the door. Murmurings. Shrieking. Crying. Sounds of moaning. Sounds of hope. What's that—hope? Yes, hope. And hope says, "What He did for her, He might do for me," and that He did.

When John awakened that morning, his mind could not have conceived just how many mercies were new that particular sunrise. I can only imagine the kinds of things that went through the mind of the young disciple. He probably tossed and turned most of the night. Perhaps he and James whispered from their pallets until they were overtaken by exhaustion and finally fell asleep.

As I imagine all that happened that Saturday and all they saw, I know one of the thoughts I'd have had if I had been John. *Is there anything the man can't do?* He watched Jesus practically bring the house down with His teaching. He watched Him confront and cast out a demon. He watched Him not only heal Simon's mother-in-law but instantly restore her strength. Then every manner of distress landed on their doorstep.

I love Matthew Henry's words of commentary on the scene at the door. "How powerful the Physician was; he healed all that were brought to him, though ever so many. Nor was it some one particular disease, that Christ set up for the cure of, but he healed those that were sick of divers [various, diverse] diseases, for his word was a panpharmacon—a salve for every sore."[1]

His Word was a panpharmacon. Ah, yes. I have yet to have an ailment God had no salve to soothe. What may be even more peculiar is that I have yet to have an ailment of soul that God's Word was not the first to point out, diagnose, then heal. His Word is far more glorious, powerful, and fully applicable than we have any idea. You very likely did not pick up this particular Bible study because you sought healing. You would surely have picked other titles. But based on my own experience and many references in Scripture, you will undoubtedly receive some fresh diagnoses and, if you cooperate, a new measure of healing. As will I. I'm counting on it.

That's the nature of His Word. As Psalm 107:20 says, "He sent forth his word and he healed them." How often God has had to send forth His Word and begin the healing to get me healthy enough to face the diagnosis! I want you to revel in something wonderful. Every time God has prepared us with His Word and gotten us to a point that we can receive a hard "pill" to swallow from Him, healing has already begun. Once He confronts us, we never need to be overwhelmed by how far we have to go. If we've heard Him through His Word, healing has already begun. Take heart. He is the Panpharmacon.

Part 2

SIGHTS AND INSIGHTS

Can you imagine walking right beside Christ? Knowing what size sandal He wore? Recognizing His accent and favorite figures of speech? Over the next ten chapters we're going to take a look at snapshot scenes in the Gospels where John accompanied Jesus. I want you to think of yourself as "Number 13." By that I mean the thirteenth disciple and one who was also invited into every scene we'll study. Remember not to spiritualize John. He was as equally flesh and blood as we are, but what he witnessed reached far beyond the natural realm. Let's stand right by this young disciple's side and gaze upon scenes that marked him forever. May we be marked as well.

Chapter 6

A SOLITARY PLACE

Very early in the morning, while it was still dark, Jesus got up,
left the house and went off to a solitary place, where he prayed.
Simon and his companions went to look for him. (Mark 1:35–36)

Sappy. Cheesy. Mushy. Whatever you want to call it, I confess to it. As I stared at these passages, before I had any idea what God would lead me to write, a lump welled in my throat. In these pages you and I are going to walk up on a scene with a few of Christ's first disciples and find Him praying. All by Himself. Or with invisible company that we can't even grasp. I love the alone moments we find of Christ in Scripture. As I continue to learn of Him, my concept of the public Jesus develops more and more; but I am still deeply drawn to the mystery of the private Jesus.

I suppose I've always been a bit drawn to the mysterious in a person. My husband Keith is a man whom very few people know intimately. Somehow knowing him makes me feel special. I am also indescribably drawn to the mysterious side of Christ. What I do know about Him gives me an insatiable desire to know what I don't . . . and for now can't.

We all have our concepts of heaven, and goodness knows our images don't change it one bit. Still, I long for heaven to be not only a place of magnificent corporate worship with myriads of saints and hosts but a place of quiet, private encounters with Jesus Christ. I can't wait to be with all my siblings in Christ and to sit around the table with Moses, Paul, and the apostle John. But as selfish as this may seem, I've got to be honest with you. I want Jesus. Alone. At least for a few minutes each millennium! My dearest times with Him on this planet have been in the secret places. That's heaven to me.

Like the disciples we'll study, I want to walk up on a scene and suddenly find Him there. Unlike them, however, I don't want to drag Him back to the masses. I want to keep Him to myself for a moment. I like to picture that He might turn around, see me, and reach out His hand for mine. I like to think He might gently draw me to sit beside Him and allow me to share what has momentarily captured His attention. Maybe a mountain view of the crystal sea. Or the sight of children playing in a flowery meadow with furry lion cubs (Isa. 11:6).

Do I have too much imagination for you? Maybe I do, but I believe heaven will be far more creative than most believers seem to picture it. Surely a God who created this world with all its magnificence, diversity, and experiences does not have an eternal home that is like a one-act play. I hardly think so. Nor can I buy that we'll always be in one huge corporate gathering. How in the world could private encounters happen with millions of the redeemed in heaven? The way I see it, that's one reason we have eternity. Plenty of time for each of us to have Jesus all to ourselves. Oh, I think we have lots of surprises in store.

Like me, you may have memorized Mark 1:35: "Very early in the morning, while it was still dark, Jesus got up, left the house and went off to a solitary place, where he prayed." Mark does not tell us what morning, so we cannot dogmatically assume, but might this have been the next morning after the healing at Peter's house? After that kind of day, had I been Him, I might have considered sleeping in. Not Jesus. While the others may have whispered from their makeshift beds about all they had seen, Jesus got up while it was still dark, left the house, and went off to a solitary place to pray.

Don't you imagine Jesus had trouble feeling at home anywhere? Perhaps that's one reason He said, "The Son of Man has no place to lay His head." He slept plenty of places . . . but none of them were His true home. He slipped out of the house that morning after the Sabbath because He had a Sunday morning service to attend. The dark wood placard that hung on the wall right above the organist at my first church would have read: "Today's Attendance: 2."

In Revelation 22:16, Christ said, "I am the Root and the Offspring of David, and the bright Morning Star." The Morning Star is the bright planet Venus seen in the eastern sky before or at sunrise. I've seen it many mornings. When I get up to have my morning prayer time, outside is still as black as night. I love the comfort of knowing that the sun will rise during the course of that precious time with God.

I often step out on the porch, look at the sky, and behold one star that shines far brighter than the rest. That morning not far from the lapping waters of Galilee's shore, the bright Morning Star rose while it was still dark and lit the desolation with the lamp of Glory. Only God saw. "Oh, child," our heavenly Father asks us today, "would you rise for only Me to see?"

Mark tells us Jesus went to a solitary place. The original word for "solitary" *(erhmos)* means being in a state of isolation . . . of an area isolated, unfrequented, abandoned, empty, desolate.[1] Just outside of Capernaum stands a place many locals through the centuries have called Eremos ("solitary") Heights. The area has rugged rocks of red granite and naked, wind-swept cliffs.

In Matthew 6:6, Christ taught, "When thou prayest, enter into thy closet, and when thou hast shut thy door, pray to thy Father which is in secret" (KJV). He had no home of His own, but when the One who spoke the earth into existence prayed, the entire Eremos Heights could be His closet if He wanted it to be! I hope you, like Jesus, have a favorite place to pray.

Jesus went to the Eremos for one reason: to be alone with His Father. Oh, how I would love to know how He prayed! What He said! How long He talked! And then I wonder if He could hear His Father's response . . . with His ears or His heart? Christ's prayers from Earth were unique, unlike anyone else's. He had a freedom and familiarity that others cloaked in human flesh could not comprehend. Surely that's one reason why the disciples later pleaded with Him, "Lord, teach us to pray" (Luke 11:1).

Hebrew men were taught to pray from the time they could speak. They recited benedictions and petitions off and on all day long. They knew how to pray as men taught to pray, but when they beheld Christ captivated by the presence of His Father for hours at a time, I believe they meant, "Teach us to pray like that!" At Lazarus' tomb Jesus prayed, "Father, I thank you that you have heard me. I knew that you always hear me" (John 11:41–42).

One wonderful reason why Christ was so drawn to prayer and could pray for hours was because He had such confidence.

Really give this some thought for a minute as we talk reality and not just theology. How differently would we pray if we were convinced of two critical factors: (1) that our Father is the omnipotent Creator and Sustainer of the universe and (2) that He always hears us?

Do we not find our minds wandering and ourselves even a tad bored in prayer at times because—if the truth were known—we wonder if our words are bouncing off the ceiling? How differently would we pray if Christ chose to manifest His presence? Would we pray differently if He sat in a chair right across from each of us, leaning forward to concentrate on what we're saying?

Beloved, if only we would realize that though He's invisible to our sight, that's in essence what He does! He intercedes for us at the right hand of the Father. When we pray, He is so close to us, He may as well be leaning over the edge of heaven and bending down to hear. His presence through His Holy Spirit literally surrounds us as we pray. His eyes are fixed on our face. On every word we're saying. On every expression we're making. Can you imagine how the angels marvel over our boredom at times when we pray, as their faces behold our Father in heaven who is listening intently to every word?

I want to give you a personal prayer assignment for you to practice in your own "prayer closet." Every time you pray for the next week, begin your prayer with Christ's words straight out of John 11:42: "I know You always hear me." Then conclude it with Christ's words in John 11:41: "Father, I thank you that you have heard me." Practice God's presence! Pray as if He's really listening because He is!

In Mark 1:35–37, the disciples were far too immature in their walk with Christ to consider the enormity of the scene. Instead, they blurted out, "Everyone is looking for you!" Ah, here we have an insight into their present state of mind. Forget what Jesus did in private! They wanted to be seen in public with the popular Jesus! We're not going to be too hard on them because they were demonstrating a normal part of adolescent Christianity. We are the same way in our spiritual immaturity. At first we are far more excited about corporate worship than we are private worship.

One reason is because frankly we don't know Him well enough to have as much to say one on One. We love the excitement of being in the masses of those who are enthralled by Christ, and we always will. However, as we mature and Jesus becomes a greater and greater personal reality to us, I think we come to treasure time in the solitary places with Him more than anything.

Mark 1:36 tells us that Simon and his companions went to look for Jesus. The only companions we've met thus far in Mark's Gospel are Andrew, Peter, James, and John, so we can be almost certain our John was among them. Notice they weren't called disciples yet. I'm not sure they qualified as learners and pupils yet! Whoever the companions were, the terminology of the original language tells us they were tracking Jesus down, almost like a manhunt. The Greek word *katadiōkō*, translated "to look," is often used in a hostile sense.[2]

I'm not suggesting they were hostile toward Jesus but that they were quite anxious and maybe even a little put out with Him that He wasn't where all the people were. We see no indication from the text that they hesitated for a moment of respect or awe when they found Jesus praying. They barreled on the scene with, "Everyone is looking for you!"

I would like to offer a little conjecture that the companions tracking down Jesus may have been Peter, James, and John. Later in His ministry, these three men were chosen by Christ to watch Him on several different occasions in the inner places. Something caused Jesus to single them out. I believe Scripture will prove that it wasn't their spiritual maturity. I think two primary motivations compelled Christ to draw the three into several intimate places:

1. The fact that they just didn't "get it" at times.
2. The fact that Jesus knew once they did "get it," they'd really get it!

In other words, I wonder if Christ might have thought, *So you're not the boundaries types, are you? OK, I'll take you behind some ordinary boundaries, but I'll hold you responsible for what you learn while you're there.* Just food for thought.

I have a friend whose little boy thought he was the teacher's pet because she seated him in class right in front of her desk. He didn't realize for years that she was motivated by his discipline problems. Why didn't she just send him to the principal instead of expending so much energy on him? Because she knew the child had a student in him, and she was determined to find it. And she did. We're going to see Peter, James, and John get their desks moved to the front of the class. Just like children, at times they might be tempted to think the Rabbi moved them there because they were the Teacher's pets.

Chapter 7

THREE AND ONE

After six days Jesus took Peter, James and John with him and led them
up a high mountain, where they were all alone. (Mark 9:2)

$\mathscr{I}$ want to remind you of our objective. You may otherwise be frustrated over my leapfrogging from place to place in Scripture. Although I wish we could go through every step the disciples took with Christ, the purpose of this journey is to draw riches from the life and letters of John. We've taken the first steps of his encounters with Jesus rather slowly because he was among those first chosen to follow Christ. For a time we will pick up the pace rather dramatically as we leapfrog from scene to scene. As we focus on the synoptic Gospels, our objective is to concentrate on the settings where John is named or known to be present.

Keep in mind that Jesus had many followers, but He chose twelve from the many to walk nearest to Him. The next chapter will center on events that happened very close to the last Passover Jesus and His disciples observed together. Every moment the twelve spent with Jesus was significant, but now we're going to look at two scenes with some common denominators that no doubt had a profound effect on John. Try your best to view each occurrence from his point of view. Keep in mind that John was probably the youngest of the apostles and younger brother to one. Think of him as flesh and blood, and imagine what each experience might have been like for him.

We find scene one in Mark 5:35–43. The synagogue ruler named Jairus had requested that Jesus heal his daughter, and they were on the way to his home. Men met them and told Jairus not to bother the Rabbi because the girl had already died. Jesus told Jairus, "Don't be afraid; just believe" (v. 36).

I am fascinated by what Jesus did next. First, "He did not let anyone follow him except Peter, James and John" (v. 37). This reduced number proceeded to the home. The mourners had already gathered. In fact, they laughed when Jesus said the girl was not dead. He drove the crowd out of the house. He took the three disciples and the girl's parents into the room with Him. Jesus then raised the girl from the dead with a mere verbal command.

I can't help wondering what went through the minds of the three men when they were allowed to follow Jesus to a place the others weren't invited. I know what would have gone through my feminine mind. Women tend to be so relational. . . . I hardly would have been able to enjoy the privilege without fretting over the others being left out. Then, of course, I would have worried about whether they would be mad at me when we got back. I would imagine for days that they were acting a little weird. In fact, knowing I would have fretted myself half to death, Jesus wouldn't have bothered letting me come. No telling how many things I've missed because I make a knot out of the simplest string.

I would have hated to miss the eyeful the three got that particular day. Raising the stone-cold dead is nothing less than divine. This scene was not business as usual no matter how many miracles the three had seen and even performed.

I have been with several people right around their times of death, and I was utterly amazed each time how quickly the body grew cold. In spiritual terms, the soul is what keeps a body warm. Physical death occurs when the soul (meaning the immaterial part of a person, soul and spirit) departs the body. At its exodus, the warmth of life departs as well. We can be comforted by the fresh realization that the spiritual life is in the soul, and the soul continues living. We talk about the finality of death, but it has relatively little finality to the believer.

I'm so glad Jesus didn't listen to those who discouraged Jairus from "bothering" the teacher any more. Their reason was because the girl was dead. The death of a loved one is no time to quit "bothering" Jesus. No,

He's not very likely to raise our loved one from the dead, but He can do countless other things to get us through our losses. Comfort is the most obvious need, but we have others.

I often talk to people who are hamstrung by a death that left issues or answers unresolved. If I may be so bold, sometimes the missing person is not a loved one but an unforgiven or unforgiving one with whom we needed to make peace. Hopelessness often ensues. Depression can result. Sometimes we are convinced that all parties must be alive and kicking for us to gain peace in a situation.

Needless to say, the ideal time to make peace with others is while everyone's still breathing. But if it's too late, bother the Teacher! He doesn't have our limitations or rationalizations. Has a death left you with unfinished business? Finish it with Jesus.

Now travel with me to scene 2 in Mark 9:2–10. Jesus took the same three disciples with Him to the Mount of Transfiguration. There they saw Jesus' clothes become glowing white before them. They heard a voice from heaven, and they saw Moses and Elijah talking with Jesus.

Much time elapsed between the two scenes we're studying. Significant events occurred between these two dates, such as the feeding of the five thousand and Jesus walking on the water. What makes these two scenes priorities for our study is the inclusion of only three disciples. Christ does nothing haphazardly. He undoubtedly had reasons for appointing their observation.

In Mark 5:37, the three were listed as "Peter, James and John the brother of James." In this scene, John is no longer named like a tagalong brother. At this point, we see his identity in Scripture undoubtedly emerging. Also note that Jesus didn't just let Peter, James, and John come along. He took them.

God's will (Greek *thelema*) always expresses divine intention. Just as Jesus was intentional toward the experiences and exposures of the three, Christ is intentional toward us. He never bosses us or appoints us to something for the sheer sake of presuming authority. His will always has purpose. Sometimes we go our own ways, and God still has mercy on us and shows us something there. Other times we beg Him to allow us to go a certain place and He consents. Still other times God takes us places we never intended to go. Those are places He will reveal Himself to us in ways we didn't even know He existed.

All three synoptic Gospels record the transfiguration. Matthew's Gospel supplies the detail that the three disciples fell facedown to the ground. I am convinced that the people of God miss many appropriate opportunities to fall facedown to the ground, not in an emotional frenzy, but in complete awe of God. We don't have a clue who we're dealing with. I believe one of Jesus' chief reasons for transfiguring Himself before the three disciples was to say, "I am not like you. This is just a glimpse of who I am."

Remember, Jesus had equipped them with supernatural power to perform some of the same miracles He performed. What would keep them from thinking that just maybe in time they might be His peers? God forbid the thought! Jesus is not a superhuman. He is God. The beloved, divine Son of Him who occupies the throne of all creation. In Psalm 50:21 God says, "You thought I was altogether like you." One primary reason He takes us places we've never been is to show us He's not like anyone else. Where has God taken you personally to transfigure your perception of Him?

Glory came down on the mountain that night. When the cloudy pillar enveloped them and the voice of the Almighty became audible, they clung to the dirt of earth in terror. Rightly so.

Mark's Gospel shares at least two additional facts. First of all, he tells us Christ's clothes dazzled with a whiteness whiter than anyone in the world could bleach them. You and I can't fathom whiter than white. Our finite minds can only embrace nature's rendition of white . . . like fresh falling snow. The divine white goes much further than the whiteness of snow.

In Psalm 51:7 David appealed to God to wash him whiter than snow. Anything we are and anything we have that is whiter than snow comes from Christ alone. I have lived long enough to sin against many people. I have sought forgiveness from those God has brought to my mind. I've been forgiven many times, but no one could make me clean. No one except Jesus, whose dazzling glories are whiter than anything in the world.

Mark also tells us that Peter made the daft suggestion of building three tabernacles because he did not know what to say. He was too frightened. Have you ever noticed how often we say something completely ridiculous when we don't know what to say? Oh, that God would have put our brains in our tongues! In His wisdom He did, however, give us twice as many ears as we have mouths, but we seem to have missed the point. God responded from the heavens, "This is my Son, whom I love. Listen to Him!" My translation: "Shut thee up!"

One of Luke's primary inclusions is the fact that Moses and Elijah were there discussing Christ's departure. A more literal translation would be "exodus." That puts chills all over me. If any two former mortals knew anything about distinctive departures, Moses and Elijah did. One died alone with God and was buried by Him, and the other was taken up in a whirlwind with chariots of fire. Jesus' assignment was far more radical, and the effects would be completely revolutionary. They had much to discuss.

We've studied two scenes in which John observed. Both involved profound miracles. Both involved Christ's power over the dead. Christ raised Jairus' daughter from the dead. Neither Moses nor Elijah returned to their mortal bodies on Earth yet, they were very much alive.

Mark 9:9–10 tells us Jesus commanded the three disciples to say nothing until after He was also raised from the dead. The three descended, debating what Jesus meant.

Beloved, Jesus is Lord over the living . . . and the dead.

Chapter 8

RIGHT-HANDED DISCIPLES

They replied, "Let one of us sit at your right hand and the other
at your left in your glory." (Mark 10:37)

$\mathcal{W}$e last saw John, his brother, and his buddy Peter as they viewed sights the others could hardly have imagined. Christ made them His inner circle. They beheld revelations of His glory both in raising the dead and conferring with those long supposed dead. One might say you'd have to be dead to be unaffected by such sights, but obviously in both cases the dead were highly affected! No one remained unchanged. But how were the disciples changing? That's the question.

Before we take a look at how the three dealt with their private invitations, let's make sure we're prepared to apply some of these truths to ourselves. Paul didn't write the Book of Ephesians to the twelve disciples. It was intended for all of us who would place our faith in Jesus. Ephesians 1:3 tells us that Christ has "blessed us in the heavenly realms with every spiritual blessing." Later on Paul described how he prayed that the Father "may give you the Spirit of wisdom and revelation, so that you may know him better" (Eph. 1:17).

Scripture clearly teaches that those of us who have trusted Christ are also chosen (Eph. 1:4) and called (Eph. 1:18). He leaves us on this earth so that our lives will have an effect for the kingdom of God. The primary way He equips us for our tasks is to reveal Himself to us. If you want to serve Christ, don't just get busy. Get to know Him intimately and you'll have a head-on collision with your calling! God wants to give us a Spirit of wisdom and revelation so we'll know what to do with what He reveals.

We know that we've been chosen and called to various kinds of ministries. God wrapped these concepts up in the difficult package we call election. At the risk of more simplicity than my biblically intellectual friends can stand, my personal belief is that God will call anyone who will come. He looks upon the heart. God has been so merciful to me that I cannot imagine how He would withhold His grace from anyone who sought Him. I believe He chooses those who He knows have the heart to choose Him.

Can I answer all the questions such a stand invariably raises? Not on your life! Neither could Paul. Check out Romans 11:33–34. I will defer to someone who was far brighter than I will ever be. In the classic book *The Pursuit of God,* A. W. Tozer wrote:

> God will not hold us responsible to understand the mysteries of election, predestination and the divine sovereignty. The best and safest way to deal with these truths is to raise our eyes to God and in deepest reverence say, "O Lord, Thou knowest." Those things belong to the deep and mysterious profound of God's omniscience. Prying into them may make us theologians, but it will never make us saints.[1]

God chooses us to reveal Himself to us. He intends His revelation to bring about such a Spirit-empowered representation of what He's about that it will transfigure the world He so loves. Our reactions to God's revelation (through His Word, nature, and circumstances) are tell-tale signs of our maturity. Even the most mature believers could be enticed by the enemy and their own egos to be puffed up by the election of revelation. Paul said it best in 2 Corinthians 12:7: "To keep me from becoming conceited because of these surpassingly great revelations, there was given me a thorn in my flesh, a messenger of Satan, to torment me."

Somebody might have needed to stick a thorn in Peter, James, and John as well and burst their balloon egos. We're going to see that they obviously struggled with election and revelation as well. Did you notice in our previous chapter that the three didn't fall facedown on the ground until God spoke from the cloud (Matt. 17:5–6)? Can you imagine still being able to stand on your feet and talk while Christ dazzled with glory and

Elijah and Moses popped onto the scene? Nope, the three weren't thinking very clearly. Sometimes we don't when our heads are too heady.

As you read Matthew 17, the voice of God seems to come almost as a divine interruption saying, "You three just don't get it, do you? You can't 'see' what you're seeing, so shut up and listen!" That they didn't exactly assimilate the revelation with maturity is crystal clear in our next passage. In the same chapter recording the transfiguration, Luke reports three scenes. The disciples misread election and revelation in each one.

In Luke 9:46–48 the disciples were arguing about which of them would be greatest. Jesus took a child and said, "Whoever welcomes this little child in my name welcomes me; and whoever welcomes me welcomes the one who sent me. For he who is least among you all—he is the greatest" (v. 48).

In Luke 9:49–50 John told the Master, "We saw a man driving out demons in your name and we tried to stop him, because he is not one of us." Jesus forbade them to stop such men, "For whoever is not against you is for you."

In Luke 9:51–55 James and John asked permission to call down fire on a Samaritan village that failed to welcome the group. Luke simply noted that Jesus turned and rebuked them.

I'm sitting here shaking my head. Oh, not just at them. At myself. At the whole lot of us. Sometimes I wonder why God doesn't give up on us when we cop attitudes like these. Only His mercy keeps us from being consumed (Lam. 3:22–23). I constantly thank Him for hanging in there with me. I would have given up on myself a long time ago. I am so grateful that God is both nearsighted and farsighted. He sees us as we really are, and He sees how we'll really be. I'm pretty convinced that only the latter keeps the former alive.

Perhaps John's age didn't help. Life simply hadn't had time to beat him over the head with humility. Forty years on the far side of the desert followed by a flock of aggravating people was enough to humble the exclusivity right out of Moses. In a wonderfully peculiar account in Numbers 11:24–30, Moses faced a similar situation. He took the elders of Israel into the tent of meeting. There the Spirit of God came upon them, and they prophesied. Two of the elders, however, did not come with the group. Those two also began to prophesy in the camp.

When Joshua heard what was happening, he asked almost the exact question as John in our incident above. He asked if he should stop the two. Moses responded, "Are you jealous for my sake? I wish that all the LORD's people were prophets and that the LORD would put his Spirit on them!" (Num. 11:29).

I'll never forget standing in the resource room of my office with a friend who asked, "What does it feel like to look at all these books with your name on them?" My face screwed up into a knot, and I said, "All they represent to me is one holy beatin' after another!" I am sad to say that much of what I've learned has come with the rod of God, but things are beginning to change, aren't they, Father?

After the three strikes recorded in Luke 9, Christ's enduring love and patience is obvious in His unwillingness to throw His thumb back and yell "Out!" Particularly since He knew what was coming next. Mark tells us how James and John came to Jesus and said, "We want you to do for us whatever we ask" (Mark 10:35). They painted a pretty good picture of spiritual toddlerhood, didn't they? But here's the painful part. We can relate too much to want to judge James and John harshly in their approach, can't we? Let's face it. All of us have to go through spiritual toddlerhood and adolescence to get to a place of maturity. We don't ordinarily leap up. We grow up. The danger is when we refuse to grow. To get stuck in this stage is about as appealing as an adult that still acts like a two-year-old.

For a few moments, James and John did nothing but descend deeper and deeper in the quicksand of their own self-absorption. (Never doubt, it is quicksand.) In this scene, James and John made only three statements.

"Teacher, we want you to do for us whatever we ask" (v. 35). "Let one of us sit at your right and the other at your left in your glory" (v. 37). The last statement we'll consider in a moment. First meditate on these statements and try to capture the emotions and attitudes behind them. Do you see a growing audacity with each statement?

Don't think for a minute they wouldn't have dug themselves deeper given the opportunity. Had Christ told them He might consider one on

His right and one on His left, how long do you think it would have taken them to rumble over who would sit where? Oh, brother! Their famous last two words almost slay me. After Christ asked, "Can you drink the cup I drink or be baptized with the baptism I am baptized with?" they answered without hesitation: "We can." They didn't have any idea what they were talking about because they didn't have any idea what Christ was talking about. Soon they would. And one day in the distant future they would sip from the cup and know the baptism of His suffering, but in their present state, they needed a baby bottle, not a cup.

Our problem is often the same as theirs. We let the human image of Christ mislead us into downsizing Him. "If He'd just stoop a little and we stood on our tiptoes, we'd be just about side by side. One at His left. One at His right." Negatory, good buddy. When the Word became flesh to dwell among us, human flesh wrapped its way around "the fulness of the Godhead bodily" (Col. 2:9 KJV).

I am convinced if we, present company included, really "got" the concept of being chosen and called by Jesus Christ the divine Son of God, like the prophet Ezekiel, the Spirit of God would have to set us on our feet for us to get off our faces (Ezek. 2:1). Yes, we've been chosen and, yes, we've been called, and we'll know we're grasping the concept when our humanity is cloaked in humility.

"Teacher, we want you to do for us whatever we ask."

or

"Teach us to do for You whatever You ask."

Chapter 9

RECLINING NEXT TO HIM

One of them, the disciple whom Jesus loved,
was reclining next to him. (John 13:23)

*T*he final week of Christ's life as the God-man started exactly like the disciples preferred: with the fanfare of a triumphal entry. No little excitement had surrounded them since the booming voice of Jesus awakened a four-day-old dead man. The longer the chief priests "let" Christ get away, the more complicated their schemes became. John 12:10–11 tells us they planned to kill Lazarus, too, for on account of his being raised from the dead, many of the Jews were going to Jesus and putting their faith in him.

The week of the great feast arrived, and so many Jews were in Jerusalem that a donkey couldn't even hear himself neigh. Surely the disciples had joined their families in many pilgrimages to the Holy City to observe the Passover, but this year they attended with One who appeared to be the Master of Ceremonies. Their impatient, ambitious feet seemed finally about to enter the big world on pay dirt. They were about to be important. Or at least that's what they thought.

My most recent memory work has been out of James 3. I keep thinking of the words of James: "Who is wise and understanding among you? Let him show it by his good life, by deeds done in the humility that comes from wisdom" (James 3:13). One thing I have learned about the wisdom of humility is that if you're riding high on the horse one day, you'd be wisest not to feel too uppity lest you be rolling in the manure the next. I hope that wasn't too plainly stated for you, but sometimes all the words in Webster's can't say it the way my country heritage can.

Circumstantially the disciples didn't have the least hint that trouble was coming. Wisdom might have warned them differently had they been listening. Christ had told them on several occasions what awaited Him, but they, like we do, cut and pasted the parts of His sermons they liked on their mental files and deleted the rest.

Word traveled quickly that Jesus was on His way to the city, so a crowd gathered to meet Him. They waved palm branches and shouted, "Hosanna! / Blessed is he who comes in the name of the Lord! / Blessed is the King of Israel!" (John 12:13 NKJV).

The disciples should have had a tip-off that this week was going to be unlike anything they had ever experienced with Jesus. Right in the middle of a parade approaching Jerusalem, Jesus took a good look at the landscape of the city and wept loudly. Luke 19:41 simply tells us that Jesus wept over it, but the Greek uses the strongest word for grief in the New Testament text. The wording suggests that His grief was not only deep, it was demonstrative.

Luke relates Jesus' words, which explain such emotion. He said, "If you, even you, had only known on this day what would bring you peace— but now it is hidden from your eyes. The days will come upon you when your enemies will build an embankment against you and encircle you and hem you in on every side. They will dash you to the ground, you and the children within your walls. They will not leave one stone on another, because you did not recognize the time of God's coming to you" (Luke 19:42–44).

Imagine Peter, James, and John standing close by and glancing at one another. Perhaps they even shrugged their shoulders. Just about the time they thought He had pulled Himself together, however, He entered the temple and began to drive out the merchants.

Obviously, the week of Christ's passion began almost as passionately as it ended. In between, only Jesus could have retained the presence of mind to perform some of the duties that meant the most to Him. Luke 19:47 tells us that between the Sunday of the Triumphal Entry and the actual observance of the Passover meal, Jesus taught every day at the temple.

All the people hung on His words. How soon they would yell, "Crucify Him!" and He would hang on theirs.

Unlike the disciples, Jesus knew what was coming and became the embodiment of the humility that comes from wisdom. Because the disciples brought knapsacks full of selfish ambition to town, they no doubt felt the disorder James 3:16 says the ambitious are bound to experience: "For where you have envy and selfish ambition, there you find disorder and every evil practice." Life can be so confusing when "it's all about us."

Between Luke 19:47 and Luke 21:38, you'll find a sampling of the teachings Christ offered in the temple on Monday, Tuesday, and Wednesday. Luke 22:1–6 follows with Satan's possession of Judas and the subsequent deal he made with the chief priests and officers of the temple. Then, according to Luke 22:7, came the Day of Unleavened Bread on which the Passover lamb had to be sacrificed. Jesus sent Peter and John to prepare for the Passover meal.

Christ's appointments are never haphazard. He can accomplish anything He desires by merely thinking it into existence. That He assigns men and women to certain tasks implies that the experience of the servant or beneficiary is often as important as the accomplishment. Sometimes more so. God can do anything He wants. He sovereignly chooses to employ mortals to flesh out an invisible work in the visible realm . . . even Jesus the perfect Word made flesh.

I believe that Peter and John were not only chosen for the job of preparing the Passover but that the job was chosen for them. When I considered this scene in *Jesus the One and Only,* I shared what I believe is far more than a coincidence: Peter and John's repetitive references in their letters to Christ as the Lamb. They seemed to have understood the concept of the Paschal Lamb like none of the other writers of the New Testament. I believe a tremendous part of their understanding came in retrospect after their preparation for the last Passover with Christ.

God added an insight in our present study as I became more deeply aware of the early influence John the Baptist had upon Peter and John. We know that each was either directly discipled by the Baptizer or indirectly influenced through their brothers. John 1:29 tells us that these disciples first encountered Jesus through the words of the Baptizer: "Look, the Lamb of God, who takes away the sin of the world!"

Jesus would not rest until He taught Peter and John exactly what that title meant. The pair didn't run by the Old City market and grab a saran-wrapped package of trimmed lamb for a buck fifty a pound. They picked out a live lamb and had the sweet thing slaughtered. Very likely they held it still for the knife. Most of us can hardly imagine all that was involved in preparing for a Passover, but you can be sure that none of it was wasted.

That's one of the things I love about Christ. He's not into waste management. If He gives us a task or assigns us to a difficult season, every ounce of our experience is meant for our instruction and completion if only we'll let Him finish the work.

The other day I came across a verse that causes me to stop, meditate, and ask big things from God every time I see it. Psalm 25:14 says, "The LORD confides in those who fear him." I desperately want God to be able to confide in me, don't you? The King James Version puts it this way: "The secret of the LORD is with them that fear him." I want God to tell me His secrets! I believe these hidden treasures are not secret because He tells them only to a chosen few but because not many seek to know Him and tarry with Him long enough to find out.

I believe as Peter and John prepared the Passover meal that day, they were privy to many secrets that became clearer and clearer to them as time passed. Ecclesiastes 3:11 says that God makes everything beautiful in its time. I truly believe that if we're willing to see, God uses every difficulty and every assignment to confide deep things to us and that the lessons are not complete until their beauty has been revealed. I fear, however, that we have such an attention deficit that we settle for bearable when beauty was just around the corner.

Surely many years and Passover celebrations passed before Peter and John fully assimilated the profound significance of the one in which Jesus became the Lamb. John never could get over it. From the pen of an elderly, shaking hand, we find over twenty references to the Lamb in the Book of Revelation. And it was Peter, his sidekick, who wrote:

> For you know that it was not with perishable things such as
> silver or gold that you were redeemed from the empty way of life

handed down to you from your forefathers, but with the precious blood of Christ, a lamb without blemish or defect. (1 Pet. 1:18–19)

Look at the expression again: "from the empty way of life handed down to you from your forefathers." When I think of a Jewish heritage, I imagine it to be anything but empty! We Americans are such a hodge-podge of cultures that many of us lack the rich traditions of other less alloyed cultures. And who could have enjoyed richer ways of life and more tradition than those handed down by Jewish forefathers to their sons and daughters? Yet Peter called them empty. Why? I think because once He saw their fulfillment in Jesus Christ, he knew they were empty without Him. Once he knew the true Passover Lamb, an Old Testament Passover meant nothing without its fulfillment in Jesus. Christ became everything, and all former things were empty without Him.

Thank goodness for the patience of Christ to make all things beautiful over time. How can we be sure they didn't fully grasp the significance of their Passover experience that evening? Luke 22:24 tells us that "a dispute arose among them as to which of them was considered to be greatest."

Hmmmm. Sounds like a good time for a pitcher and a towel to me. We'll push the hold button on the washing of the disciples' feet until we consider the uniqueness of John's Gospel. I wonder how many times the disciples looked back on that argument with humiliation. I can relate. I have had my share of moments when I said something so entirely ludicrous that I cannot even think about it without my whole face screwing up in a knot. You, too? I have a feeling we're going to have to take some good-natured ribbing about some of those things in heaven. I hope they are funny by then.

Let's conclude this chapter with a snapshot moment that precipitated the dispute over who among the disciples was the greatest. Jesus told them that one among them would betray Him. At this exact moment, John's Gospel adds an important tidbit of information. Assuming "the disciple Jesus loved" is our John, his place at the table was "leaning . . . against Jesus" (John 13:25).

John's location constitutes one of the chief reasons many scholars believe John was the youngest disciple. At the traditional Jewish Passover, the youngest child at the table who is able to talk often sits nearest the father or father figure and asks the traditional questions that prompt the father to tell the story of deliverance from Egypt. The room was small enough for Peter to ask Jesus a question even if he was seated at the opposite end of the table. The fact that he prompted John to ask the question suggests that John may have assumed the role as the official petitioner that evening.

I also love imagining that the youngest among them might have had the least protocol and acted as he felt and not just according to what was proper. Hence his leaning against Jesus. Glory! You see, there's just nothing doctrinal about John's leaning on Jesus. It wasn't the law. It wasn't in the proverbial Passover book of rules. John didn't have to lean on Jesus to talk to Him. Christ could hear him just fine. John leaned on Him because he wanted to. Because he loved Him. Because He was . . . leanable. Approachable. Downright lovable.

Both of my daughters are very affectionate, but my older is without a doubt more proper. My youngest wouldn't know the word *protocol* if it were tattooed on her forehead. (I hope I don't give her any ideas. She's threatened a tattoo before.) I have often said if she is *with* me, she is some-how *on* me. As my mother would say, attached to my person. From the clues we gather here and there, I like to think that John was somehow the same way with Jesus. Very likely, he was the baby of this family. And his affection for Jesus wasn't encumbered by silly things like protocol. I love that about him.

One of our primary tasks through this journey is to explore the deep affection that flowed like a teeming brook between Jesus and John. I'll just be honest with you. I want what they had. I want what God and David had. I want what Christ and Paul had. If a mortal can experience it with the Immortal Invisible, I want it. I want to know this love that surpasses knowledge that I may be filled to the measure of all the fullness of God (Eph. 3:19). All else is just an empty way of life handed down by bored and unmotivated forefathers. No thanks. Give me Jesus. If I make someone else uncomfortable, that's too bad.

Chapter 10

FROM THE EDGE OF A GARDEN

He took Peter and the two sons of Zebedee along with him, and he began
to be sorrowful and troubled. (Matthew 26:37)

$\mathcal{W}$hen Peter and John prepared the Passover, they could never have imagined the events that would fall like one domino upon another. They prepared a table for thirteen. They had no idea they were preparing a table before their enemy. At that point, they didn't even know an enemy sat among them.

Few things startle and shake us to the core like the sudden revelation of a Judas. Maybe because we can't believe we didn't see it. Maybe because we're terrified that if one of us could be Judas, couldn't we all? Aren't we all self-centered, vain, and ambitious? Did he seem altogether different than us? Didn't he say, "Surely not I," like the rest of us? We are terrified by our similarities! And rightly we should be. But one thing sets us apart. He sold his soul to the devil.

John's Gospel tells us something none of the Synoptics include. Jesus told them one at the table would betray Him. Peter prompted and John asked who the betrayer would be. Jesus answered, "It is the one to whom I will give this piece of bread when I have dipped it in the dish" (John 13:26). He then gave the bread to Judas.

John 13:28 tells us no one at the meal understood. Over the course of years and countless replays of the scene in the mind of the apostle John, he knew the devil entered into Judas at that table right before their very eyes.

How did he know? Christ taught in John 14:26 that the Holy Spirit is also the Holy Reminder. He can reveal the truth even in something past and remind us what He was teaching us at the time that we were unable to grasp. Jesus often teaches us lessons that He knows we won't fully assimilate until later.

Try to grasp that Judas was not inhabited by any old demon from hell. Satan is not omnipresent. He can only be one place at a time, and for that time, he was in Judas. The prince of the power of the air flew like a fiery dart into the willing vessel of one of the Twelve. We can follow. Closely. And still not belong to Jesus. We can talk the talk. We can blend right in. We can seem so sincere.

I believe through the videotape of his own retrospect, John saw the devil in Judas's eyes. I think he saw Satan in his hands as he reached for the dipped bread. Think about it. For the briefest moment, two hands held the same bread. One soiled by silver (and not nearly enough). The other only a thin glove of flesh cloaking the hand of God. John saw the devil in Judas's feet as he walked away, . . . for if we are ever truly with Christ, we cannot leave Christ (see 1 John 2:19).

Two-thirds of a century later John would write, "They went out from us, but they did not really belong to us. For if they had belonged to us, they would have remained with us; but their going showed that none of them belonged to us" (1 John 2:19). We learn some of our best, and worst, life lessons at the table. He learned that lesson at the table. He learned all too well.

Later the same hands that betrayed Christ would tie a knot in a rope and loop it around his own neck. Those same feet would spasm and jerk, then dangle lifelessly. I think perhaps Judas took his own life because the same devil he betrayed Christ to please then betrayed him. The devil used him and left him just as surely as Judas used Christ and left Him. Judas did not even have the dignity of a warrior of hell. He was discarded like a soiled rag. Less than nothing. That's Satan's way. He is friend to no one. He only pretends. He is Judas. The Betrayer. I wonder, . . . has the devil ever betrayed you? Has he ever talked you into anything and used you, then left you dangling? He has certainly betrayed me.

Soon after Christ confronted Judas and he departed their midst, Christ and His disciples observed the ordinance of the New Covenant, sang a hymn, and went out to the Mount of Olives (Matt. 26:30). Again, what they could not assimilate in the teaching of the bread and the wine, the Holy Reminder would later explain to them.

The Mount of Olives was perched east and directly across from the Old City overlooking the temple. The view was so good that several decades later the Roman commander Titus set up headquarters on its northern ridge, successfully planned the city's destruction, and named it Mount Scopus, or Lookout Hill. In ancient times the whole mount must have been heavily wooded. As its name implies, it was covered with dense olive groves. It was from this woodland that the people, under Nehemiah's command, gathered their branches of olive, oil trees, myrtle, and palm to make booths when the Feast of Tabernacles was restored after their years of captivity in Babylon[1] (Neh. 8:15).

According to Luke 22:39, Jesus had obviously been often to the Mount of Olives. Unlike the disciples who took the steep walk beside Him, as Jesus climbed that hill, He knew its significance both past and future. No wonder He had been there so many times. On the previous Sunday He had stood on Lookout Hill over His beloved city and baptized the Mount of Olives with His tears. "If you, even you, had only known on this day what would bring you peace. . . !" This most profound of all Passover nights, He would baptize the Mount of Olives with sweat like drops of blood falling to the ground.

Matthew 26:36–46 tells the familiar story of Jesus' ultimate struggle in the garden called Gethsemane. During Jesus' agony there, Peter, James, and John were once again drawn out from the others. Gethsemane is the third time Scripture documents them as eyewitness to a scene the others did not observe. I've mentioned all three. I think we can rest assured the disciples had never seen Jesus like the three saw Him in Gethsemane.

I have studied this scene many times before but never from the point of view of the disciples. Imagine that you are one of the three. Consider what Jesus represented to the disciples for the past three years. He certainly represented security and strength to them. Grown men don't follow for three years with virtually no income unless they are completely taken with the leader. I believe Jesus was their whole lives. In Him their pasts made sense. Their present was totally immersed in Him, and all their hopes for the future rested in His faithfulness to do what He promised. And indeed He would . . . but never in a million years would they have expected how.

"My soul is overwhelmed with sorrow to the point of death. Stay here and keep watch with me" (Matt. 26:38).

Wait a second! This was their Rock! Their Strong Tower! "What in the world is wrong with Him? Why is He on the ground like that? Why is He writhing in anguish? Why is His hair drenched in sweat? It's freezing out here! And why does His sweat look like blood drops falling to the ground? Why does He keep asking for a cup to be taken from Him? What cup? He's crying 'Abba!' [Mark 14:36]. What's He so upset about? Is it because one of us betrayed Him? Why won't He stop? I hate seeing someone cry like that. I thought nothing could get to Him. Why won't He stop?"

Have you ever seen someone you consider to be a rock in unabashed anguish, virtually inconsolable, and overwhelmed with sorrow? If so, think how you felt. Then multiply that feeling by the total dependency on Jesus these men had learned.

I believe the disciples experienced many emotions as they watched their Strong Tower fall to His knees with His face to the ground. Luke 22:45 tells us that the three disciples finally fell asleep from the exhaustion of their own sorrow.

The disciples may not have realized that Jesus was no less God that moment than He was on the Mount of Transfiguration or when He raised the dead. Their Rock and their Strong Tower was not falling apart. He was falling on His knees. That takes strength. I always wonder how the mountain kept from splitting in two when the weight of the Word made flesh fell with knees upon it. Oh, how creation must have groaned!

There in the garden, the Son of God bore His private cross. Very soon He would bear it publicly, but when He rose from knees bruised with anguish, His face, dusted with earth, was set like flint. I want you to see one last point that I find critical to our understanding about the heart of God. Christ knew what He was going to have to do when He came to earth. Remember? He is the Lamb slain from the foundation of the world. He was as good as dead from the beginning. Jesus lived for one purpose alone: to do the will of His Father. Yet He still felt.

Jesus is the precise image of His Father, who also feels. God is holy. God is righteous. Our salvation necessitates a cross. Our poor decisions necessitate chastisement. The refusal of the lost to believe necessitates judgment. But God still feels. Beloved, God still feels.

And so will we. Sometimes obeying God in a matter will be the hardest thing we've ever done in our lives. We are not wrong to feel. We are wrong to disobey. Hash it out with God. Ask for the cup to be removed. But resolve to do His will. No matter what. Glory is at stake. That's why He drew the three close enough to see. To teach them to pray . . . not sleep . . . in their anguish. This time they slept. They had little power to do otherwise. But a time would come when each would rise from his own Gethsemane and bear his cross.

Part 3

DEFINING
MOMENTS

Are you keeping up with our pace? Catching up with the youngest disciple is rather like catching up with any adolescent boy. He practically has us out of breath. At least we're not likely to get bored! The Word of God is alive, and God wants to ignite a fresh passion in us through perhaps the most familiar accounts in the life of Christ.

In the latter half of our study, we'll consider many truths that are far less familiar to us, but we can only get there by way of the cross. Before this study I had never looked at the events surrounding the cross and glorious resurrection over the shoulder of one of the disciples. It profoundly affected me. I hope you gain an entirely new perspective as well. Ask God to free you from any bondage that familiarity can breed, then completely immerse yourself in every scene.

Chapter 11

STANDING NEARBY

*When Jesus saw his mother there, and the disciple whom he loved standing
nearby, he said to his mother, "Dear woman, here is your son," and to the
disciple, "Here is your mother." (John 19:26–27)*

$\mathcal{H}$ave you ever looked around you at circumstances you could never
have imagined experiencing and thought, *How did we get here?*
I remember feeling that way when I sat with Keith's family in the ICU
waiting room while his beautiful twenty-three-year-old sister lay dying
with an aneurysm. Just a few nights earlier we all had been laughing until
our sides split. Just that morning Keith, Amanda (a toddler at the time),
and I had been to church and shared a pizza for lunch. Suddenly in a
string of events that happened with staggering velocity, our entire lives
changed. No Broadway stage could have captured the raw, gaping emotions of real-life drama. Those times when you want to scream, "No! This
isn't really happening! This can't be happening!" Days that you desperately wish you could drop off the calendar so you can just go back to life
as it was.

I believe that such experiences give us some concept of the way John
must have felt in the scene depicted by John 19:17–27. Jesus hung on the
cross. Pilate placed a sign over Jesus' head. The soldiers gambled for His
clothing.

Can you imagine how John's head must have been spinning? Don't you
know he wished someone would wake him up from his nightmare? Then
came a profoundly tender and emotional interchange between Jesus, John,
and Mary. Jesus assigned John to care for Mary, but take care that you don't

65

tag it a warm and fuzzy moment and try to snuggle up to it. The events John observed were horrific. We can only appreciate the depth of the tenderness against the backdrop of the horror. Most of us have studied the cross of Christ many times, but let's attempt to capture it from the exact angle where the apostle John's sandals flattened the dirt.

Let's rewind the events to place John accurately in the scenes. We know without a doubt that John was an eyewitness to the arrest.

Mentally recapture what we studied in our previous chapter as John, James, and Peter most closely witnessed Christ's agony in the garden of Gethsemane. Their witness dissolved into sorrow, then sleep. They were awakened by the voice of their Leader saying, "Are you still sleeping and resting? Look, the hour is near, and the Son of Man is betrayed into the hands of sinners. Rise, let us go! Here comes my betrayer!" (Matt. 26:45–46).

You've been jolted from sleep. Like me, you've probably also fallen asleep at a time when you should have been awake and alert. Imagine John trying to shake off the numbing weariness and feeling guilty that he hadn't stayed awake. Then picture his young face as he panned the mountainside and saw an entire detachment of soldiers ascend the hill carrying torches, lanterns, and weapons.

To me one of the most amazing moments in the final hours of Christ's life happened when He answered the soldiers' demand for Jesus of Nazareth by saying, "I am he," and the crowd drew back and fell to the ground. In the most literal rendering of His response, the word *he* doesn't appear in the original Greek. I believe they experienced a compulsory buckling of the knees because the Son of God announced the name by which God said He'd be remembered throughout all generations: "I Am!" (Exod. 3:14). John himself recorded this scene. You can bet he knew it by heart. John also saw a sword take the ear off the high priest's servant and was the only Gospel writer who divulged Peter as the swordsman.

We are told another important detail in John 18:15: "Simon Peter was following Jesus, and so was another disciple. Now that disciple was known to the high priest, and entered with Jesus into the court of the high priest" (NASB). Many scholars believe the description of *another disciple* refers to John.

If we're accurate in what seems an obvious assumption, while several of the disciples followed from a distance, John appeared to have been the closest eyewitness of the Twelve as the final hours unfolded. Whether or not he saw the trial before Pilate, he very likely stood close enough to hear.

Camp on 19:16. "Finally Pilate handed him over to them to be crucified." Finally??? Hadn't these events happened so quickly that John's mind could hardly fathom what he had seen? Hadn't they just accompanied Christ down the Mount of Olives a few days earlier as the masses waved palm branches and proclaimed Jesus as Messiah? Obviously the wording means that Pilate finally handed Christ over after they had tossed Him back and forth from court to court like a tennis ball in a fixed match. I'd like to interject, however, an additional kind of *finally*. Read each Scripture below and meditate on the word *finally* after each.

I will put enmity
between you and the woman,
and between your offspring and hers;
he will crush your head,
and you will strike his heel. (Gen. 3:15) FINALLY.

I will make you into a great nation
and I will bless you;
I will make your name great,
and you will be a blessing.
. . .
and all peoples on earth
will be blessed through you. (Gen. 12:2–3) FINALLY.

Go down and bring Aaron up with you. But the priests and the people must not force their way through to come up to the LORD, or he will break out against them. (Exod. 19:24) FINALLY.

King Solomon and the entire assembly of Israel that had gathered about him were before the ark, sacrificing so many sheep and cattle that they could not be recorded or counted. (2 Chron. 5:6) FINALLY.

Then came the day of Unleavened Bread on which the Passover lamb had to be sacrificed. (Luke 22:7) FINALLY.

Finally a public road was about to be paved from the Holy Place, through the Holy of Holies, out into the courts of the Jewish men, the Jewish women, and finally to the courts of the Gentiles—right up to your door and mine. Finally a perfect, unblemished Lamb would be sacrificed to fulfill the righteous requirements of the temple's blazing altar. Finally something would happen to reconcile believing man to God once and for all. After thousands of years of man's folly, someone in a cloak of flesh did it right. Finally! Glory to God!

Retrospect and the recorded Word make us much smarter than the disciples had the privilege of being several thousand years ago. In the immediacy of the moment reflected in John 19:16, *finally* simply meant that Pilate made a definitive decision after a long, excruciating night; but to us it represents the best of good news. We don't know how distant John was forced to remain, but can you imagine the verdict filtering through the ranks? "Jesus is going to be crucified!" "The verdict is in: crucifixion!"

Mind you, the verdict was illegal. But it was certainly lethal. They all knew too well what crucifixion entailed. It was the worst nightmare of anyone alive in that part of the world. John could not possibly have assimilated the information calmly. Imagine the hot knife of shock searing through his stomach. Try to imagine what kinds of things must have gone through his mind as he heard the verdict.

After beating Jesus within inches of His life, they held His hands and feet against the crude wood and fastened Him there with a hammer and three long nails. Whether or not John saw the pounding of the hammer, heaven could hear the pounding of his heart. At a time when any thinking man would want to run for his life, the youngest of all the disciples stayed.

Near the cross. That's what the Gospel of John says. Above the young man hung his world. His hero. His attachment. His future. His leader. Love of his life. Three years earlier he had been minding his own business trying to gain his daddy's approval with a boat and a net. He hadn't asked for Jesus. Jesus had asked for him. And here he stood. Isaiah's startling prophecy tells us that by the time the foes of Jesus had finished with Him, His appearance was disfigured beyond that of any man, and His form marred beyond human likeness (Isa. 52:14).

"When Jesus therefore saw his mother and the disciple standing by, whom he loved, he saith unto his mother, Woman, behold thy son!" (John 19:26 KJV). Don't take it lightly. Hear it. Not the way the passion plays do it. Hear the real thing. Hear a voice erupting from labored outburst as Jesus tried to lift Himself up and draw breath to speak. Every word He said from the cross is critical by virtue of the fact that Jesus' condition made speaking harder than dying. Chronic pain is jealous like few other things. It doesn't like to share. If a man is in pain, he can hardly think of anything else, and yet Jesus did. I think perhaps because the pain of His heart, if at all possible, exceeded the pain of His shredded frame. The look of His mother's face. Her horror. Her suffering.

Jesus gazed straight upon the young face of the one standing nearby. Less than twenty-four hours earlier, this face had nestled against His chest in innocent affection. John, like our Melissa, was the baby of the family . . . and he knew it. He no doubt reveled in its privilege. If anyone had an excuse to run from the cross, perhaps it was John, and yet he didn't.

Jesus saw the disciple whom He loved standing nearby. I believe indescribable love and compassion hemorrhaged from His heart. "Then saith he to the disciple, Behold thy mother! And from that hour that disciple took her unto his own home" (19:27 KJV).

If the cross is about anything, it is about reconciliation. "For he himself is our peace, who has made the two one and has destroyed the barrier, the dividing wall of hostility" (Eph. 2:14). The unbelief of Christ's brothers had raised a wall of hostility between them and His disciples. As Christ gazed upon His beloved mother and His beloved disciple, He saw His own two worlds desperately in need of reconciliation and a woman who no doubt was torn between the two. Simeon's prophecy to Mary was fulfilled before Jesus' very eyes: "A sword will pierce even your own soul" (Luke 2:35 NASB). How like Jesus to start stitching a heart back together even as the knife was tearing it apart. One day soon His family and His disciples would be united, but the firstfruit of that harvest waved beneath the cross of Christ. "From that time on, this disciple took her into his home."

How perfectly appropriate! Right at the foot of the cross we're about to discover the very quality that set the apostle John apart from all the rest. I am a huge fan of the apostle Peter and can relate to him far more readily than John, but the inspired words the Holy Spirit later entrusted to the Son of Thunder suggest a profound uniqueness. I am reminded of an Old Testament saint about whom God said, "But my servant Caleb has a different spirit and follows me wholeheartedly." God didn't mean a different Holy Spirit. All we who are redeemed have the same Holy Spirit. God referred to something wonderful about Caleb's own human spirit that made him unique. I believe John had something similar. These were fallible men prone to the dictates of their own flesh just like the rest of us, but they had something in them that was almost incomparable when overtaken by the Holy Spirit. They were simply different.

You and I have arrived at a red-letter moment on which much of the remainder of our journey hinges. I am convinced we've stumbled on the thing that set John apart and made him the fertile soil into which God could sow the seeds of such a Gospel . . . such epistles . . . and such a revelation. John remained nearby Jesus whether his leader was on the Mount of Transfiguration or in the deep of Gethsemane's suffering. John leaned affectionately upon Him during the feast but also followed Him into the courts for the trials. John clung to Jesus when He raised the dead, and he clung to Jesus when He became the dead.

John was found nearby when human reasoning implied his faithful Leader's mission had failed. He could not have comprehended that the plan of the ages was going perfectly. Yet he remained. He who looked upon a face that had shone like the sun (Matt. 17:2) was willing to look upon a face bloody and spit upon. He stayed nearby during both Christ's brightest and darkest hours. The young disciple knew Jesus in the extremities. John was willing to look when others would have covered their eyes, and he beheld Him. How can we behold what we are unwilling to see?

We cannot claim to know anyone intimately whom we've not known in the intensity of both agony and elation. Anyone with eyes willing to truly behold Jesus will at times be confused and shocked by what he sees. You see, if we're willing to be taken to the extremes of His glory where intimate knowledge is gained, we will undoubtedly see things of Him we cannot explain and that sometimes disturb.

Then comes the question: Will we walk away from Jesus when from human understanding He looks weak and defeated? Do you know what I mean by that question?

What do we do when we can't explain what Jesus is doing?

Will we remain nearby when He hasn't stopped a tragedy?

When based on earthly evidence, human reasoning is left to one of two harrowing conclusions: He is either mean or weak. Think, beloved, about what I'm saying. Will we cling when our human reasoning implies evil has defeated Him? Or that evil seems to be found in Him? Will we stand by faith when human logic says to run?

That's what will make us different.

Chapter 12

A RACE TO THE TOMB

So Peter and the other disciple started for the tomb. Both were running,
but the other disciple outran Peter and reached the tomb first. (John 20:3–4)

*A*fter this, Jesus, knowing that all things had already been accomplished, to fulfill the Scripture, said, 'I am thirsty.' . . . Therefore when Jesus had received the sour wine, He said, 'It is finished!' And He bowed His head, and gave up His spirit" (John 19:28, 30 NASB).

Sometimes violent circumstances shake the earth beneath our feet. We feel as if a canyon has suddenly appeared and we've been hurled into it. Our emotions swing wildly, and we think we'll be torn in two. Those like Mary and John who loved Jesus most must have felt such a dichotomy of emotions at the finality of His death. They must have almost shut down like a breaker on an overloaded circuit. Reflecting on the events of the previous three years for John and thirty-three years for Mary, hear the echo of those words again: "It is finished." Imagine the feelings they must have experienced.

Watching someone suffer violent pain causes most loved ones to feel relief when it ends, even if death bid it cease. Then true to our self-destructive, self-condemning natures, relief often gives way to guilt. To add to the heap, the finality of the death ushers in feelings of hopelessness. Why? Because humanity has bone-deep indoctrination in the following statement: Where there is life, there is hope.

Not in God's strange economy. That day of all days, where there was death, there was hope. What mind could have fathomed it? And strangely, even now for those of us in Christ, our greatest hope is in what lies beyond our deaths. We stand on the edge of our cliff-like emotions looking into the deep cavern of our grief, and we're sure that the jump will kill us. For those of us who entrust our feeble selves to our faithful Creator, in ways I can neither explain nor describe, it doesn't. In Jesus, when death of some kind comes and we are willing to take it to the cross, remain nearby, and suffer its grief, we will also experience the resurrection.

We say, "But part of me has died with it." And indeed it has. Hear the words of Christ echo from the grave: "I tell you the truth, unless a kernel of wheat falls to the ground and dies, it remains only a single seed. But if it dies, it produces many seeds" (John 12:24). As a child bearing the name of Christ, if a part of you has died, in time it was meant to produce many seeds. Has it? Have we lived long enough and cooperated thoroughly enough to see tender shoots come forth from the barren ground? Oh, Beloved, don't give up!

We hear so much talk about the phases of grief: the shock, the anger, often depression, then, finally, acceptance . . . if we're lucky. We're led to believe that acceptance of death is the final stage of grief, but if we're in Christ, the final stage has not come until we've allowed God to bring forth resurrection life and many seeds from the kernel of wheat that fell to the ground. Yes, we have to come to acceptance but not just acceptance of the death. Acceptance of the resurrection life. Don't stop until you experience it. Though it tarry, it shall come!

In chapter 20 of his Gospel, John gives his own account of the events that occurred early on the first day of the week. Again, we are pretty safe to assume that the disciple in the scene with Peter is John himself. Mary Magdalene went first to the tomb. When she found it empty, she went to tell the others.

We have no idea where Mary found Peter and John, but she found them together. As usual. They were dear friends, weren't they? They had most likely known one another all their lives. Since we so often see them paired without James, I wonder if Peter was closer to John's age than the older brother's. They'd known each other through the awkward years when their voices began to change and were probably already working together in Zebedee's fishing business. One of them grew a beard, in typical adolescent patches, before the other. Surely they teased each other about girls.

We don't know whether John was married, but without a doubt he celebrated heartily at his buddy's wedding supper. They walked away from their nets on the same day and followed this magnetic man from Nazareth. For the last three years they had lived the Great Adventure together. They had seen things people would not even believe. And now they had seen something they themselves couldn't believe. Their fearless leader beaten to a bloody pulp and nailed to a criminal's cross. Jesus was dead. And to top it off, missing.

"They have taken the Lord out of the tomb, and we don't know . . ." Their feet began moving before their minds could think. They were running. Harder. Faster. Hearts pounding. Adrenaline pumping. Fear surging. Butterflies catching. "Where is He?" For crying out loud, "What is He? WHO is He?" So many questions. So many doubts. Flashes of hope. But why? It was hopeless after all. Wasn't it?

They had walked side by side for years. Now they ran side by side. I realize I'm reading something into the picture that wasn't intended by the author, but at this emotionally heightened moment in Scripture, I am amused at the man in John to incidentally tell us that he outran Peter. Ever competitive, aren't they? Then the same youth that outran Peter appeared to have chickened out on going into the tomb. Both instances seem to indicate his younger age. We're told in John 20:8, "Finally the other disciple, who had reached the tomb first, also went inside." Can you just imagine Peter saying, "Come on, John! It's OK. Mary was right. No one's here. But look at this!"? Strips of linen were lying there, and the one that had been wrapped around Jesus' head was folded up all by itself.

Now who in the world do you think folded up that napkin (v. 7 KJV)? If you figure Jesus probably rose right out of those grave clothes, I wonder if one of the angels God summoned to guard the tomb and tell the news had picked it up and folded it.

Peter later wrote of how the angels desired to understand the great salvation provided for humans (1 Pet. 1:10–12). As glorious as the celestial beings are, I don't think they can comprehend the greatness and grace of so radical a salvation. The angels were created to praise the very One that we rejected . . . and killed.

Surely the angels were horrified that the Father didn't summon them to stop the madness. If the archangel Michael and the devil disputed over the body of Moses (Jude 9), can you even imagine the confrontation over this Body? The whole plan must have seemed preposterous to them. Two of them were assigned to watch over the body of the Beloved One. One at His head. One at His feet. Total silence. Not a twitch. Weeping endured for a long winter's night. Would joy ever come in the morning?

The Father had waited long enough. He didn't even let the sun come up. He created the day. He'd say when it was morning. After all, the darkness is light to Him (Ps. 139:12). Suddenly the Lord God Omnipotent raised His mighty arm and unleashed strength beyond comprehension. Somehow I don't think the lifeless body of Christ gradually grew warm. No, I'm convinced the blood flashed red-hot through His veins and He stood to His feet so fast the grave clothes couldn't stick to Him. Clothed in resurrection raiment, Christ Jesus the Savior of the world stepped out of the tomb before the stone had a chance to get out of the way.

According to Matthew 28:2, what happened next shook the ground. "A severe earthquake had occurred, for an angel of the Lord descended from heaven and came and rolled away the stone and sat upon it" (NASB). More than a few times I've been called the Drama Queen. May I have the honor of presenting to you His Truly, God Almighty, the King of Drama? Compared to Him, I'm nothing but a knot on a log. Yep, He's got the drama thing going, and I for one don't want to be caught sitting when a standing ovation is in order.

Meanwhile, back at John 20, Mary returned to the tomb after telling Peter and John. She tarried long enough to see the resurrected Lord Jesus face-to-face. How I thank God that He appointed His Son to bring such dignity to women. Especially one like me who had been so defeated and disturbed in her past. In a tender way, Mary was the very first one Christ sent forth to bring the best news of all: Jesus is alive! Oh, that we would not be like the stone. May we be moved every time the news hits us afresh.

Now picture the scene in John 20:19–20. Mary took the news just as Christ instructed. The clock ticked slowly through the daylight hours as the disciples tried to assimilate Mary's report. Somewhere in this time frame Jesus appeared to Peter in an encounter that I believe was so private, we are intentionally left without a single detail (1 Cor. 15:5). We have no reason to believe John had yet laid eyes on the resurrected Lord.

The disciples are gathered in a room "for fear of the Jews" (John 20:19). Imagine the situation. Feel the oppression of the fear of man in the air. Picture the bars across the doors and the captives inside who only a short time before had wielded power to cast out demons and heal the sick. Had they been stripped of their authority? Of their abilities? No, indeed. Powerlessness is always the message the enemy sends fear to bring.

Suddenly Jesus walked right through their barriers and appeared among them. I've been there. I bet you have, too. Like a father has compassion on children, so Jesus has compassion on us (Ps. 103:13). He knew what their finite minds needed, so He showed them His hands and side. Have you ever noticed how we constantly expect people to heal up from the beatings of life and lose their scars? I'm somehow comforted to know that Christ still has His. In a very real sense the scars from the wounds of the very friends that surrounded Him . . . and all the rest of us He will ever call friend.

Picture the expressions on their faces. Feel the oppression lift in the glorious imposition of electric life. Now look around the scene of your imagination and find our friend John. Wait for a moment, even a few seconds, when Jesus' eyes may have fastened on him alone.

Somehow in my imagination, I see young John's eyebrows pinned to his hairline, eyes as big as saucers. I think he probably froze for a second until the love of Christ melted him like butter. Then I wonder if he broke out in such a toothy grin that Jesus wanted to laugh. Someone as young as John probably was not only thinking the same things as the others, he might have been thinking, perhaps even saying, "We won!" And indeed they had. They had won Christ.

Chapter 13

WHAT ABOUT HIM?

When Peter saw him, he asked, "Lord, what about him?" (John 21:21)

One of the postresurrection images of Christ I love most is in John 20:17. Jesus has to tell Mary Magdalene to peel herself from Him so both of them can do what God had called them to do. The moment she recognized Jesus, she obviously latched on to Him for dear life, as if to say, "Now that I've found You, I will never let You go!"

Although you and I have never seen Christ face-to-face, we're not altogether different. We sometimes receive a fresh revelation of Christ in a moment of crisis and don't want to budge from it for the rest of our days. Christ seems to say to us, "Yes, this revelation is a gift to you, but be careful not to get stuck here. Don't cling to your 'sightings' of Me. Let those moments be fuel for your future. Walk by faith and not by sight in what I've called you to do. There's work to be done! Rest assured I'll always be with you because now that I've found you, I will never let you go."

I don't doubt that once they saw their resurrected Savior, the disciples wanted to hang on to Him just as tightly as did Mary Magdalene. They were just as unable. Acts 1:3 tells us Christ revealed Himself for forty days after He rose from the dead.

Come with me. Let's sit on the shore of the Sea of Galilee, also called the Sea of Tiberias, and watch one of the last encounters Christ appointed to the disciples before He returned with them to the Mount of Olives. Our eyes will be on the events recorded in John 21. Although the disciple-oriented spotlight seems to be on Peter, we will focus on John's role in the events described.

John 21:2 tells us that Simon Peter, Thomas, Nathanael, James, John, and two other disciples were all gathered in a fishing boat. My husband would tell you that seven men in your average boat is at least five too many, but Peter and the others had obviously returned to the commercial vessel where Peter had earned his living for years. He seems to have ascribed to this philosophy: when you don't know what to do, do what you used to do. Even though the disciples must have been ecstatic to have Christ in their midst, I believe He purposely let those days become an identity challenge for them. Notice Jesus didn't hang around with them every minute He was back. He had appeared to the disciples twice before this encounter (John 21:14).

The fact that Jesus didn't bind Himself to them during His brief post-resurrection tenure must have been confusing to them. I'm not sure they knew how they fit into Christ's plans from this side of the grave. Surely the thought occurred to them, "What need does anyone powerful enough to walk out of a tomb have for the likes of us?" They didn't understand that Christ's primary purpose during those forty days was for people to understand that He was God. Keep in mind, Jesus had more on His agenda than appearing only to the apostles. First Corinthians 15:5–7 lets us know Jesus appeared to over five hundred disciples.

Psalm 46:10 tells us what to do when we're not sure where we fit in God's action plan. The psalm says, "Cease striving and know that I am God" (NASB).

Yep. Be still and know it ourselves. Don't default into our past. Don't jump the gun for our future. Just behold and know. Instructions will come when the time is right. In the meantime, *being* is so much harder than *doing*, isn't it? Thankfully, Jesus knew where to find His disciples anyway, and He interrupted their doing with His own being. John seemed to have a better grasp of what Christ had come to be than any of the others at this point. John is only attributed four words in this scene: "It is the Lord."

Oh, that you and I would come to recognize what is the Lord and what is not. The second John announced Jesus, Peter jumped from the boat and swam to Him with all his might. I realize our primary attentions are on John in this study, but I can't let this moment pass without putting the flashlight on one of Peter's sterling moments. In our Christian circles we so often surround ourselves with people of similar practice of faith. We have our unspoken codes. Spiritual practices that we consider acceptable. We also agree on things that are not. Things that are weird. Behaviors that are just . . . well . . . overboard. Then someone jumps ship and decides he or she doesn't care what the rest of us think. Nothing is going to get between him and Jesus. Glory! As much as I love John, in this scene I want to be Peter!

Actually, I remember well when I began to break the unspoken code of just how far my church compadres and I would go with this "spiritual thing." Years ago those closest to me charged me with going overboard far more disapprovingly than others. Do you know what, Beloved? I wouldn't climb back in that boat for anything. How about you? Have you jumped out of the boat of what is most comfortable and acceptable and decided you want Jesus even if you have to make a fool of yourself to get to Him? If not, are you ready? What's holding you back?

Let me warn you. Intimacy with Christ doesn't always feel warm and fuzzy. Just ask Peter. That water was cold! This scene would have taken place during the latter part of our month of May. The days are very warm in that part of Galilee, but the temperature drops dramatically during the night. Mind you, this fishing trip took place before breakfast (John 21:12). No wonder the rest of the disciples followed in the boat! I believe Jesus esteemed Peter's impetuous determination to get to his Lord. I am also convinced that this act was an important part of Peter's restoration. Notice he didn't ask to walk on water. He was willing to dog paddle in ice water to get to Jesus this time.

I am convinced Peter's solo pursuit set the stage for Christ to single him out in the redemptive scene that followed. His leap from the boat may have suggested that at this point Peter truly loved Christ more than these. John 21:15–23 records the famous scene when Jesus recommissioned Peter after his denial. I love this scene because it represents something of a do-over. In verse 19 Christ told Peter, "Follow me!"

Three years earlier Peter heard the same words and, to his credit, he had done it. But he had done it in his own strength and with his own agenda. His own ambition. The result was "Woman, I don't know him" (Luke 22:57), and that was the last time Peter warmed himself by a fire.

Ambition could not supply the motivation to follow Jesus where Peter would have to go. In John 21 Jesus repeated the one motivation that would suffice. Jesus said to him the third time, "Simon, son of John, do you love Me?" (John 21:17).

Oh, beloved, can you see the significance? No other motivation will last! We might feed the sheep or serve the flock based on other motivations for a while, but only one thing will compel us to follow the Lord Jesus Christ faithfully to the death: love! No one had more spiritual tenacity than the apostle Paul, and he made no bones about what kept him on the path amidst unparalleled pain and persecution. In 2 Corinthians 5:14, he wrote, "The love of Christ controls us" (NASB). James 1:12 says the Lord has promised the crown of life "to those who love him."

You see, our callings may differ, but if we're going to follow Jesus Christ in the power of the crucified life, our compellings will be the same. Only love compels to the death. Dear one, life is hard. Opposition is huge. Circumstances will inevitably happen in all our lives that will defy all discipline, determination, and conviction. Love keeps burning when everything else disintegrates in an ashen heap. Pray for this one thing more than you pray for your next breath. I am convinced love is everything.

I wasn't the first one convinced. I simply follow in a long line of believers who failed their way into the discovery that love is the highest priority and motivating force in the entire life of faith. Generations before any of us wised up, a young disciple named John was so drawn to Christ's discourse on love that he couldn't help but listen as Jesus and Peter walked away from the others to talk. I am convinced the conversation recorded in John 21:15–23 began in the group of eight. Perhaps in the course of the question and answer, Jesus quite naturally stood up, brushed Himself off, and took a few steps away from the small circle of men. Peter, unnerved by his own interpretation of the repetitive question, probably jumped to his feet and followed.

The New American Standard tells us that Peter was hurt because Jesus questioned his love a third time: "Lord, you know all things; you know that

I love you." Mind you, he was still drenched to the bone from his zeal. Jesus then prophesied the reason why Peter's love for Him would be so critical. Peter would be asked to glorify God by giving his own life. Only love would make him willing.

Then, as if to say, "Knowing all this and with your eyes wide open," Christ reissued the call, "Follow me!" Don't downplay it for an instant. The cost of the call was huge. We don't know what caused Peter to suddenly look behind him and see John following them. Perhaps John stepped on a branch that had fallen to the ground. Perhaps he groaned audibly when he heard Christ foretell his closest friend's future.

I don't believe John trailed them out of selfish curiosity. I think he sensed the enormity of the concept the risen Teacher was teaching through this emotional interchange. This was no tiptoed eavesdropping. I think he was drawn to the conversation like a magnet. I believe Scripture will prove that John, perhaps like no other disciple in that circle, assimilated the profound implications of what his beloved Savior was saying. "You are My called ones. You have tough futures ahead of you, but the glory God will gain will be immeasurable. Love is the only motivation that can afford this kind of cost."

When Peter saw John, he asked, "'Lord, and what about this man?'"

At times like these I wish we had the Bible in its completely inspired and original form on videotape! We would be far better equipped to interpret a scene accurately if we could see the expressions on the face of the speaker and hear his tone of voice. Since we have no such help, words like Peter's may have as many different interpretations as I have commentaries. I'm looking at two different commentaries right this moment, and each says something different about Peter's motivation for asking this question. Here's the good news: that means we can speculate without getting too far off base. What do you think was in Peter's voice? Do you think his question was out of deep concern for John as one of my commentaries supposes, or did it arise out of jealousy or some other negative emotion as the other suggests?

No matter what your interpretation may be, I think we all can admit that the question plagues us as well at times, no matter what our reason for asking. Perhaps you have served near someone else, and God has called you to suffer some pretty difficult circumstances while he or she seems to flourish in relative ease. Or perhaps your heart has broken for someone who works so hard and serves so diligently, but difficulty is her constant companion. Maybe one of your children has seemed so blessed and gifted by God and you keep looking at the other and asking, "Lord, what about him?"

Whatever your experience or mine, I know we can benefit from Jesus' command in John 21:22: "If I want him to remain alive until I return, what is that to you? You must follow me!" Does His response speak to you as strongly as it does to me in times when I wonder what God is doing in someone else's life?

Beloved, over and over Jesus tells us, "You can trust Me!" In this scene He is saying to His present-day disciples, "You can trust Me with you, and you can trust Me with them. I am the same God to all of you, but I have a different plan for each of you. You won't miss it if you keep following. Remember, I've been a carpenter by trade. Custom blueprints are My specialty. God's glory is My goal. Now fill your canteen to the brim with love and follow Me."

Chapter 14

IF AND WHEN

You will receive power when the Holy Spirit comes on you. (Acts 1:8)

$\mathcal{L}$et's not work up to something profound in this chapter. Let's just get started with it. Before we go a moment further, try to grasp this: They saw Him. They touched Him. The disciples came face-to-face and hand to nail-scarred hand with the resurrected Lord of hosts. Yes, we walk by faith, but do you realize that our faith is based on Rock-solid fact? We are going to stand on the sidelines and watch the disciples experience some pretty wild things, and yet they happened just as Scripture says they did.

You see, the testimony of the incomparable Word of Truth makes what seems incredible perfectly credible. We begin with Acts 1:1–12. You are probably very familiar with the scene described in these verses, but sometimes overfamiliarity can be the biggest treasure thief of all. Rewind the verses again, and let's replay them in slow motion.

Luke begins the Book of Acts, the companion volume to the Gospel of Luke, at the end of Christ's earthly tenure. Luke tells us Jesus had showed Himself to be alive "by many convincing proofs, appearing to them over a period of forty days, and speaking of the things concerning the kingdom of God" (v. 3 NASB). Now at the end of that time, Christ and His disciples gathered at the Mount of Olives (v. 12).

Jesus spoke these final words: "You will receive power when the Holy Spirit comes on you; and you will be my witnesses in Jerusalem, and in all Judea and Samaria, and to the ends of the earth" (v. 8). I am convinced we can as readily apply Jesus' promise of power as did Christ's original disciples. The Holy Spirit comes no other way but in power. His omnipotence is part of His essence. The Spirit of Christ cannot come to us weak or fragile. He comes with power.

Before our chapter's conclusion, we'll also see that when we receive what the Holy Spirit is fully equipped to apply to us, the effects show. In fact, that's the point. Paul said we have this treasure in earthen vessels (2 Cor. 4:7). The "treasure" Paul is touting is the Holy Spirit. Besides the multifaceted ministries of the Holy Spirit to each believer, according to the verse, God's goal in giving us this treasure is "that the surpassing greatness of the power may be of God and not from ourselves."

Beloved, God wants to hang out all over you! Don't you see? That's why our circumstances and challenges are often beyond us! If life were completely manageable, we'd manage on our own strength, and no one would see the living proof of God's existence in us. We were left here for the distinct purpose of becoming witnesses to an injured world in desperate need of a Savior.

Do you belong to Jesus Christ? If so, the Holy Spirit dwells in you (Rom. 8:9), and He did not cheat you of a single ounce of His power. He came to show off in you. As He does, your whole life will become a living witness just like the disciples. Our assignments may differ, but you and I have exactly the same Holy Spirit that Christ promised to His first disciples. If we only knew what we had, our lives would be so different!

After Christ gave them the assurance of the coming power of the Holy Spirit, we are told He was taken up "before their very eyes, and a cloud hid him from their sight" (Acts 1:9). Try to imagine being one of the eleven on the Mount of Olives that day. Verse 11 seems to imply they were all standing, so imagine that they were basically eye to eye with Jesus, not letting a single word from His mouth fall to the ground. Jesus promised them the power of the Holy Spirit; then without warning the disciples realized that they were glancing somewhat upward as He seemed a tad taller. As He rose a head above them, surely some of them looked down and saw that His feet were no longer on the ground. Luke 24:50 tells us Christ was blessing them as He lifted off the ground. Can you imagine what they were thinking and feeling?

Perhaps by now your imagination has drawn a rough sketch of the apostle John on the canvas of your mind. Picture him and the others bug-eyed with their mouths gaping open. Had my grandmother been one of the disciples (a frighteningly funny thought), she would have stood there saying, "Now, don't that just beat all?" I feel sure they said something comparable in Aramaic.

Just about the time they might have tried to rub the supernatural sight out of their eyes, God threw a cloudy cloak of shekinah glory over His beloved Son and swept Him home. Oh, don't you know the Father had been watching the clock of earth for that precious moment to finally arrive? While Christ was no prodigal, He was most assuredly a son who had journeyed to a foreign land. I can almost hear the Father say to His servants, "Quick! Bring the best robe and put it on him. Put a ring on his finger and sandals on his feet. Bring the fattened calf and kill it. Let's have a feast and celebrate. For this son of mine was dead and is alive again!" (see Luke 15:22–24).

Had the angels not broken the stare, the remains of eleven stiff carcasses might still be on the Mount of Olives today. The angels said, "Men of Galilee, why do you stand looking into the sky? This Jesus, who has been taken up from you into heaven, will come in just the same way as you have watched Him go into heaven" (Acts 1:11 NASB).

I wonder if their words about the return of Christ stirred up memories of a very recent conversation between Jesus and Peter, overheard by John. You'll remember Jesus said to Peter, of John, "If I want him to remain alive until I return, what is that to you? You must follow me" (John 21:22). The implication of Christ's words may have led both Peter and John to wonder if the younger son of Zebedee would live to see Jesus return. We know for a fact that such a rumor spread. Whether or not Peter and John temporarily mistook Christ's *if* for a *when,* plenty of others did. (Remember, the Gospel was written years later when retrospect made statements like these much clearer.) Beloved, few words in Scripture are bigger than *if.* Watch for it and be careful not to make it a *when.* The Word of God is full of unconditional promises, but plenty of other statements of biblical fact hinge on an *if.* In this very chapter we've discussed a priority promise Christ gave in Acts 1:8. It's a *when* statement: "when the Holy Spirit comes on you."

Those of us in Christ may keep wondering *if* we have the power to be victorious in the challenge before us, but God's wondering *when* we're going to believe Him!

Scripture tells us the disciples' return to the city was a "Sabbath day's walk," which would have been about three-fourths of a mile. I have walked that brief trek a number of times, and it is straight downhill until you ascend back up the temple mount to the city gates. You can hardly keep from walking fast due to the incline, but somehow I'm imagining their mouths were traveling faster than their feet. (You're imagining that mine was too!)

We read that the disciples went upstairs to the room where they were staying (Acts 1:13). The definite article and the emphatic arrangement of the words in the Greek sentence structure indicate that the location was well-known and highly significant to the disciples.[1] In the days that followed, the now eleven apostles were joined for prayer by several women, Mary, and Jesus' siblings. Acts 1:15 shows Peter speaking to that first New Testament cell group that numbered 120 people.

You may attend a church about this size and wonder with frustration what God could do with such a small group of people. Dear One, when the Holy Spirit falls on a place, it doesn't matter how small the group— things start happening! Remember, the Holy Spirit comes in order to get results! Let's find out what can happen when the Holy Spirit interrupts a prayer meeting. You and I are about to behold the disciples' *when!*

Now I want you to come with me on one of my favorite journeys. Look at the headings in Leviticus 23. This awesome Old Testament chapter records the annual feasts God appointed to Israel. I am convinced every one of them is ultimately fulfilled in Jesus Christ. In the context of this chapter, we'll emphasize three.

The most important of the Jewish feasts was (and is) Passover (Lev. 23:4–8). I so love the last few words in 1 Corinthians 5:7: "Christ our Passover also has been sacrificed" (NASB). We can easily see the connection that Jesus is the fulfillment of all the Passover lambs slain in history.

The feast that immediately followed Passover was Firstfruits, when a sheaf of the first grain of the harvest was waved before the Lord for His acceptance (Lev. 23:11). This was the day after the Passover Sabbath, obviously falling on a Sunday. First Corinthians 15:20–23 clearly says that the resurrection of Jesus was the firstfruits. "Now Christ has been raised from the dead, the first fruits of those who are asleep" (v. 21 NASB).

Fifty (pente) days after Passover came the Feast of Weeks, later called Pentecost. It was the celebration of seven weeks of harvest. The one sheaf waved on Firstfruits turned into an entire harvest celebrated seven weeks and one day later. "Christ the first fruits, after that those who are Christ's at His coming" (1 Cor. 15:23 NASB). The Feast of Weeks was the presentation of an offering of new grain to the Lord (Lev. 23:16). In other words, it was the celebration of harvest reaped.

Now do you see the significance of what happened on Pentecost? Fifty days earlier Christ, the Passover Lamb, had been crucified. On the day of Firstfruits, that very Sunday morning, His life was waved acceptable before God as the firstfruit from the dead. Fifty days after Pentecost, the Holy Spirit came just as Christ promised. And He came to show off! He revealed His all-surpassing power in simple jars of clay that day. The Holy Spirit never comes just to show off, however. He comes to show off and bring results: "The Lord added to their number daily those who were being saved" (Acts 2:47).

Beloved, I present to you the first harvest reaped by the life, death, and resurrection of Jesus Christ our Lord. That's Pentecost! And even now I believe we are still living in the continuing harvest of Pentecost. Christ tarries only so that the harvest can reach its peak ripeness and be reaped to the glory of God. He does not will for any to perish but for all to come to repentance (2 Pet. 3:9). He desires everyone. He forces no one. He will not wait forever.

One day the ultimate Feast of Trumpets (Lev. 23:23–24; 1 Thess. 4:16) will come, and we will meet Jesus in the air. Then one day the books will be opened and closed for the last time, and the final judgment will take place (Rev. 20:11–15). The Day of Atonement will be past (Lev. 23:26–27; Rom. 3:23–25). Those who were covered by the blood of the Passover Lamb will tabernacle (Lev. 23:33–34) with God forever and ever . . . and so shall we ever be with the Lord (1 Thess. 4:17).

"But the father said to his servants, 'Quick! Bring the best robe and put it on him. Put a ring on his finger and sandals on his feet. Bring the fattened calf and kill it. Let's have a feast and celebrate. For this son of mine was dead and is alive again. . . .' So they began to celebrate" (Luke 15:22–24).

I feel like getting started a little early. I'm going to go put on some praise music, and I may just put on my dancing shoes!

Chapter 15

JUST A HANDFUL

Then Peter said, "Silver or gold I do not have, but what I have I give you.
In the name of Jesus Christ of Nazareth, walk." (Acts 3:6)

*S*cripture sends me. That's all there is to it. We have an appointment with Peter and John in just a few minutes at Solomon's Temple, but first I need to run ahead and do what Psalm 50:14 says: "Sacrifice thank offerings to God, / fulfill your vows to the Most High." The rocks will cry out if I don't stop and make a thank offering. My heart overflows with inexpressible gratitude to God for the treasure of His Word. He has singlehandedly used His Word to heal me, free me, thrill me, and lead me. I love it so much that sometimes when I finish reading a segment that has opened a fresh spring in the deep well of my soul, I cannot help but gently, reverently kiss the page.

The Word is the only truly divine substance that is touchable and tangible in this earthly realm. I do not worship a book. I worship the One who breathed life onto the page in the form of human vocabulary so that mortal creatures like me could hear the very voice of Jehovah God. I could weep at the thought. Often a dear sister who has been touched by one of the Bible studies will thank me for writing them. A lump wells in my throat as I try to articulate to you what I want to say to her:

Beloved, I thank you. Do you realize that your desire for these studies is the very thing God uses to keep this woman who was once so broken and self-destructive in a perpetual state of healing and filling? Life in the Word has released me from life in the pit and caused my soul to dance in meadows of wildflowers and swim in coral reefs! I trek to exotic places on the other side of the globe and step back in time to an ancient civilization and all without leaving my office! I am awash with gratitude to God and to this small slice of the body of Christ that gives me such invitation.

At the conclusion of our previous chapter, you and I celebrated the Pentecost of three thousand souls. Added to the strong cell group of 120, Solomon's Temple would have paled in comparison to the gleaming harvest. Before we get to the heart of this chapter's study, consider the description of the early church in Acts 2:42–47. The following is my paraphrase: They were devoted to both the apostles' teaching and to the fellowship of fellow believers. They regularly saw wonders and miraculous signs done by the apostles. They shared their wealth and livelihoods, giving to anyone who had need. They met together daily for prayer and fellowship with glad and sincere hearts. Finally, people were being saved and added to the church.

Now that's a church I want to attend! Let's get to our appointment with Peter and John. Acts 3:1–13 tells of the two entering the temple. Peter healed a lame beggar, which drew a crowd. Then when the crowd had gathered, Peter preached a powerful sermon pointing the people to the Jesus they had crucified.

Can you believe the change in Peter already? Primarily the difference is the anointing of the Holy Spirit, but I believe Peter's former failure was a huge part of his present victory. We wonder why God allows some of us, yours truly included, to be sifted like wheat. Then when we see the difference in Peter, the reason is clear. God only allows servants to be sifted who have something that needs sifting!

If we feel like we're going through a sifting season because God has allowed the enemy to play havoc in our lives, we are wise to cut to the chase and find out what God wants sifted. God saw the same thing in my earlier ministry that I believe He saw in Peter's. You spell it P-R-I-D-E. Let me assure you, God's methods of separating the chaff from the grain are very effective.

What you have in this chapter of Scripture is a pair of mighty fine servants. Allow me to highlight a few things I love about Peter and John in this scene.

1. They cherished their heritage. Please don't miss the fact that the New Testament church was Jewish! According to Acts 2:46 the believers met daily in the temple courts. Acts 3 opens with Peter and John on their way to the three o'clock prayer time at the temple, which coincided with the evening sacrifice. The thought never occurred to them to cast off their Judaism for their new faith in Christ. For heaven's sake, Jesus was Jewish! Nothing could have been more absurd. Their Messiah had fulfilled their Jewish heritage. They were no longer obligated to the letter of the Law because Christ had met its righteous requirements. They were free, however, to enjoy its precepts and practices as expressions of their faith in Jesus.

Can you imagine how belief in Christ and their newfound knowledge of Jesus as the answer to every symbolic practice spiced up their participation? Suddenly the black-and-white of their ritual prayer services turned Technicolor with the life of the Spirit. I snicker when I think of observers at Pentecost thinking the disciples must have been drinking. Don't you know they secretly wanted a sip of whatever the believers were having?

Last year I stumbled on a definition of a Hebrew word that I want to share with you. Take a look at the well-loved Scripture, Jeremiah 29:11, " 'For I know the plans I have for you,' declares the LORD, 'plans to prosper you and not to harm you, plans to give you hope and a future.'" According to the Old Testament Lexical Aids of the *Key Study Bible,* the Hebrew word for *future* includes the following explanation: "Its general meaning is after, later, behind, following. The Hebrew way of thinking has been compared to a man rowing a boat; he backs into the future while looking toward where he has been. Therefore, what is 'behind' and what is 'future' come from the same root, 'ahar.'"[1]

Try to grasp this: God cherishes your heritage, too. You may balk, "What are you talking about? My past is horrible!" Listen carefully, Beloved. We are no longer under the law and authority of our pasts, but like Peter and John we are also free to use them as they lend expression to our faith in Jesus. As much as you might not want to hear this, you couldn't become the servant God is calling you to be without the threads of your past being knitted into the Technicolor fabric of your future.

If your heritage had absolutely nothing to do with your future, God is far too practical to have allowed it. I am convinced this is true in my own life. When Satan begged to defile my young life, I don't believe he would ever have gained an ounce of permission from God had my faithful Father not known without a doubt how He could use it. God is never more glorified than when He brings an oak of righteousness (Isa. 61:3) out of what once was so damaged a root.

I love the image of the rowboat in the definition. Don't read more into the definition than you should. Certainly we want to keep our eyes on Jesus. The word picture is simply giving us food for thought. Some of us are so focused on our past, we're not rowing to our futures. Others are trying to turn their backs on their pasts with such denial that no matter how hard they row, they can't make any progress. If we're going to become the effective servants God desires us to be, we need a balance of dealing with our past and facing our future.

Still not convinced? Perhaps you're thinking, *I'd take Peter and John's Jewish heritage over mine any day!* Wonderful! Because in addition to your own, you have their heritage, too! Behold what Galatians 3:29 says about you: "If you belong to Christ, then you are Abraham's seed, and heirs according to the promise." I love that Peter and John cherished their heritage.

2. Peter and John understood true religion. They were not so busy getting to prayer meeting that they missed the beggar at the gate. Don't miss the significance of the location at the gate called Beautiful. Leave it to God to appoint a bitter reality in our "beautiful" scene. Try as we may to avoid the misery, misfortune, and injustice around us, they will find us. My city is filled with gated and extravagant "planned communities" with walls around them to keep the niceties in and the unpleasantries out.

I don't have a single problem with great wealth as long as folks still have a clue about the rest of the world. God is too faithful to let us hide forever. We have to come out from behind those pristine walls sooner or later, and when we do, one of these days we're going to have a head-on collision with reality. The kind of reality that begs the question, "What are you going to do about this?"

Peter and John could have glanced at the nearest sundial and said, "Oops! We're almost late for prayer meeting. Beg on, brother!" Instead, Peter looked straight at the man as did John (Acts 3:4). Refreshing, isn't it? I'm not much for looking suffering and poverty straight in the face. I'll face it, all right. But I like to look slightly to one side or the other. Not Peter and John. They looked straight at him and likewise demanded that he look straight at them.

Peter may have had many reasons for telling the beggar to look at them, but several things occur to me. We are told the man was crippled from birth. Actually "from the womb" would be a more literal translation of the Greek. We also are told he was taken to the temple every day. Verse 3 tells us the beggar saw Peter and John, but the inference is clear he didn't really look at them. I think the man had begged so long, he saw himself as nothing more than a beggar. He had ceased to look "normal" people in the eye. He didn't want to look in the face of anything that made him feel more inferior than he already felt.

I'm also convinced that the man's begging had become tragically rote. Completely mechanical. Dear One, I want to say something that may seem harsh. Sometimes we decide God is mean because He won't give us what we're begging for, but we don't realize He has a higher mercy toward our crippled estate. We want a Holy Enabler. God wants to be our Healer. Have you ever begged for something that in retrospect you realize would have done nothing but help keep you in your crippled condition? I sure have!

3. *Peter and John gave what they had.* I love the words in the King James: "Silver and gold have I none; but such as I have give I thee: In the name of Jesus Christ of Nazareth rise up and walk" (Acts 3:6). God never asks us to give what we don't have! Somehow I'm relieved by that assurance. Recently this verse came alive for me. Soon after the terrorist attack on the Twin Towers, clergy and church leadership in New York City found themselves overwhelmed by the task of ministering to their flocks after such unprecedented disaster. The American Association of Christian Counselors was asked to come to the city to lead a training conference for dealing with grief specifically caused by trauma. The AACC quickly pulled together

their most experienced Christian counselors and also asked a handful of Christian speakers to join them. I'm still mystified to have been among them.

On my way in the airplane, I poured out my heart to God and told Him I did not begin to know how to tell them to deal with such inexpressible tragedy. I kept saying, "Lord, I'm over my head here. I'm out of my league. I don't know what I'm talking about, and I have nothing in my catalogue of experience to draw from!"

The Holy Spirit reminded me of this Scripture. God seemed to say, "Beth, I'm not sending you to New York City as a Christian counselor. Don't try to be what you're not. Go and do what I've taught you to do. Teach My Word." Although I was still very intimidated by the task, God's reminder was profound to me. I began my message with Acts 3:6. I confessed my tremendous lack of experience and credentials but pledged that "such as I have give I thee." I was so relieved not to have to try to be something that I'm not, or do something that I don't.

4. *Peter took him by the hand and helped him up.* I love this part of the story. Peter and John knew better than anyone that the power to heal the man came solely from the Holy Spirit. The man wasn't healed because Peter took him by the hand and helped him up. To me, the tender representation here is that Peter offered the man a handful of faith to help him get to his feet. After all, this man had been crippled all his life. What reason did he have to believe he could be healed? All he thought he wanted was a little money. When the beggar grabbed on to Peter's hand, he felt the strength in his grip. The confidence of his faith. In one clasp, Peter offered a handful of faith, and that was all the man needed to come to his feet.

Oh, Beloved, can you see him? Close your eyes and watch! Watch the beggar jump to his feet, his tin cup tumbling down the temple steps and the few measly coins spinning in the afternoon sunshine. Look at the expression on his face! Watch him dance on legs thin from atrophy. Look! Look straight at him! That's him jumping and praising God through the temple courts. Laugh over the horrified expressions on pious faces. Look for the others in the crowd who are ecstatic with joy and decide to grab a handful of faith for themselves.

People recognized him as the same man who used to sit begging at the temple gate called Beautiful, and they were filled with wonder and amazement at what had happened to him. Yep, it was his past that made his present so miraculous.

5. Peter and John took no credit for the miracle. After all, if man can do it, it really isn't a miracle, now is it? Miracles are from God . . . for the likes of crippled man. Someone reading today has been begging God for trivial things like silver and gold when God wants to raise her to her feet to jump, dance, and praise Him. Why do we want God to help us stay like we are? Grab a handful of faith and be changed!

Part 4

BEYOND THE LIMITS

As I first walked the journey you are presently taking through God's Word, I had never given any significant thought to John's place in the early church. Neither had I considered the tremendous impact the benchmark events had on his individual life. The Word of God never gets old to me because no matter how often I've studied a scene, fresh insight can always be gained from a new perspective. The Bible is like a priceless gem held up to a light. If you tilt it and look from a different angle, you see all sorts of new colors. May God grant each of us a new depth of understanding into the Spirit of God piercing the soul of man.

Chapter 16

A NEW FIRE

Then Peter and John placed their hands on them, and they
received the Holy Spirit. (Acts 8:17)

*W*ith the unfolding of the fourth division of our study comes the dramatic start of a new chapter in the lives of Christ's first followers. We just witnessed the New Testament church gathering often for prayer in the temple courts. They savored their Jewish heritage and viewed their faith in Christ as an extension and perpetual fulfillment of their former practices. However, the disciples soon faced a virtual end to their freedom to practice their faith unafraid on temple grounds. Acts 4:13–20 tells how the religious leaders felt threatened by the power of Peter's words. They threatened Peter and John "not to speak or teach at all in the name of Jesus" (v. 18).

Over the next several chapters in the Book of Acts, persecution increased like stones pummeled from the fists of a crazed mob. The reality of the religious establishment's intentions rose frighteningly to the surface as Stephen fell to his knees. I am convinced he was bloodied and bruised by a gnawing and growing paranoia in their souls: What if they were wrong about Jesus of Nazareth? What if they did crucify the Son of glory? They would do everything they could to silence the mouths of those who made them question their own actions.

The Sanhedrin underestimated the tenacity of Christ's unschooled and ordinary followers, who in effect inverted their muzzles and made them megaphones. Acts 8:1–4 tells of God's unusual method of spreading the gospel. Saul embarked on a project to persecute the followers of Jesus and to bring them in chains to Jerusalem. I can't wait for you to read a fitting quote out of a book that's over a century old. In *The Two St. Johns of the New Testament,* James Stalker wrote, "Not infrequently it was by persecution that the new faith was driven out of one place into another, where, but for this reason, it might never have been heard of; so that the opposition which threatened to extinguish the fire of the Gospel only scattered its embers far and wide; and wherever they fell a new fire was kindled."[1]

What amazing providence! When Christ told His disciples that they would receive power and become witnesses not only in Jerusalem but to the uttermost parts of the earth, they never expected His means! No, His ways are not our ways. Our ways would always be comfortable. Convenient. Certainly without hurt or harm. We would always ask that God use the favor of man to increase our harvests. Not the fervor of opposition.

If you've walked with God very long, I have little doubt He has used what you perceived as a very negative means to achieve a positive result. I suspect that God has allowed you to experience a fence pushed down painfully in your life to expand His horizon for you. God is faithful, isn't He? Even when He turns the ignition on a holy bulldozer to plow down a confining fence.

Next in the Acts account, God used Philip to start a revival in Samaria. When the Jerusalem church leadership heard about it, they sent our dynamic duo of Peter and John to find out what was going on.

If we were studying the Book of Acts, I would explore the disciples' encounter with Simon the Sorcerer with you; but since our goal is to study the life, heart, and spirit of the apostle John, something else seizes my attention in this scene. Does the location of Samaria and its relationship to John ring a bell of any kind to you?

The first bell this reference probably rings is the word Christ spoke over the eleven disciples in Acts 1:8 before His ascension. I'd like to suggest that when Christ made the proposal that His disciples would be witnesses in Samaria, He raised a few eyebrows. Jerusalem? No problem. Judea? Absolutely. Ends of the earth? We're Your men, Jesus. But Samaria? Jews despised the Samaritans! If Gentiles were the target of the Jews' prejudices, then the Samaritans were the bull's-eye. And the feelings were mutual.

Samaritans were considered by most Jews to be a mongrel breed. They were border people who lived in the strip of land between the Jews and the Gentiles. The Jews didn't associate with the Samaritans (John 4:9).

The idealists among us might be thinking, *But surely since they followed Christ, the disciples didn't have those kinds of prejudices toward people. After all, they were Christians.*

Luke 9:51–56 gives a far more realistic picture. Our friends James and John wanted to call down fire on a Samaritan village because of a small slight. Don't assume they were being overdramatic and didn't really mean what they were saying. That Jesus took great offense to their suggestion is clear as He turned on His heels and gave them a swift rebuke.

Had Jesus granted their request, all of those Samaritans of age would have perished in their sins. Believers often charge the lost with not taking hell seriously enough, but I'm not sure we take it very seriously ourselves. To hope someone "burns in hell" is profoundly offensive to God and proves we lack His heart (Ezek. 33:11; 2 Pet. 3:9). James and John didn't volunteer to call fire down from heaven to save Jesus the trouble. They wanted the head-trip of wielding that kind of power. They wanted to be hosts of a firework spectacular.

Scripture tells us Jesus looks upon the heart. I wonder if Jesus saw something in young John's heart that was even more lethal than his big brother's. You see, instead of threatening His childish followers with a dose of their own medicine, Jesus chose a far more effective route. In Acts 8:14 Jesus arranged to assign John to be an ambassador of life to the very people he volunteered to destroy. Don't think for an instant John's assignment was coincidental. Even as the words fell from Jesus' lips in Acts 1:8, He may very likely have looked straight at John when He said, ". . . and Samaria."

Earlier I mentioned our naïveté to think followers of Christ are automatically void of prejudices. Whether our preferred prejudices are toward denominations, people of other world religions, colors, or economics, they are usually so deeply ingrained in us that we see them far more readily as the way we are rather than as sin. Prejudice is sin. The prejudgment and stereotype of a grouping of people is sin. James and John used a key word in Luke 9:54: "Lord, do you want us to call fire down from heaven to destroy them?" Prejudice destroys. Entire world wars have been fought and multiplied millions slain over nothing more than what many would term "harmless" prejudice.

One of God's most redemptive tools for dealing with prejudice is appointing His guilty child to get to know a person from the group she or he has judged. I was reared in one denomination and had very few if any relationships in my young life with anyone outside that denomination. Much prejudice evolves from pure ignorance, and I grew up judging some groups of people that I simply didn't understand. God wasn't about to let me stay in my bubble because He intended to develop in me a heart for the entire body of Christ. His redemptive way of accomplishing His goal was to place me in the position of getting to know others who practiced their Christian faith in ways that differed from mine.

The most obvious work God did in my life involved a woman from one of those churches that my old church would have considered maniacal and unsound. We didn't make our judgment from firsthand knowledge, of course. The church simply got dumped into one huge category.

I was in my twenties and "accidentally" developed a friendship with her before I knew where she went to church. I fell in love with her heart for God. She had such a love for His Word, and we boasted in Him often and developed a deep friendship. When I found out her denomination, I was stunned. She wasn't crazy. She wasn't a maniac. She wasn't unsound. When my other friends would make fun of people from that church, I couldn't bring myself to join in anymore. The jokes weren't funny. I learned a very important lesson I hope never to forget. Do we even know the people personally whom we stereotype and judge? Perhaps the better question is, Would we be willing to get to know someone and take the chance of God changing our prejudicial minds?

I don't think for a second John missed the point when the apostles sent him and Peter to the Samaritans. He came face-to-face with them. They, too, were created in the image of God. They, too, loved their children and worried over their welfare. They, too, bruised when they were hit and wept when they were sad. They seemed so different from a distance. Somehow, up close and personal, they didn't seem nearly so . . . weird.

Mind you, these were the same people upon whom John was so anxious to call down destruction. Have you ever noticed it's much easier to hate from a distance?

Acts 8:15 tells us Peter and John prayed for the Samaritans. Persistent prayer is a prejudice-buster every time if we'll let it be. Then something really amazing happened. "Then Peter and John placed their hands on them, and they received the Holy Spirit" (Acts 8:17).

Well, well, well. They got their wish after all. They did call down fire on the Samaritans. The kind of fire that destroys things like hate. Meanness. Prejudice. For those who let this Holy Fire consume them. The kind of fire that destroys the old and births the new. Our God is a consuming fire, and that day He lit the hearts of Samaritans at the hands of Jews.

I want to say something that sounds simple, but it is so profound to me right at this moment: How I praise God that we—sinful, selfish, ignorant mortals—can change. John wasn't stuck with his old prejudices. God neither gave up on Him nor overlooked the transgression. God was gracious enough to push the envelope until change happened. Acts 8:25 concludes the segment with the words, "Peter and John returned to Jerusalem, preaching the gospel in many Samaritan villages." How like Jesus. He turned John's prejudice into a fiery passion.

If one keeps walking with Christ, he can't stay the same. We can cease cooperating, but we'll have to cease walking close to Jesus to do it. We can fake the walk but only for so long. If we truly pursue intimacy with Christ, change will happen. Praise God, it will happen. Beloved, I want to ask you a question as I ask myself the same. What is a way God has dramatically changed your attitude toward a target of your own personal prejudice? If you don't have an answer to that, I'd encourage you to seriously consider your heart.

I'd like to conclude with a look at a fascinating account in Mark 8:22–26. This account is one of the only times in Scripture we see an incomplete healing that necessitated a second work of Christ. Jesus encountered a blind man. First he spat on and touched the man's eyes. The man then said he could see but that people looked to him like trees walking around. When Jesus again touched the man's eyes, the healing was completed, and the man saw clearly.

Since Jesus knew just what He was doing, He obviously had a point to make to the blind man or perhaps His observers. I like the King James Version of Mark 8:24. When asked if he saw anything, the man looked up and answered, "I see men as trees, walking." I am convinced that no matter how many Bible studies we attend and no matter how we serve our churches, we have not known the deep healing of Christ and the restoration of our souls until the way we view others has dramatically changed. Until we see everything clearly (v. 25). Just as Christ sees them. Christ didn't see men as trees, walking. The blind man wasn't healed until he saw men the way Christ saw them. We need to imitate Paul who said, "From now on we regard no one from a worldly point of view. Though we once regarded Christ in this way, we do so no longer" (2 Cor. 5:16).

Beloved, do we still see men as trees, walking? Do we see them as distortions of who they really are? Would we be willing to allow God to change our minds and adjust our sight? We're only half healed until then.

Chapter 17

DEVASTATION

He had James, the brother of John, put to death with the sword. (Acts 12:2)

J had no idea when I began this Bible study how profoundly different the scenes would look when viewed through the eyes of John. The series I wrote prior to our present journey was *Jesus the One and Only.* I have researched some of the same scenes, but the perspective has changed dramatically as I've attempted to look over John's shoulder rather than Jesus'. Had God not appointed us to walk specifically "beside" John, I would never have viewed the next dramatic scriptural account from his point of view. May the Holy Spirit help us grasp the significance of these events in his regard.

Acts 12 tells us that Herod began to persecute the church because such actions bought him favor with the Jewish leaders. His action undoubtedly impacted John more than the other believers because Herod had James "put to death with the sword" (v. 2).

We may have to untangle a maze of Jameses and Johns in the chapter. Herod killed our John's brother James. Then he arrested Peter. An angel delivered Peter from prison, so Peter proceeded to the home of Mary, the mother of John. This was John Mark, the cousin of Barnabas and the writer of the Second Gospel.

We have no way of knowing for certain whether or not John the apostle was among those gathered and praying at Mary's house. He may have been among those referenced in Acts 12:17 whom Peter told to "tell James and the brothers" about his deliverance from prison. The "James" referenced in this passage is the younger sibling of Jesus, and the "brothers" in this passage may have been Christ's other biological half-brothers. They became believers after the resurrection and were active participants in the prayer meetings recorded in Acts 1:14. Keep in mind, John may have been with the group at John Mark's, but another possibility exists. From the cross Jesus said, "Here is your mother." And "from that time on, this disciple took her into his home" (John 19:27).

Now that we have untangled the Jameses and Johns, let's return to the presenting issue. Herod had John's brother killed. Let the weight of it fall on you. "James, the brother of John." Inseparable as boys. John, the younger, always tagging along. His entire early identity was wrapped up in his brother's: James son of Zebedee and his brother John.

The other day I sat on an airplane next to a mom with two little boys. The older couldn't have been more than three and the younger about eighteen months. As a mother, I knew how hard keeping a hat or cap on a toddler can be, yet the little guy kept a baseball cap firmly on his head the entire flight. Would you like to know why? Because big brother wore a baseball cap just like it. Don't you know James and John were the same way? Almost every little brother wants to be just like the big one.

My daughters love each other dearly, but they were raised differently than my older sister and I. Amanda and Melissa had their own rooms and could use the word *mine* and mean it. Raised on a shoestring, from our early adolescence my sister Gay and I shared the same small room and the same double bed. Beyond our underwear, I am hard-pressed to think of a single thing either of us could have called "mine." We whispered late into the night and would laugh until the bed frame shook. We'd hear Major Dad stomping down the hall to warn us, and we'd immediately fake a dual snore . . . which brought on uncontrollable laughter and a good (but useless) scolding. We were inseparable.

I remember the call that came to our home informing us that Gay had flipped our old Volkswagen bus on the highway pulling out of a local burger joint. She was practically unscathed, but I remember having one of my first realizations that we were indeed two separate people and that one of us could live and the other die. I wept almost as if it had happened.

I have studied and even taught Acts 12 many times. I love the story of Peter's deliverance from prison, but until today I have never regarded the events from John's point of view. How devastated he must have been! By this time in the Book of Acts, the disciples all knew the Jews could make good on their threats. They had crucified Christ and stoned Stephen. They told Peter and John to stop speaking in the name of Jesus or else. They chose "or else."

Acts 8:1 tells us that earlier a persecution had scattered the believers, but the apostles remained in Jerusalem. Yes, John and Peter trekked to Samaria, but the ministries of the apostles remained intact in Jerusalem for this period of time. I assume that they simply did not yet feel released by the Holy Spirit to center their ministries elsewhere.

Now in a terrible wave of persecution, James was arrested. I wonder if John saw them seize his brother. If not, who broke the news to him? Can you imagine the sear of terror that tore through his heart? Remember, John was the apostle who'd had connections when Jesus was arrested and was able to get into the priest's courtyard. Don't you know he tried to pull every favor and call on every connection he had?

He probably couldn't sleep. He couldn't eat. He no doubt fell facedown on the floor and begged God to spare his brother's life. Beloved, don't hurry past this scene. James was John's flesh and blood. All the disciples were terrified, but none of them could relate to John's horror. Surely prayer meetings took place. Don't forget, these were men with the power and authority of the Holy Spirit to heal diseases and cast out demons. No doubt they named and claimed James's release and demanded his life in prayer. For all we know, James claimed his own life before his jailers and forbade them to harm one of Jesus' elect. After all, the disciples were promised power and were told they would be Christ's witnesses all over Jerusalem, Judea, Samaria, and the uttermost parts of the earth. His ministry had just begun! No, this couldn't be the end. He would surely be delivered!

Then they killed him. I pity the person who came to John with the news. In 2 Samuel 1, David was so horrified by the report of Saul and Jonathan's deaths that he had the bearer of bad news slain. Although John had no such authority or desire, don't you imagine he wanted to shake the bad news out of the bearer's mouth and demand a different ending? Don't you also imagine that he tried his hardest to shake the reality out of his own head? James was the first of the disciples martyred. Reality must have hit like an unsuspected tidal wave, crashing on the shores of servant lives.

More than any of the other ten, John must have replayed the events a thousand times in his mind, wondering if his big brother had been terrified or calm. Did he think of their parents? Hadn't Zebedee been through enough? How was he going to tell his mother? Had James felt any pain? Was it quick? Was he next? Then before he had time to steady from reeling, he learned he was not next. Peter was. Have you ever felt like a percussionist slammed king-size cymbals on both sides of your head? Not Peter! This was too much! Not James *and* Peter! Not both of them, Lord! Please, please, no, Lord!

> When he arrived at the house of Jairus, he did not let anyone go in with him except Peter, John, and James. (Luke 8:51)

> About eight days after Jesus said this, he took Peter, John and James with him and went up onto a mountain to pray. (Luke 9:28)

> Jesus sent Peter and John, saying, "Go and make preparations for us to eat the Passover." (Luke 22:8)

> He took Peter and the two sons of Zebedee along with him, and he began to be sorrowful and troubled. (Matt. 26:37)

> So she came running to Simon Peter and the other disciple, the one Jesus loved, and said, "They have taken the Lord out of the tomb, and we don't know where they have put him!" (John 20:2)

> Peter turned and saw that the disciple whom Jesus loved was following them. . . . When Peter saw him, he asked, "Lord, what about him?" (John 21:20–21)

"Yeah, Lord! What about me? How will I go on with all of this without James and Peter? What are You doing? What aren't You doing? Will You let them kill all of us?" John had good reason to believe Peter might never make it out of that prison. But then he did. God granted him a miracle . . .

scarcely before they had mopped the blood of John's big brother off the floor. Can you imagine the mix of emotions John must have felt if he was anything like the rest of us?

I believe something huge happened for John in this traumatic turn of events. I think the young apostle came to the startling reality that when all comes down, we are each on our own before God. Every life is separate and distinct. We may think we have partnerships in life or in ministry that we cannot exist or operate without. We may think that everything in the Christian experience is about "body life," but it's not. Yes, we're all parts of the body of Christ, and we function in each generation as parts of a whole, but until we each stand before our God with a shocking awareness of our solitary standing, I'm not sure we have a clue about our "part."

I don't believe any one of us who is serious about God will forego this test. And this test is no thirty-minute quiz. It's a lifelong essay test written on the tablets of our hearts. Will we loose our hold on anything and anyone else as prerequisites of our followship and follow Him in the intensity of aloneness? If you can answer quickly, I'm not sure you grasp the seriousness of the issue. Even the question makes me feel insecure. Would we be willing to live . . . and die . . . alone with Christ?

I have a wonderful staff of coworkers at Living Proof Ministries. I would not trade them for anything! I'm crazy about my husband and get a bigger kick out of my two young adult daughters than anyone in the world. I am very involved in my church. I am often surrounded by scores of people. Yet moments come unexpectedly when the awareness of my solitary estate before God so radically overwhelms me that I fall to my knees and weep. Bitterly. Frighteningly. The feeling is so intense at times I can hardly bear it. I heard an internationally known speaker say something the other day that I, in my much smaller world of ministry, could totally understand. She said, "I'm so far out on a limb with God now, if I even think of walking by sight instead of faith, I'm dead." Amen.

That goes for all who have truly chosen to follow Jesus Christ. Size of ministry makes no difference whatsoever. How much of your life you've banked on Jesus is the issue. Have we held some back for ourselves . . . just in case? Just in case He's not as real, as powerful, as active as we thought?

Just in case He doesn't come through? Just in case He really can't be taken at His Word? Or have we bet the farm? Meaning everything we have and everything we are is banked on the reality of Jesus Christ as Lord of all the earth. We will never fulfill our destinies until our hope is built on nothing less. How about you? Do you have a "just in case" contingency plan, or are you totally out on a limb with God?

We can lock arms with fellow servants just like the disciples did, and we will experience a measure of God's anointing and perform some significant works. For the parts of the whole to work as God intended them, however, each part is tested and tried as its own whole before a highly personal God. If we insist on a sandbox full of company, we'll miss the waves of the ocean where man can only walk one at a time. When a wave of loneliness suddenly erupts, ride the thing. Let your stomach rise and fall with fear and peculiar excitement. Don't fight the feeling. Don't just busy yourself. Ride the wave straight into the presence of God and experience the strange adventure of feeling you're the only one there.

The intensity of your solitary estate is often most obvious when you fight to reconcile the facts of life with the words of faith. When you grapple with questions like, "Why did God let the blood of my brother spill but performed a miracle for my best friend?" And the explanations of others only frustrate you more. In fact, often we only bother asking so we can release a little anger in the demand of a better answer. Rarely will it come. I'm not sure John ever figured this one out. Goodness knows he was thankful his friend's life was spared, but why was James's life seemingly less significant? Why was he the first to go? Why, Lord? And what about me?

Solitude is not so much the place we find answers. It's the place we find our own square foot of earth from which to grapple with heaven and decide if we're going on . . . possibly alone . . . without our answers. And many of us will. Why? Because the privilege of wrestling with such a holy and mysterious God still beats the numbness—the pitiful mediocrity—of an otherwise life. Sometimes we don't realize how real He is until we've experienced the awesomeness of His answerless Presence. He knows that what we crave far more than explanations is the unshakable conviction that He is utterly, supremely God.

110

Chapter 18

THE RIGHT HAND OF FELLOWSHIP

James, Peter and John, those reputed to be pillars, gave me and
Barnabas the right hand of fellowship when they recognized
the grace given to me. (Galatians 2:9)

$\mathscr{I}$f you read the background Scriptures, you noticed a new character in Acts 12:25. You may wonder what the persecutor-turned-preacher named Saul had to do with our protagonist. Actually, Paul's testimony will offer us several important insights into the apostle John and also will supply us with a very valuable time line.

In Galatians Paul tells that after his conversion he went to Arabia and then returned to Damascus. Only after three years did he travel to Jerusalem. The three years encompassed his original stay in Damascus, his flight to the desert, his return to Damascus, and his travel time to Jerusalem.

Acts 9:26 tells us that when Paul came to Jerusalem, "he tried to join the disciples, but they were all afraid of him, not believing that he really was a disciple." Position John among the disciples in Jerusalem at this time.

Don't miss the words in Acts 9:1: "Saul was still breathing out murderous threats against the Lord's disciples." Peter, John, and the others had plenty of reasons to take Saul's actions personally. Furthermore, they hadn't received the same vision God had given to Ananias in Damascus concerning the validity of Saul's conversion. Saul could have faked his conversion as a means of getting close to them and exposing their unrelenting evangelism after the warning to cease.

Acts 9 and Galatians 1 may seem to contradict each other in reference to Paul's time with the apostles. Galatians 1:19 tells us he saw only Peter, but I believe the intent of the reference is the time he spent getting acquainted. The rest of the apostles may have heard Barnabas's apologetic for Paul, but the only one who really got to know the new convert was Peter. John did not get to know Paul at this time and may have even purposely remained somewhat distant from him.

Fast-forward your thoughts on the time line now to the events we studied in the previous chapter: the death of James, John's beloved brother. We have no reason to believe much time passed between Paul's conversion and the martyrdom of James. We know that Stephen was martyred before Paul's conversion and that Paul in fact gave approval to his death. James was martyred after Paul's conversion. Even though several years had passed according to the time line in Galatians 1 and 2, don't you imagine that if John were anything like most of us, he had some pretty strong feelings about Paul? His threats against the lives of the disciples prior to his encounter with Christ were described as murderous. Paul was among the most radical activists that existed among the haters of "the Way."

Even though Paul dramatically gave his life to Christ before James was seized and killed, had I been John, I would have had a fairly difficult time embracing him. I'm afraid I might have had thoughts like, "If not for people exactly like you, my brother might still be alive." Maybe John felt none of what I'm describing, but I believe Christ's first ragtag band of followers were like us. Yes, the Holy Spirit had come to them and, yes, they had matured somewhat, but grief and loss don't always perpetuate extremely rational feelings. None of the rest of the apostles had lost a blood brother at this point. I just have to wonder how John felt about Paul those first several years.

Now let's pick up with the time line in Galatians 2 where the apostle John appears. Paul says that fourteen years later he went up again to Jerusalem. Acts 15 describes this trip in greater detail. The meetings are often called the "Jerusalem conference" or "council." When it comes to

John, we know nothing of the years falling between the last mention in Acts and the events described in Galatians 2. For now all we know is that he continued to serve faithfully and obviously retained Jerusalem as home base, just as Peter did. We do know from Paul's testimony that John held a primary role in the Christian church in Jerusalem because Paul listed him as a "pillar" of the church (Gal. 2:9).

The James to which Galatians 2:9 refers is Christ's younger half-brother who became part of the backbone of the infant church after the resurrection. He was also the one who wrote the New Testament book that bears his name. James the brother of John had been slain about a decade earlier. A different James now joined with Peter and John to form what Paul called pillars of the church. According to Galatians 2:2, Paul approached the leaders privately for fear that they would reject the Gentile Christians. He was not unsure of the revelation God had given him, but he did not know whether they would accept it.

Acts 15:6–19 describes the outcome of the meeting. Peter appealed to the leaders not to put a yoke on the necks of the Gentiles that they had not been able to bear. Then James delivered the verdict: "We should not make it difficult for the Gentiles who are turning to God" (v. 19).

Paul used far fewer words to describe the outcome in Galatians 2:9. He simply said, "James, Peter and John, those reputed to be pillars, gave me and Barnabas the right hand of fellowship." Mrs. Fanett, my high school English teacher, would be appalled at the poor English Paul used when he said "me and Barnabas," but in Greek the reference of first person comes first.[1]

Picture the five men mentioned in Galatians 2:9 conferring together and giving approval to one another: James, the unbelieving mocker turned preacher; Peter, the one sifted like wheat, denying Christ three times then having enough faith to return and strengthen his brothers; John, the Son of Thunder, who asked if he could sit at Christ's side in the kingdom and destroy the Samaritans with fire from heaven; Paul, a former religious mad-man who approved the murder of Stephen and helped fuel a persecution that resulted in James's death; Barnabas, the son of encouragement, who risked getting hammered by the early church by building a bridge between unlikely brothers.

That's just it. We're all unlikely brothers. In Christ's church the pillars were never designed to match. Each one is distinct. What need would cookie-cutter disciples meet? Not only does Christ choose variegated pillars, everything else within His church is marked by His creative distinctiveness as well. None of us were meant to match. We were meant to fit together. Two identical puzzle pieces don't "fit." Oh, that we would celebrate that difference on one ultimate basis.

Do you remember what Paul said James, Peter, and John recognized in him that caused them to extend the right hand of fellowship? They "gave me and Barnabas the right hand of fellowship when they recognized the grace given to me" (Gal. 2:9).

First Peter 4:10 echoes the same concept: "Each one should use whatever gift he has received to serve others, faithfully administering God's grace in its various forms." Beloved, we don't have to agree on every single point of doctrine. We don't even have to always get along.

Galatians 2 continues with the record of a fairly heated argument between Peter and Paul. God does, however, expect us to respect one another and acknowledge the grace of God extended to all who are in Christ. Paul came to the leaders in private, but the inference of the right hand of fellowship tells us they gave him a very public stamp of approval. One he needed and one I believe God would have held the pillars in the church responsible for not extending.

To fulfill our kingdom purposes on earth, we could all use a right hand of fellowship from another in ministry, couldn't we? When I think back on those God so graciously appointed to extend such a hand to me, I am deeply humbled and awed. I have been asked countless times how John Bisagno, the longtime pastor of my home church, handled this ministry coming out of his church. Beloved, he didn't just handle it. He pushed it! For years the only reason people invited me to come to their church was because they trusted him!

Did Brother John know I had a lot to learn? Perhaps more than anyone else. So did my mentor, Marge Caldwell. Did he agree with everything I taught or did? I doubt it. Yet they both continued to work with me, give me a chance to grow, and let me develop into my own person and not cookie-cutter images of them. They each extended me the right hand of fellowship for one reason. They recognized the grace of God in my once broken life. Boy howdy, has there been a heap of it.

I want to share one more personal example with you. When LifeWay approached me with a contract to tape the first series, *A Woman's Heart: God's Dwelling Place,* I was pitifully wet behind the ears. I don't know much about what I'm doing now, but I assure you I knew nothing then. I was petrified. The enemy came against me with such conflict and fear, I think I would have backed out had I not signed a contract. I felt like I needed advice desperately and needed someone to tell me whether my feelings were normal. I still feel like an idiot over what I did next, but I was desperate. I called Kay Arthur's office and asked to speak to her. I had no idea what I was doing. I had never seen her in person or had the privilege of taking one of her courses. Don't get the idea that I in any way saw a comparison. I just wanted to talk to a woman who had taught the Word on videotape no matter what gulf of knowledge and experience separated us.

God wasn't about to let me get in touch with Kay Arthur. First of all, He wanted me to rely on Him alone. Furthermore, He knew He had already extended the right hand of fellowship to me through sufficient people. I also believe God knew how extremely impressionable I was at that time and that I had not yet allowed Him to fully develop my style. I have so much respect for Kay that if I could have, I would have wanted God to make me just like her. What need whatsoever would God have had for such a thing? Kay does an excellent job of being Kay, so why on earth would God have wanted me to approach Bible study in exactly the same way? He already had her!

Today I could pick up the phone and call Kay, and we could laugh and talk for an hour if we had the time. I will never see myself worthy enough to help her with her heels, but I call her a friend. We met privately five or six years ago, but through the years both of us felt the call of God to do something far more public.

Each of us has gone out of our way to demonstrate publicly that we are united in Christ Jesus and we serve the same God . . . albeit with different styles. I have taught some of her books. Kay has invited me to several of her conferences to lead prayer and to speak. She has extended to me something more precious than gold: the right hand of fellowship. She knows I have a lot to learn. We wouldn't agree on every interpretation. She is simply a woman who recognizes grace when she sees it. I am so grateful.

Fourteen years lapsed between the time Paul first tried to fit in with the apostles and when he finally received the right hand of fellowship. I'd like to suggest the hand didn't come a moment behind schedule. What use would God have had for Paul if he simply turned out to be another James? Another Peter? Another John? His mission was distinct. And so, Beloved, is yours. God knows what He's doing! Trust Him. God is busy making you someone no one else has ever been.

Chapter 19

LESSONS FROM OBSCURITY

From that time on, this disciple took her into his home. (John 19:27)

$\mathcal{N}$ext we arrive at a very intriguing place. One characterized not by John's appearance but by his conspicuous absence. In the next chapter we will begin turning our attentions to John's writings, but let's not hurry. First let's glance at the great apostle's role in the Book of Acts then tarry over his disappearance from the pages. I am convinced that what John didn't do may have nearly as much to say as what he did.

Acts 12:2 is the last mention Luke makes of John as he refers to his brother's death. I am very intrigued by the fact that Luke mentions John only a handful of times in the annals of the early church, and he never quoted John. Our dear protagonist appears only as an aside to Peter. While the Book of Acts traces almost every move of a converted persecutor named Saul, after James's death, John's ministry continues with very little notice.

I wonder what the apostles thought about Paul gaining so much of the spotlight. I think we'd be pretty naïve to think they didn't notice. Galatians tells us John was a pillar of the church in Jerusalem, but we are told very little about him. John was in the audience of twelve when Christ told Peter He would build His church upon the foundation poured by the chip-off-the-old-block's testimony. After the resurrection John had also heard Christ tell Peter what his future held.

John may have felt that Peter at least had an important future . . . even if it ultimately required his life. John, on the other hand, knew nothing about his own. All he may have known was that Peter's ministry was sky-rocketing, and no one would argue that Paul was a household name.

John? Christ simply asked him to take care of his mother. Goodness knows he loved her. He took her into his home just like he promised, but somehow in the midst of the responsibility, neither Scripture nor traditions give us any indication he ever had a family of his own. Of course, to have known Mary so well was to gain priceless insight into Christ. After all, who knew Him better? Surely she recounted stories as the evening oil in the lamp grew scarce. Scripture paints John as curious, so I can't imagine that he failed to ask a thousand questions through the years. "What did Gabriel look like when he brought the news? Did you know instantly he was an angel? What was his voice like?" Or, "Did you almost lose hope that James and your other sons would ever believe?" Luke 2:19 tells us that "Mary treasured up all these things and pondered them in her heart." She certainly must have had much to say.

If Mary was like most aging mothers, I imagine she told the stories all the more and perhaps even repetitively as her life hastened toward its end. Many of the early church historians agree that John resided in Jerusalem until Mary died. I don't think I've ever meditated on Mary's death before. The New Testament records very little about the deaths of the members of the infant church. The Old Testament on the other hand bears many records of the deaths of saints. I can't help but wonder if—from God's standpoint—the cross and the resurrection made the deaths of His servants of little importance in the face of sudden glory.

Still, I wonder what Mary's home-going was like. If John and Christ's half-brothers had any notion she was dying, they were no doubt by her side. A natural death must have been so different to the eyewitnesses of the resurrected Lord Jesus. They knew firsthand the reality of life beyond the grave. Though they may have felt pain, they probably experienced little fear. Hebrews 2:14–15 tells us that Jesus shared our humanity so that "by his death he might destroy him who holds the power of death—that is, the devil—and free those who all their lives were held in slavery by their fear of death."

Can you imagine how anxious Mary was to see her firstborn son? I have little doubt that those nearby reassured her through her final hours with words of their imminent encounter. Like all of us, God counted her steps and kept her tears in a bottle. Both were full and it was time. As He narrowed that solitary life to an earthbound close, He could easily see beyond the weathered face lined by time.

Surely God grinned as He remembered the astonishment on her adolescent face when she realized she had been chosen over every other woman who lived. A girl of most humble means would bear the Messiah. Then perhaps He laughed out loud as she broke into the praises recorded in Luke 1:46–55. The Greek translation of her words, "My spirit rejoices in God my Savior," intimates she was exulting with her whole inner being. The years that followed were tumultuous but exquisite. She had the unspeakable privilege of being a player in the plan of the ages.

I like to think Mary was surrounded by loved ones as she inhaled her last ounce of earthly air. I imagine her sons gathered around her. All of them. The one she adopted at the cross. And the One she surrendered to the grave. I wonder if they knew their Brother was right there among them . . . more present in His invisibility than they could ever be. Mary bid farewell to mortality and was ushered to immortality on the arm of a handsome Prince. Her Son. Her God.

John's job was done. What now? Perhaps he did what we sometimes do. When I am confounded by what I don't know, I rehearse in my mind what I do know. He knew that the last thing Christ told the apostles was that they would be witnesses in Jerusalem, Judea, Samaria, and the uttermost parts of the earth. I am of course offering supposition, but I wonder if he thought to himself, "I've served here in Jerusalem for years. I've preached to Samaritans, and I know Judea like the back of my hand. I'm no longer a young man. Who knows how much longer I have? I'm heading to the uttermost."

Beloved, listen. Christ's early followers were adventurers! They were pioneers! If they listened to us sit around and decide whether we had time to work in a Bible study with prison inmates around our nail appointments, they'd be mortified. In our postmodern era, church life is associated with buildings and programs. Church life to them was moving in the adrenaline and excitement of the Holy Ghost at the risk of life and limb. They were willing to do things we would reason couldn't possibly be the will of God (i.e., risking our necks) for the sheer joy of what lay before them. They ran the race. They didn't window shop.

I'm not meaning to be harsh, but I fear they might look at all of us and think virtually none of us looked like disciple material to them. But you know what I'd want to say to that first motley crew? "None of you looked like disciple material either when Christ dragged you from your safe little lives." My point? We can still become disciple material! I desperately want to! I want to live the Great Adventure. Don't you? Even if that Great Adventure leads me into virtual obscurity for a while. Stay tuned to see what I mean.

Most historians and scholars believe John moved to Ephesus but also traveled to Rome at some point. Some historians believe his trip to Rome came soon after his departure from Jerusalem, but I am inclined to believe the opposite order carries more circumstantial support. I think John settled in Ephesus first of all and that his venture to Rome happened before his exile in Patmos and probably led to it. R. Alan Culpepper, who is considered by many to be a modern-day expert on the life of John, wrote:

> While the New Testament never mentions the activities of the apostle John in his later years, early Christian writers, though not unanimous, furnish strong evidence that he spent several decades in residence in Ephesus. The critical testimony is furnished by Irenaeus, bishop of Lyons (around A.D. 180–200): Afterwards, John, the disciple of the Lord, who also had leaned upon His breast, did himself publish a Gospel during his residence at Ephesus in Asia. (Against Heresies III. I. 1)[1]

In *The Two St. Johns,* James Stalker added:

> This is the statement of Irenaeus, who must have known the fact perfectly well, because he was a disciple of Polycarp, the martyr bishop of Hierapolis, and Polycarp was a disciple of John.
>
> The latter part of St. John's life was spent in this region; and the city with which the unanimous tradition of early times associates him is Ephesus.
>
> This city was situated on the Aegean coast, and it was one of the great centres of human life in that age; for Christianity, at its

inception, had a predilection for large cities, whence its influence might radiate into the regions with which they were connected. Ephesus contained a great population and was a place of enormous wealth and activity.[2]

Those familiar with the life of Paul may recall that he spent several crucial years ministering in Ephesus. Most scholars agree that John's time followed Paul's by a matter of years, but Luke's record of Paul's encounters adds important insights as we imagine John ministering there. Acts 19:8–20, 23–41 tells of the highly unusual supernatural works God performed through the apostle Paul. When I researched the study *To Live Is Christ*, the reason why God chose to do such astonishing works in Ephesus became clearer to me. Ancient Ephesus was one of the most pronounced centers of black magic in the entire world, so God made sure to perform works that wouldn't simply impress. They would baffle. James Stalker wrote of Ephesus:

> Being connected by both land and sea with Syria and the countries beyond, it swarmed with those professors of black arts whom the East in that age poured in multitudes into the great cities of the West; and these preyed on the strangers from every shore who entered the harbor. The center, however, of degradation was the temple of Diana. This was reckoned one of the seven wonders of the world. It was larger than any known structure of the kind . . . its worship was maintained by innumerable priests and priestesses . . .
>
> Obviously this was a place where the Gospel was urgently needed; and before it was visited by St. John the work of its evangelization had been vigorously begun. It had been the chief center on the third missionary journey of the Apostle Paul, to it he had devoted three whole years. At the end of that time he was violently driven forth; but his work remained, and St. John, when he arrived, entered on the heritage left by his predecessor.[3]

Nothing is said about John's specific ministry after James's death, and nothing at all is recorded about his tenure in Ephesus. Though we have much information about Paul's ministry there, we know virtually nothing about John's. As far as we are concerned, John served in biblical obscurity for a measure of years. And, Beloved, that is precisely the most important point of this chapter.

Did John start doubting his identity and his significance somewhere along the way? Peter was no doubt the front-runner in Jerusalem and the early church. Next to him, the Book of Acts implies James, the half-brother of Christ, was most prominent. Furthermore, John went to Ephesus and built on the foundation laid by none other than Paul, the former persecutor and latecomer onto the scene.

You may be thinking, *But what difference does that make?* In an ideal world, none. But this is no ideal world. In the dead of the night when insecurities crawl on us like fleas, all of us have terrifying bouts of insecurity and panics of insignificance. Our human natures fall pitifully to the temptation at times to pull out the tape measure and gauge ourselves against people who seem far more gifted and anointed by God.

John went on to outlive every other apostle while all of them were counted worthy to give their lives for the sake of Christ. Did he ever wonder if he were too unimportant to even be considered a threat enough to kill?

We may want to think he was surely too mature and filled with the Holy Spirit to have such thoughts, but keep in mind this is the same disciple who asked to sit at one of Jesus' sides in the kingdom. Yes, John was a new creature, but if Satan worked on him anything like he works on me, he targeted his weak times and hit him again with the same brand of temptations that worked in the old days. John's old fleshly desires for significance had been goliath. I can't imagine Satan not trying to pinpoint them again. How about you? When you're weak, down, or tired, doesn't Satan occasionally try to awaken some of the temptations of the old man of flesh in you?

One way we have to respond is by choosing to believe what we know rather than what we feel. If John struggled with his identity in the era of the early church, that's exactly what he must have done. We know because of the virtually incomparable fruit produced after years of relative obscurity. In spite of others seeming more powerfully used by God and in the midst of decades hidden in the shadows, John remained tenacious in his task.

Beloved, there is no such thing as obscurity to Christ Jesus. The eyes of El Roi ("the God who sees me" Gen. 16:13–19) gaze approvingly upon every effort you make and every ounce of faith you exercise in Jesus' name. You have not been forgotten! You have no idea what may lie ahead! No doubt remains in my mind that God spent this time testing and proving John's character so that he could be trusted with the greatest revelation. The answers God is willing to give us in our tomorrows often flow from our faithfulness when we have none today.

Chapter 20

THE ONE JESUS LOVED

His disciples stared at one another, at a loss to know which
of them he meant. One of them, the disciple whom Jesus loved,
was reclining next to him. (John 13:22–23)

I stumbled upon a quote in Culpepper's book on John that I can't shake
out of my head. "Saints . . . die to the world only to rise to a more intense
life."[1] I've turned the quote over in my mind a hundred times, and I'm convinced it's true. John may be the perfect example. I believe God had something so divinely unique to entrust to this chosen apostle that He had to
slay the call of the world in him. Mind you, not the call *to* the world but
the call *of* the world.

I don't think John was so unlike Abraham or Moses. God chose these
men but refined them for their tasks through the crucible of time and challenged trust. The obvious difference is that God used John mightily soon
after his calling, but I'd like to suggest that his latter works fall into the category we'll call "greater works than these." In terms of John's recorded
works, the earlier and latter works were separated by critical years of further
preparation.

As God sought to kill the world in His chosen vessels and crucify them
to their own plans and agendas, their terms in waiting were not emptied
and lifeless. Rather, their lives greatly intensified. Our callings are not so
different. We will never be of great use to God if we do not allow Him to
crucify us to ourselves and the call of the world. Our consolations are
exceedingly great, however! We trade in the pitifully small and potentially
disastrous for the wildest ride mortal creatures could ever know. We don't

just die to self to accept nothingness. We lay down our lives and the call of the world to receive something far more intense. The call of God! The time spent awaiting further enlightenment and fuller harvest are meant to bulge with relationship.

Months then years then even decades may have blown off the calendar of John's life in biblical obscurity, but don't consider for an instant that they were spent in inactivity or emptiness. No possible way! Please do not miss the following point: During the interim years of biblical obscurity in John's life, *one of the most intense relationships in the entire Word of God developed.* Please turn up the volume on this entry and read the italicized words again because the point is so critical I'm typing this standing up!

Yes, Christ used John to cast out demons, heal the sick, and spread the good news through word of mouth. But somewhere along the way God built a man to whom He could entrust some of the most profound words ever recorded on parchment. What kind of man writes, "In the beginning was the Word, and the Word was with God, and the Word was God"? What semblance of humanity is entrusted with the love letters of 1, 2, 3 John? And who in the world could ever be chosen for the penning of the incomparable Revelation? Yet all were indeed entrusted to a man once simply known as the "brother of James."

Something happened, Beloved. Something big. Something intense. No one knows for certain the exact order of John's writings, but I am most comfortable with the theory of many scholars who believe the order was given to John in the order they appear in Scripture. Most scholars believe the weightiest evidences suggest they were all written within a matter of years anyway. This time frame would fall in the A.D. 80s and 90s. If so, decades passed while John the apostle served in places like Jerusalem and Ephesus while the other disciples were each martyred one by one.

Can you imagine being John as news traveled the miles like a newspaper landing with a thud on his doorstep with one obituary after another? Firm tradition places Peter in Rome in the A.D. 60s, where he and Paul were martyred under the reign of Nero.[2] One was crucified. The other beheaded. How John must have grieved! But they were neither the first nor last. One by one each was translated through the crimson door of violent death to everlasting life until only one remained. What kinds of things do you imagine the apostle John felt as the solitary remaining apostle?

We don't know much about what happened between Christ and John in those biblically obscure years, but one thing is certain. A thing so significant that I believe it was the single hinge from which hung the fulfillment of all the remaining works of God in John. Somewhere in the midst of those years and decades, John formed his identity as the beloved disciple. By the time the words of his Gospel were transferred by the Holy Spirit to him, this identity was intact.

Do you realize that John alone called himself "the disciple Jesus loved"? Do you find that at all peculiar? If we believe the Gospel of John was inspired, however, then we also must accept that the detail of John's self-identity was also inspired. Not because Jesus' love for John exceeded the others but because God purposed the reader to know how John saw himself. At first glance we might be tempted to think John a bit arrogant for terming himself such, but God would never allow a man who received such revelation to get away with that kind of self-promotion.

I'd like to suggest that John's evolving identity over the course of those decades came out of the opposite kind of heart. God is far too faithful not to have greatly humbled John before giving him such surpassing revelation. (See a parallel concept in 2 Cor. 12.)

I believe quite possibly the heightened positions of Peter and Paul in the era of the early church coupled with the impending martyrdom of each apostle fed abasement in John rather than exaltation. Surely he struggled with terribly perplexing feelings of fear that he, too, was doomed to martyrdom and yet fear that he wasn't. Does that make sense?

When one person remains after all the others have been counted worthy to die and yet no profound purpose has been revealed, all sorts of insecurities could arise. We don't even have to wonder if Satan was after him. Surely the devil saw the martyrdom of all the others as a victory even though in reality through their willingness to die, he was defeated. John no doubt became the bull's-eye on hell's target. Among plenty of other assaults, don't you imagine Satan taunted John with survivor's guilt? Believe me, I know personally how debilitating survivor's guilt can be.

I have lived with a man for twenty-five years who lost his older brother and his younger sister and suffered terribly with false guilt for a time. It's a powerful deception.

As the years went by and the virile, youthful fisherman grew old and gray, I am convinced John's weakening legs were steadied and strengthened on the path by the constant reassurance, "Jesus, You chose me. You keep me. And above all else, You love me. You love me. No matter what happens or doesn't, Jesus, I am Your beloved."

Perhaps the reason why this theory (which I didn't get from any book) is so plausible to me is because the times I have most identified myself as loved by God have without exception been the difficult times. Not the flourishing times. I went through such a terrible time of loss and attack while writing *Breaking Free*, I could hardly stand it. I survived a two-year period of tremendous difficulty by repeating over and over, "Oh, God, I am so thankful I am loved by You. You love me so much. I am Your beloved. The apple of Your eye." Isaiah 54:10 became my absolute lifeline. "'Though the mountains be shaken and the hills be removed, yet my unfailing love for you will not be shaken nor my covenant of peace be removed,' says the Lord, who has compassion on you."

Psalm 90:14 began my mornings because I couldn't face the day without it: "Satisfy us in the morning with your unfailing love, / that we may sing for joy and be glad all our days." The lines of my journals through those difficult months are replete with confessions of love. Not so much mine for God, mind you. But God's for me!

I grabbed at His love like a starving refugee scavenging for food one day and like a selfish child snatching sweets the next. Not only was I desperate; certain circumstances had made me desperately insecure. I was so needy that all my loved ones could have done was throw a bucket of water in a cavern. I needed more love than a person could spare. I needed the mammoth love of God.

Beloved, you and I are not on love rations! At this particular point in your life, are you desperate for a surplus of love and acceptance? Human nature seeks to get—one way or the other—what it feels it needs most. How do you try to grab on to an extra measure of love and acceptance?

Have you already discovered that your need exceeds mortal fulfillment? I've learned the hard way that when I am in a crisis of insecurity or pain, no one has enough of what I need. The attempt to retrieve it from human resources will ultimately result in my despising them and their despising me. God is our only source. He will never resent us for the breadth, depth, and length of our need. I love the quote in Deuteronomy 33:12: In the promise to Benjamin, Moses said, "Let the beloved of the LORD rest secure in him, / for he shields him all day long, / and the one the LORD loves rests between his shoulders."

We will all have seasons like I'm describing because their divine purpose is too vital. Much of our identity is developed right there. In the aloneness. In the search for purpose. In the fear of being passed over. In the terror that somewhere along the way we crossed the line of no return.

We learn who we really are in times when we're faced with the prospect of believing God loves us even if He never greatly uses us. Do we believe He proves His love by His blatant use of us? If so, had any of us been John during the years conspicuously silent in Scripture, we might have given up. Or at least dropped into a lower gear.

Not John. He knew two things, and I believe he grabbed on to them for dear life. He knew he was called to be a disciple. And he knew he was loved. Over the course of time, those two things emerged into one ultimate identity. "I, John, the seed of Zebedee, the son of Salome, the brother of James, the last surviving apostle am he: the one Jesus loves." Beloved disciple. Somewhere along the way, John, that Son of Thunder, forsook ambition for affection. And that, my friend, is why he was sitting pretty when some of the most profound words ever to fall from heaven to earth fell first like liquid grace into his quill.

Part 5

RECEIVING HIS FULLNESS

I had a blast studying the highlights from the Gospel of John that you have before you for the next ten chapters. When I first began my research for this journey, I knew we would consider John's Gospel, but I had no idea how I would ever choose which aspects to emphasize. His Gospel is unique in so many ways and provides endless insights. As I approached this part of the study, I felt overwhelmed by the task of picking and choosing one text over another. God mercifully and clearly spoke to me through His Word and told me exactly how to approach it in order to meet our study goals. I'll explain our approach in chapter 21. In each of these chapters, I learned something that I believe will mark my walk. I hope you do too!

$Chapter\ 21$

MORE LIFE

*The Word became flesh and made his dwelling among us. We have
seen his glory, the glory of the One and Only, who came from the Father,
full of grace and truth. (John 1:14)*

$\mathcal{W}$e have arrived at the blood-pumping heart of our study. We now turn
our attentions on the Gospel of John. We will comprehend little about the
man who wrote the brief epistles of 1, 2, and 3 John and the incomparable Revelation if we don't grasp the emphasis of the inspired apostle in his
unique Gospel. John's Gospel is like his spiritual EKG—it reveals the state
of his heart.

As I stated earlier, I am more convinced by the evidences of the later
dating of John's writings during the reign of the Roman emperor
Domitian, placing them between A.D. 81 and 96. If I'm on target, decades
passed, as did the lives of the other apostles, until John was the only one
with feet still planted on planet Earth and not without purpose. We discussed in our previous lesson how John's relationship with God only
swelled with intensity through the obscure years. I believe we discovered
something that will prove pivotal to us in our journey: John forsook ambition for affection. To love and be loved became his lifeblood.

The more I study John's life, the more I am convinced that intensity
breeds extensity. The more intense John became in his relationship with a
then invisible Jesus, the more God extended the boundaries of revelation.
God broke the sound and sight barriers of this apostle and allowed him to
experience a length, breadth, and depth that others never saw. We will see
evidence of both intensity and extensity as we behold the concepts that

mold John's Gospel to such a unique shape. Our purpose, however, is not only to marvel over John's beloved relationship with Christ but also to be indelibly marked in our own. The same Spirit, the same Truth, and the same Lord also work in us.

John 1:16 introduces a key concept that will carry us through this vital part of our journey. I want to encourage you to memorize it! "From the fullness of his grace we have all received one blessing after another." If you will receive what this verse is saying to you, you won't be changed just for the course of this study. Your entire life experience with Jesus will be transformed.

The original word for blessing is *charis,* often translated "grace." This explains the King James rendering: "And of his fulness have all we received, and grace for grace." *Charis* means "grace," "particularly that which causes joy, pleasure, gratification, favor, acceptance, . . . a benefit, . . . the absolutely free expression of the loving kindness of God to men finding its only motive in the bounty and benevolence of the Giver; unearned and unmerited favor."[1]

Based on John 1:14, 16, and this definition, I believe we can accurately draw the following conclusions:

1. Jesus is full of grace and truth. He's the One and Only.
2. All of us get to receive from His fullness! Not just John the apostle. Not just John the Baptist. Jesus is full and overflowing with everything any of us who believes could possibly need or desire, and we get to receive from it!
3. These grace gifts flowing from Christ's fullness are not only beneficial, but they are expressions of God's favor that cause joy and pleasure!

It's high time I made a blatant confession. I am a Christian hedonist. Have been for years even before I knew what the term meant. I wish I had better words for it, but let me just say it like it is: Jesus makes me happy! He thrills me! He nearly takes my breath away with His beauty. As seriously as I know how to tell you, I am at times so overwhelmed by His love for me, my face blushes with intensity, and my heart races with holy anticipation. Jesus is the uncontested delight of my life.

I never intended for this to happen. I didn't even know it was possible. It all started with an in-depth study of His Word in my late twenties and then surged oddly enough with a near emotional and mental collapse in my early thirties. At the end of myself I came to the beginning of an intensity of relationship with an invisible Savior. No one had ever told me such a relationship existed. Now I spend my life telling anyone who will listen.

I thought I was just weird. I knew so many believers who wore Christ like a sacrifice that I thought I missed something somewhere. Don't get me wrong. Plenty of believers in the world make huge sacrifices in the name of Jesus Christ, but I'm not sure American believers can relate, . . . and we can be a little nauseating when we try.

By far the biggest sacrifices I've ever made were times I chose to pursue myself and my own will over Jesus and His. I'd be a liar to tell you Jesus has been some big sacrifice for me. He is the unspeakable joy and love of my life. In crude terms, I think He's a blast.

While still in the closet, I began stumbling on other Christian hedonists. Perhaps Augustine is the most blatant historical example. Of his conversion in 386, Augustine wrote, "How sweet all at once it was for me to be rid of those fruitless joys which I had once feared to lose! . . . You drove them from me, you who are the true, the sovereign joy. You drove them from me and took their place, you who are sweeter than all pleasure."[2] My heart leaps as I read words that I, too, have lived!

Jonathan Edwards was another. In 1755 he wrote, "God is glorified not only by His glory's being seen, but by its being rejoiced in. When those who see it delight in it, God is more glorified than if they only see it."[3]

C. S. Lewis was also a fine Christian hedonist. He wrote:

> If there lurks in most modern minds the notion that to desire our own good and earnestly to hope for the enjoyment of it is a bad thing, I submit that this notion has crept in from Kant and the Stoics and is no part of the Christian faith. Indeed if we consider the unblushing promises of reward and the staggering nature of the rewards promised in the Gospels, it would seem that our Lord finds our desires not too strong, but too weak. We are half-hearted creatures, fooling about with drink and sex and ambition when infinite joy is offered us, like an ignorant child who wants

to go on making mud pies in a slum because he cannot imagine what is meant by the offer of a holiday at the sea. We are far too easily pleased.[4]

Meditate on John 1:14 and 16 again. Grace is God's favor looking for a place to happen! From His favor we can receive one blessing after another! Beloved, I don't care who you are or how long you've known Jesus, I am convinced we have hardly scratched the surface. So much more of Him exists! So much more He's willing to give us! Show us! Tell us! Oh, that we would spend our life in furious pursuit! That's exactly what John Piper has done. He's my favorite example of a holy hedonist from the early twenty-first century. Although you could almost pick any of his works for evidence, he draws his hedonistic conclusions best in one statement: "God is most glorified in us when we are most satisfied in Him."[5]

Don't get me wrong. I'm not saying our motive for pursuing God is strictly for our own delight and satisfaction. We pursue Him because He is the point and essence of all existence and His glory is the sole purpose for our creation (Isa. 43:7). However, when we pursue Him feverishly and desire to love Him passionately, we will have an unexpected and stunning collision with joy and fulfillment. If you're not convinced, you just wait and see as we study together in the chapters ahead.

Long before Augustine graced the page with his confessions, inspired men such as Moses, David, and Paul proved holy hedonists.

Faced with the chance to go on to the promised land with great blessings but without the presence of God, Moses declared, "If your Presence does not go with us, do not send us up from here" (Exod. 33:15).

David wrote, "Because your love is better than life, / my lips will glorify you. . . . / Because you are my help, / I sing in the shadow of your wings" (Ps. 63:3, 7).

Paul found the secret that only Jesus can truly satisfy. He said he considered "everything a loss compared to the surpassing greatness of knowing Christ Jesus my Lord, for whose sake I have lost all things. I consider them rubbish, that I may gain Christ" (Phil. 3:8). In fact, Paul believed greater joy lies in suffering with Christ than a pain-free life without Him. He wrote,

"I want to know Christ and the power of his resurrection and the fellowship of sharing in his sufferings, becoming like him in his death" (Phil. 3:10).

Yes, the Word of God is full of godly hedonists who testified in one way or another that seeking God zealously and jealously was the best thing that ever happened—not to God but to them. God stated it Himself when He said to Abram in Genesis 15:1, "I am . . . your very great reward." In the same vein, I dearly love Hebrews 11:6 that tells us we must not only believe God lives but that He "rewards those who earnestly seek him." Our God is worth loving with all our passion because the more we seek Him the more He rewards us—with more of Himself.

Is finding Him not reward enough? Yet God superabounds in His giving! Many inspired men in Scripture confessed the glorious gain of pursuing God, but few can compete with our very own apostle John. I plan to prove it to you. I'm no proficient Bible scholar, but I have learned to make use of a few study tools and have performed a little research of my own. In the totality of John's writings and in a comparison of his Gospel with the three synoptics, John has more to say about the concepts of life, light, love, truth, glory, signs, and belief than anyone else in the entire New Testament.

John has overwhelmingly more to say about God as Father than any other inspired writer. In fact, out of 248 New Testament references to God as Father, John penned 130. In impressive balance, John also has more to say about God and the world than any other inspired writer. Of the New Testament references to the world, 103 out of 206 are John's. I could go on with many examples.

My point? It's certainly not that his Gospel is better than others. Each was inspired just as God perfectly intended. The point is that in length of life and depth of love, John discovered the concept of *more*. I am convinced a nutshell explanation for John's entire experience and perspective is intimated in one of the most profound statements of Christ ever dictated to John.

Jesus said, "I have come that they might have life, and have it to the full" (John 10:10). *Perisson,* the Greek word for "full," is one we need to know by heart. It means "over and above, more than enough . . . generally, superabundant, . . . much, great."[6]

Do you realize that Christ wants you to have a great life? Am I making you nervous? Don't confuse great with no challenges, hardships, or even suffering. In fact, the greatest parts of my life experience have been overcoming the overwhelming in the power of the Holy Spirit. Christian hedonists don't discount suffering. They just don't give up until they find the gain in the loss (Phil. 3:8). When we lay down these lives of ours, God wants us to be able to say we lived them fully. We didn't miss a thing He had for us. We had a blast with God. Just like John.

Jesus offered a lot of life; John took Him up on it. Jesus shed a lot of light; John chose to walk in it. Jesus revealed a lot of glory; John chose to behold it. Jesus delivered a lot of truth; John believed it. Jesus shed a lot of blood; John felt covered by it. Jesus lavished a lot of love; John received it. Jesus is full of everything we could ever need or desire. Thankfully, many receive, but others receive more abundantly. John was one of those. I want to be another.

Beloved, with all my heart I want to know God, and I want to experience one blessing after another flowing from His favor. I want more. That's all there is to it. I am convinced that God welcomes the hedonistic approach that says, "God, You are the best thing that could ever happen to me, so happen indeed!"

We are going to concentrate on the overall invitation to abundance in the Gospel of John. In each chapter we'll meditate on concepts John emphasized more in his Gospel than any of the synoptic writers and often the other New Testament writers as a whole. In other words, we're going to study the points where the needles shot high on John's EKG.

C. S. Lewis was right. We have been too easily pleased. Somewhere along the way many of us formed a concept of Christ and settled with it. So few really grasp the invitation to great adventure. They try to reduce God to nothing but religion then grow bored with the image they created. As a result, hearts become accidents waiting to happen, for our souls were instead created to exult and dance in holy passion. If we don't find it in the Holy One, we'll search for it amid the smoldering heaps of the unholy. I have burn scars to prove it.

Chapter 22

MORE BELIEF!

*But these are written that you may believe that Jesus is the Christ, the Son
of God, and that by believing you may have life in his name. (John 20:31)*

$\mathcal{I}$n the very early years of the New Testament church, Eusebius penned
the following statement from Clement of Alexandria: "John, last of all, con-
scious that the outward facts had been set forth in the Gospels, was urged
on by his disciples, and, divinely moved by the Spirit, composed a spiritual
Gospel."[1] If Clement was accurate, John was familiar with the synoptic
Gospels and had neither the desire nor a compelling of the Holy Spirit to
repeat the biographical approach of Matthew, Mark, and Luke. The
Gospel of John shares only about 10 percent of its content with the other
Gospel writers. Clement did not mean all four were not equally inspired. He
simply suggested that the last Gospel can draw us further into spiritual truths.

While the Gospels of Matthew and Luke begin with human genealo-
gies, John's Gospel begins with the zenith proclamation of Jesus Christ, the
preexistent, eternal Word. Though John's approach is vast and deep, my
Greek teacher tells me that John's Greek is the most easily read of all the
New Testament books. Perhaps Augustine had these facts in mind when he
wrote, "John's Gospel is deep enough for an elephant to swim and shallow
enough for a child not to drown."[2] So whether we're elephants or children
in our relationship to the Word, you and I can splash to our delight in the
living water of this Gospel.

Like several other New Testament books, the end of this Gospel
explains why the book had a beginning. John inscribed two insightful passages toward his conclusion. One is the final verse: "Jesus did many other

things as well. If every one of them was written down, I suppose that even the whole world would not have room for the books that would be written" (John 21:25).

I never hear this verse without thinking about my first guide in Israel who told me that the ancient Hebrews often spoke in pictures and images. He said, "For instance, we would read John's intent in this final verse like this: 'If all the trees of the forest were quills and the oceans ink, still they could not record all Jesus did.'" Ah, yes! That's my kind of wording!

Whatever your preference in rhetoric, we can conclude from John's ending that the elements shared in the pages of his Gospel were purposefully selected by the leadership of the Spirit working through the personality and priorities of John. Knowing he could say more than the scrolls on earth could record, what caused John to choose the particular accounts recorded in the Gospel? In other words, what was he trying to achieve in his inspired choice of material? He provides the answer in John 20:30–31: "Jesus did many other miraculous signs in the presence of his disciples, which are not recorded in this book. But these are written that you may believe that Jesus is the Christ, the Son of God, and that by believing you may have life in his name."

No other Gospel writer surpasses John's determination to express Jesus' absolute deity. John wrote his Gospel so that the reader would behold truth from an utterly convinced eyewitness that Jesus Christ is the uncontested Christ. The Messiah. The Son of God. John 1:12 tells us why this belief is so critical: "To all who received him, to those who believed in his name, he gave the right to become children of God."

Like no other Gospel or New Testament writer, John presents Jesus Christ as the Son of God the Father. Out of approximately 248 times in the New Testament where God is deemed Father, 110 of those are in John's Gospel. John was the consummate evangelist, and he knew salvation could not be secured by those who did not acknowledge Jesus Christ as the absolute Son of the God. He made sure no one could miss the saving facts in his Gospel. Of course, the reader could see the facts and yet still miss the salvation because something vital is required of anyone who desires to become a child of God: belief!

In his book *Encountering John,* Andreas J. Kostenberger wrote:

> Apart from "Jesus" and "Father" there is no theologically signifi-
> cant word that occurs more frequently in John's Gospel than the
> word "believe" (pisteuo; 98 times). John's ninety-eight instances
> compare to eleven in Mark, fourteen in Matthew, and nine in
> Luke. Thus Merrill Tenney seems to be justified in calling John
> "the Gospel of belief." Another interesting observation is that
> while John uses the verb "to believe" almost a hundred times, he
> does not once use the corresponding noun (pistis, "faith"). It
> appears therefore that John's primary purpose is to engender in his
> readers the act of believing, of placing their trust in Jesus Christ.[3]

Glory to God! His statement brings us to a glorious point! Do you
remember when I told you that God would transform our lives if we would
"take God up" on some of the abundance He presents throughout the
Gospel of John? You don't need to wait a moment longer. Through our
study God is calling you and me to believe Him more. John's Gospel
doesn't just call us to belief, as if it were in the past tense and complete. In
Christ we are called to be living verbs, Beloved! We are called to the ongoing act of believing!

Yes, for many of us the belief that secures our salvation is past tense and
complete. In other words, we have already trusted Christ for salvation, and
we are now and forever secured. But tragically too many live in past-tense
belief, believing God for little more from that time forward.

I want to ask you a critical question: Is the scope of your belief in
Christ in the past-tense security of salvation, or can you be caught in the
active, ongoing lifestyle of believing Christ? In other words, are we simply
nouns—*believers?* Or are we also verbs—*believing?*

Believing in Christ and believing Christ can be two very different
things. We begin with the former, but we certainly don't want to end there!
We want to keep believing what Jesus says about Himself, His Father, and
us until we see Him face-to-face.

Think of the roll call of the faithful in Hebrews 11. As eternally vital
as it is, none of these were commended for the initial faith that enabled

them to enter a relationship with God. They were commended for ongoing acts of believing at times when their physical eyes could not see what God told them they could believe.

John's Gospel includes the word *life* more than any other Gospel. Over twice as many times, in fact, as Matthew who falls in second place. By no coincidence the same Gospel that shouts life also shouts the act of believing. Any of those in the great cloud of witnesses of Hebrews 11 would tell us that really living the Christian life is synonymous with really believing the God who created it.

I'm going to ask you a question that has my own head spinning. Who is your Jesus? Throughout the pages to come, we'll study John's Jesus, full of grace and truth, who offers us one blessing after another. But at this present time, who do we believe Jesus to be with our own lives? In reality, what we believe is measured by what we live, not by what we say. If your life were a Gospel like John's, who could people "believe" your Jesus to be? Think specifically and concretely. Based on your life, might people believe Jesus to be a Redeemer because He has obviously redeemed your life from a pit? Or a Healer because He has healed you from a certain disease? Please keep in mind these kinds of questions are to provoke our deep meditations. They will either help us see progress and reason for rejoicing or help us to see where we want to go.

John's Jesus is described throughout his Gospel. He is the same One who is meant to be ours: the preexistent, miracle-working, only begotten Son of the Father of all creation. Years ago God revealed to me that I believed in my childhood church's Christ who thankfully was a Savior for sinners, but I had hardly begun to believe in the Bible's Christ. Yes, He is a Savior for sinners and so much more! We have derived a staggering amount of our impressions of Christ from vastly incomplete if not totally unreliable sources, as sweet and respectable as they may be!

We are blessed beyond measure for every time one of these human instruments extended us reliable impressions of Jesus. I derived most of my early impressions about Jesus based not so much on what I learned at church but what I saw at church. I certainly believed Jesus saves, and that belief led me to my own salvation experience. But I believed Him for little more because I saw evidence of little more. The few marvelous exceptions marked me forever, but I wonder why so many believers believe so little of Jesus. I'm just going to say it like I see it. Either Jesus no longer does what the Bible says He did, or we don't give Him the chance.

John went out of his way to present us an all-powerful Son of God who speaks and His Word is accomplished. A Savior who not only saves us from our sins but can deliver us from evil. A Great Physician who really can heal and a God of glory who reveals His magnificence to mere mortals. And, yes, a God of signs and wonders. We've already seen John testify that one of his chief purposes in his Gospel was to testify to the signs Jesus performed so readers would believe, not in the miracles themselves, mind you, but in the Christ who performed them.

Many claim, "The day of miracles has ceased." I don't doubt that God may employ miracles less frequently in cultures where the Word of God is prevalent, but I know Jesus Christ still performs miracles. First, I know He does due to the claims of Hebrews: "Remember your leaders, who spoke the word of God to you. Consider the outcome of their way of life and imitate their faith. Jesus Christ is the same yesterday and today and forever" (Heb. 13:7–8).

The second reason I know Jesus Christ still performs miracles is because I'm one of them. I'm not being dramatic. I'm telling you the truth. The only excuse for an ounce of victory in my life is the supernatural delivering power of Jesus Christ. I was in the clutches of a real, live devil, living in a perpetual cycle of defeat. Only a miracle-working God could have set me free then dared to use me. My friends Patsy Clairmont and Kathy Trocolli testify that they are nothing less than miracles as well. You may remark, "Those are not real miracles!" but Scripture suggests no greater work exists.

According to the apostle Paul in Ephesians 3:20, God "is able to do immeasurably more than all we ask or imagine, according to his power that is at work within us." Do you see, Beloved? The most profound miracles of God will always be those within the hearts and souls of people. Moving a mountain is nothing compared to changing a selfish, destructive human heart.

Third, I know Jesus Christ still performs miracles because I've witnessed them. I have seen Him do things most people I know don't even believe He does anymore. Jesus healed a woman I know personally from liver cancer and a man I know personally from pancreatic cancer. I've seen women bear healthy children who were diagnosed inside the womb with debilitating conditions. I was in a service with a dear friend in his eighties who has been legally blind for years when God suddenly restored a remarkable measure of his sight—right on the pew of a Baptist church! Hallelujah!

Like you, I have also seen many who have not received the miracles they hoped for. I can't explain the difference except to say that God often defers to the greater glory. Sometimes the far greater miracle is the victory He brings and the character He reveals when we don't get what we thought we wanted.

On the other hand, sometimes we see little because we believe little. That's the obstacle you and I want to overcome so that we can live in the abundant blessing of Jesus Christ. When my life is over, I may not have seen Jesus perform some of the miracles the Word says He can—but let it be because He showed His glory another way and not because I believed Him for so pitifully little that I didn't give Him the chance!

Through His work on the cross and His plan before the foundation of the world, Christ has already accomplished so much for your life in heaven! If His work is going to be accomplished here on earth where your feet hit the hot pavement, however, you're going to have to start believing Him. When we received Christ as our Savior, you might picture that a pipe of power connected our lives to God's throne. Unbelief clogs the pipe, but the act of believing clears the way for the inconceivable! As much as John's Gospel has to say about believing, I'm not sure anyone recorded a more powerful statement than Mark. He tells us Jesus said, "Everything is possible for him who believes" (Mark 9:23).

Student of God's Word, the Jesus of some of our churches, denominations, family, and friends may not be able to deliver us, heal us, and stun us with amazing feats, but the Jesus of Scripture can. And He's the same yesterday and today and forever. It's time we start believing Him for more. When we've turned the last page of this Bible study, may we be found firmly embracing the powerful and believable Jesus of God's Word.

Chapter 23

MORE WINE

When the wine was gone, Jesus' mother said to him,
"They have no more wine." (John 2:3)

 esus loves weddings. No doubt about it. The preexistent eternal Word began His divine thesis with the first one in Genesis 2 and consummates it with the last one in Revelation 19. Who can count how many weddings He'll attend in between? Jesus is always the officiating preacher and the one who signs the license whether or not we asked Him to be. After all, marriage was His idea. All His excitement over a simple wedding is because His heart is flooded with anticipation over His own. With us, His bride.

Just take a good look at Ephesians 5:25–32:

> Husbands, love your wives, just as Christ loved the church and gave himself up for her to make her holy, cleansing her by the washing with water through the word, and to present her to himself as a radiant church, without stain or wrinkle or any other blemish, but holy and blameless. In this same way, husbands ought to love their wives as their own bodies. He who loves his wife loves himself. After all, no one ever hated his own body, but he feeds and cares for it, just as Christ does the church—for we are members of his body. "For this reason a man will leave his father and mother and be united to his wife, and the two will become one flesh." This is a profound mystery—but I am talking about Christ and the church.

As I write to you from the throes of middle age, am I ever glad to know we're presented without wrinkles! Incidentally, I'm almost positive that

Ephesians 5:29 implies husbands are supposed to do the cooking. One thing is certain, we're not going to have to do the cooking at our own marriage supper with the Lamb. Until then, every wedding He attends is a blessed rehearsal for the big one. For now, we have a wedding to attend in Cana, and I'd hate to walk in late.

John tells the story in 2:1–11. Jesus attended a wedding feast, and the wine ran out. Such an occurrence would have been a great embarrassment to the host. Mary brought it to Jesus' attention, but He seemed to snub her request. His mother just told the servants to do Jesus' bidding. Jesus turned six stone jars of washing water into wine.

We can readily assume the families involved in the wedding were people Jesus knew well. Don't miss the fact that Jesus was invited. We ordinarily don't invite strangers to our weddings. Furthermore, the wedding date caught Jesus at a critically busy time, just as His Father was launching His ministry. For Him to be intentional enough to attend this wedding tells us He had relationships and divine purpose there. The hosts were probably good family friends since Mary obviously helped with the wedding.

I believe Jesus had another reason why He didn't have to have His arm twisted to attend the wedding. I happen to think He loved a good party. Still does. I am convinced Jesus' basic personality in His brief walk in human flesh was delightful and refreshingly relational.

Jesus made the disciples allow children to come to Him (Matt. 19:14). His critics complained about Jesus eating with tax collectors and "sinners" (Luke 5:30) and partying rather than fasting (Matt. 9:14). Do those examples surprise you? Did you catch the similarity to John 2?

For starters, children aren't drawn to cranky people. They are very good judges of character and like people who are fun. The other references imply that Jesus in our midst is reason enough to celebrate. Why in the world have we let "partying" become associated with licentiousness? God created man and formed within him an authentic soul-need to feast and celebrate. In fact, God deemed celebration so vital, He commanded His people to celebrate at frequent intervals throughout the calendar year (Lev. 23). Let me say that again: He *commands* that we celebrate His goodness and His greatness!

I say it's time we take the whole idea of partying back. I'm always mystified that many nonbelievers think Christians must be dull, bored, and wouldn't know a good time if it socked them in the noggin. Boy, do we have a secret! No one laughs like a bunch of Christians! My staff and I roll with laughter together at times.

They aren't my only fellow partyers. A week or so ago three of my dearest friends and I scrunched on one couch together all holding hands. One of us had lost a daughter several days earlier to a drunk driver. As we held on to one another for dear life, God gave us the sudden gift of the hardest belly laugh any of us have had in a long time. Unbelievers might be insulted to know that when we go to their parties, we wonder why they think they're having such a good time. Lean over here closely so I can whisper: I think they're boring.

The primary reason why celebrations around Christ's presence are so wonderful is because they are the kind intended to be sparkling refreshment to a world-worn soul. We get to attend Christ's kind of parties without taking home a lot of baggage. We don't have a hangover later or a guilty conscience. Christ-centered celebrations are all the fun without all the guilt. That's real partying.

Throughout these chapters we are studying the concepts of more, fullness, and abundance in John's overflowing Gospel. How fitting that the writer who had more to say about abundant life and effervescent living than any other Gospel penman was also the only one inspired to tell us about the wedding in Cana: an event where *more* became the very issue at hand: They have no more wine. And, Son, You're the only one who can give them what they need—more.

One reason for John's unique insight into the wedding in Cana is that he was the only Gospel writer in attendance. Matching the chronologies of the Gospels suggests that Matthew hadn't been called yet and Luke and Mark didn't come into the picture until much later. Many scholars believe John was an adolescent when he followed Christ—a partying age if you'll ever find one! The last statement in John 2:11 intimates the wedding at Cana had a tremendous impact on him: "He thus revealed his glory, and his disciples put their faith in him."

It's one thing to follow Christ around the countryside. It's another thing to put your faith in Him. Never lose sight of the fact that Judas followed Jesus. Jesus is looking for true disciples who really place their faith— their trust—in Him. We can follow Jesus to Christian conferences all over the nation or down the aisles of every church in America but never put our faith in Him. John, the one who wrote the Gospel of belief, officially began his own great adventure of believing right there in Cana.

Yes, it was a big day for John. It was also a big day on the kingdom calendar. Any first in Scripture is huge. How Jesus chose to perform His first miracle cannot be overestimated. The scene contains more applications than we have space to discuss. Since it's just the two of us, however, let's dip the ladle into the stone water jar and draw forth two cups of wine to share:

1. God ordained that Christ's first earthbound miracle would be filling empty jars. Praise God! Does any pain rival that of emptiness? Don't miss the significance of the kinds of jars these were. They were stone jars.

I think this first miracle reveals a vivid picture of the condition God's chosen people were in at that time. Legalism had soared during the four hundred years without a fresh word from God. As we discussed in the very beginning of our study, the kind of Pharisaism Jesus found so revolting developed during the latter part of the intertestamental silence. We, too, can substitute legalism for our lack of fresh involvement with God. All the Jews' ceremonial rituals and washings had done was leave them as empty as those oversized jars and as cold as stone. Religious observances mean nothing apart from God.

Meaningless ritual and all the self-helps of personal cleansings are not the only things that leave us empty. A few chapters later Jesus ran into a woman at Sychar's well who was as empty as the stone water jars ever thought about being. She had tried to fill her empty life with five husbands (John 4:17–18).

Beloved, you can take this one to the spiritual bank: any compulsion for too much of anything is symptomatic of the horror and urgency of emptiness. Far too many people think that the "good Christian thing to do" about our gnawing emptiness is get a grip, stop whining, and live without for the rest of our lives. If that's what we do, we miss the very first miracle Jesus came to perform! John's Gospel came along to give us the best of good news. We were never meant to live with emptiness! We were meant to be full; His children were all meant to receive His fullness in one blessing after another!

Let me echo a precept underscored continually through this look at abundance. We were created to be full. When we're not filled with the good things Christ came to bring us, we will grasp at anything as a substitute. An unsatisfied soul is an accident waiting to happen.

We also see a second aspect of the first miracle. It brought new wine. To the woman at the well, He brought the living water. To the guests at the wedding, He brought new wine. He gives us what we need. And what most of us need is some new wine!

John 2:11 contains another detail we need to recognize. Through His first miracle Jesus revealed His glory. In other words, the miracle performed in the physical realm was meant to reveal something far more glorious in the spiritual realm. Though Jesus certainly met an immediate need at the wedding, the wine represented something of far greater significance.

Psalm 104:15, Judges 9:13, and Psalm 4:7 identify wine as gladdening the heart and bringing cheer. Remember the "Hmmm" passage in Matthew 9:14–17? The Pharisees blamed Jesus for partying instead of fasting, and Jesus responded with the word that one does not pour new wine into old wineskins. One reason Christ came was to fill the emptiness created by the letter of the Law, ritual religion, or any earthly substitute.

I believe that new wine is beautifully implied in Ephesians 5:18. Paul wrote, "Do not get drunk on wine, which leads to debauchery. Instead, be filled with the Spirit." The passage implies that the filling of the Holy Spirit does in full measure what we try to accomplish when we desire to be drunk with wine.

You see, one reason people drink too much wine is because it changes the way they feel and the way they behave. So does the "new wine" of Christ, but His effects are always good. Jesus came to bring the new wine of the Spirit! Something we can drink our fill of without all the negative side effects of wine and the emptiness it leaves behind in the wake of the temporary fix.

You see, throughout the Old Testament, only handfuls of people had the Holy Spirit in them or upon them because under the old covenant God gave the Spirit for empowerment more than fulfillment. John's Gospel will reveal later that one of Christ's primary purposes for coming and laying down His life was to send the Holy Spirit to us—not just to walk beside us but to dwell in us. At the first revelation of Christ's glory in Cana, they had no idea that the true New Wine was on its way! The Master of our banquet saved the best of the wine for last.

Beloved, do you realize that joy and gladness are among the many gifts and services Christ brought His Holy Spirit to grant? Check it out for yourself. "The fruit of the Spirit is love, joy, peace, patience, kindness, goodness, faithfulness, gentleness and self-control. Against such things there is no law" (Gal. 5:22–23).

Just think! No matter how much you drink of His Spirit, against such things there is no law. Further, the more you drink, the more fully satisfied you are with love, joy, peace, and all sorts of side effects we're so desperate to achieve. To top off the goblet, instead of losing self-control, we gain it. You can't beat a drink like that!

When Melissa was a toddler, she was never satisfied with a little of anything. Every time I offered her a treat, she'd cup her plump little hand, thrust it forward and say, "Can me have a bawnch [bunch] of it?" The way she saw life, why bother with a little if you can have a bunch of it. Indeed! John would agree! Dear one, how tragic for us to continue with pangs of emptiness. What a waste! Christ came to bring us a bawnch of it! Stop feeling guilty because you crave lots of joy in your life. You were made for joy! You are a jar of clay just waiting to be filled (2 Cor. 4:7). May this lesson end with the clink of our cups as we toast to a life overflowing with New Wine!

Chapter 24

MORE ABOUT THE WORLD

For God so loved the world that he gave his one and only Son, that
whoever believes in him shall not perish but have eternal life. (John 3:16)

*O*ne of the most astonishing statistical comparisons between the Gospel of John and the three synoptics is how much more God inspired him to tell us about the world. Based on an NIV word count comparison, Matthew mentions the world ten times, Mark five times, and Luke seven times. The Gospel of John? A whopping seventy-three times! In fact, the totality of John's New Testament contributions informing us about the world constitutes almost half the mentions in the entire New Testament. Obviously we will miss a very important concept in John's Gospel if we overlook what he tells us about the world.

Perhaps the most overwhelming is a concept to which we've grown inordinately casual: Jesus was sent by God to the world. Let's try to get our arms stretched a little further around this fact for a moment. John 17 tells us that the Father and Son had fellowship and shared glory before the world even existed. Jesus said, "Father, glorify me in your presence with the glory I had with you before the world began" (John 17:5). In fact, I am absolutely convinced that mankind exists out of the holy passion of the Trinity to draw others into their fellowship.

The Father, Son, and Holy Spirit, complete in themselves, desired the overflowing and exceeding joy of additional relationship so "in the beginning God created the heavens and the earth" (Gen. 1:1). Although distinctions exist between the words *earth* and *world*, they are intertwined and virtually interchangeable where creation is concerned. Genesis 1:1 says that

God created the earth, and John 1:10 tells us the world was made through Christ. *Earth* tends to encompass the physical properties of our planet while *world* encases more of the system, social and otherwise, on it and around it. You might think of the distinction this way: Our world exists on this earth.

Every time the word *world* is used in the NIV translation of John's Gospel, the Greek word is *kosmos*. The word means "world, with its primary meaning being order, regular disposition and arrangement. . . . The earth, this lower world as the abode of man."[1]

Now try to grasp this: God the Father, Son, and Holy Spirit desired the existence of humanity for fellowship. They wanted humans to have a will of their own because they wanted to be chosen. Not commanded. They knew that equipping humanity with a will would necessitate a plan for redemption because we would ultimately make some very poor choices. Thus, the plan of salvation was already completely intact before the creation of the world. When the Holy Trinity was ready, each member participated in the creation.

Genesis 1:1: "In the beginning God created the heavens and the earth." Stay with me here. The Word of God delineates between one little planet He called the earth and the entire rest of the universe. We have no idea what is out there. What little science documents and hypothesizes makes Genesis 1:1 inconceivably impressive.

Our solar system is in a galaxy called the Milky Way. Scientists estimate that more than 100 billion galaxies are scattered throughout the visible universe. Astronomers have photographed millions of them through telescopes. The most distant galaxies ever photographed are as far as 10 billion to 13 billion light-years away. The Milky Way's diameter is about 100,000 light-years. The solar system lies about 25,000 light-years from the center of the galaxy. There are about 100 billion stars in the Milky Way.[2] Imagine, 100 billion stars estimated in our galaxy alone, and Psalm 147:4 tells us God "determines the number of the stars and calls them each by name."

Impressive, isn't it? But this gets even more impressive: In the beginning God created the sun, the moon, every star, all their surrounding planets, and the earth. You and I have no idea what God's activities may have been elsewhere in the universe, but according to the Bible and as far as He wanted us to know, He picked out one tiny speck upon which to build a world. Our world. And He picked it out so that when the time had fully come, He could send His Son (Gal. 4:4).

Can you imagine the fellowship of the Trinity on the seventh day? As they rested and looked upon the very good work they had accomplished, one planet had been tended like no other to our knowledge. Perfectly placed in the universe with adequate distance from sun, moon, and stars to sustain human life, it was chosen for divine infiltration.

"For God so loved the world." Scripture doesn't tell us He loved the sun, and it is the most impressive among the heavenly bodies we can see. Nor are we told He loved the stars even though He knows every one of them by name. John goes out of his way, however, to tell us—not just that God loved the world—but that He *so* loved the world.

In a universe so vast, so incomprehensible, why does God single out one little planet to so love? Beloved, absorb this into the marrow of your bones: because we are on it. As despicable as humanity can be, God loves us. Inconceivably, we are His treasures, His prize creation. He can't help it. He just loves us. So much, in fact, that He did something I, with my comparatively pitiful love for my children, would not do for anyone. He "gave his one and only Son, that whoever believes in him shall not perish but have eternal life" (John 3:16).

Dear one, let it fall afresh. I am overcome with emotion. Elohim is so huge. We are so small. Yet the vastness of His love—so high, so wide, so deep, so long—envelops us like the endless universe envelops a crude little planet God first called Earth.

Not long ago Keith had a bench with a simple covering placed in the corner of our small backyard. Almost every morning I light a candle and head out to that bench for a predawn worship service and quiet time. Sometimes I have to pull a big blanket out of a warm dryer to wrap around me in the cold. At that time in the morning the heavens are still as dark as the blackest night, and the stars look like God lit ten thousand candles of His own. In that morning hour, I feel like He lit them just for the two of us. (And for the two of you.) I feel a million miles from the freeways of Houston.

Blessed man that he was, David the psalmist was a million miles from a freeway when he was besieged by the sight. He wrote, "When I consider your heavens, / the work of your fingers, / the moon and the stars, / which you have set in place, / what is man that you are mindful of him, / the son of man that you care for him?" (Ps. 8:3–4).

In the midst of constant discoveries, modern science hasn't even begun to discover the true wonder of God's universe. Yet even when I consider what they do know, I am overwhelmed with David's same question: who are we, God of all creation, that You would give a single thought to us? Let alone a mindful.

Amanda was one of the dreamiest and most tenderhearted toddlers you can imagine. I often stooped down to talk to her so that I could look her right in those big blue-green eyes. Every time I squatted down to talk to her, she squatted down, too, . . . and there we'd be. The gesture was so precious I always had to fight the urge to laugh. I dared not because she was often very serious about those contemplative moments between the two of us.

Of his God, the psalmist wrote, "Your right hand sustains me; / you stoop down to make me great" (Ps. 18:35). The Amplified Version says it this way: "Your gentleness and condescension have made me great." I don't think the Scripture applies to us in the modern world's terms of greatness. I think it says of us, "You stoop down and make me significant." Yes, indeed. And when the God of all the universe stoops down and a single child recognizes the tender condescension and bends her knee to stoop as well, the heart of God surges with unbridled emotion. And there they are. Just the two of them.

As you conclude this chapter, please read aloud and thoughtfully John 1:10–12 with all this in mind. Much of the world carries on as if their Creator does not exist. Oh, but He does. Bow down, dear children of God. His love has made you great.

> He was in the world, and though the world was made through him, the world did not recognize him. He came to that which was his own, but his own did not receive him. Yet to all who received him, to those who believed in his name, he gave the right to become children of God. (John 1:10–12)

Chapter 25

MORE OF WHO HE IS

"I tell you the truth," Jesus answered, "before Abraham
was born, I am!" (John 8:58)

$\mathcal{M}$uch of the lost population and unbelieving world religions attempt a show of respect by claiming that while they don't believe Jesus Christ was the Son of God, they certainly esteem Him as a good man. A true prophet. They don't realize that their summation of this historical figure reveals they are decidedly ill-informed. If Jesus is not the Son of God and indeed deity, He was either a pathological liar or mentally ill. If at best Christ was a prophet, then He had to be a false prophet because He unabashedly claimed Messiahship. In reality, if the Christ that walked among men two millennia ago was not God's Son, then He grossly misled people, and nothing good is left to say about Him.

For years I've been aware of a group of scholars who meet annually to discuss and debate matters of Scripture. Of course, that is their right. The part that baffles and even somewhat amuses me is that they come to their final conclusions by popular vote. For example, they once voted on whether or not Christ would visibly return to earth in a second coming. (They voted it down.) They have also voted on matters such as whether Mary was really a virgin and the validity of certain biblically professed miracles.

If they weren't people of influence, I would laugh my head off. Why? Because the vote of humans, no matter how arrogant, couldn't change truth an iota if our lives depended on it! If the world population took a vote as to whether Jesus is the Son of God and not a single ballot was cast in His favor, He'd still be the Son of God. Furthermore, when His Father says

"Go!" Christ's feet will touch the Mount of Olives, and it will split from east to west (Zech. 14:4). He doesn't need our permission or even our faith to be who He is. Aren't you thankful?

We are going to examine seven claims Christ made in the Gospel of John about who He is. These seven titles are by no means the totality of His claims. They simply share several common denominators in John's Gospel that we don't want to miss. As we continue with our theme of "more," we will find that the Gospel of John tells us more about the self-proclaimed identity of Christ than the others.

Note Christ's claims of identity in the following Scriptures. No matter how many times you've seen these titles, I pray you will approach them with freshness.

- Then Jesus declared, "I am the bread of life. He who comes to me will never go hungry, and he who believes in me will never be thirsty" (John 6:35).

- When Jesus spoke again to the people, he said, "I am the light of the world. Whoever follows me will never walk in darkness, but will have the light of life" (John 8:12).

- Therefore Jesus said again, "I tell you the truth, I am the gate for the sheep. All who ever came before me were thieves and robbers, but the sheep did not listen to them. I am the gate; whoever enters through me will be saved. He will come in and go out, and find pasture" (John 10:7–9).

- "I am the good shepherd. The good shepherd lays down his life for the sheep" (John 10:11).

- "I am the resurrection and the life. He who believes in me will live, even though he dies" (John 11:25).

- "I am the way and the truth and the life. No one comes to the Father except through me" (John 14:6).

- "I am the vine; you are the branches. If a man remains in me and I in him, he will bear much fruit; apart from me you can do nothing" (John 15:5).

In fairly rapid succession Christ made a point of defining Himself a perfect seven times. I see three basic common denominators in these seven titles. Consider each with me:

1. All seven titles are preceded by "I am." Of course, to make any sense, they must, but I want you to consider the impact of these two words when emitted from the mouth of Jesus the Messiah. Take a good look at John 8:48–59. This passage is so important that I'm providing all of it for you:

> The Jews answered him, "Aren't we right in saying that you are a Samaritan and demon-possessed?"
>
> "I am not possessed by a demon," said Jesus, "but I honor my Father and you dishonor me. I am not seeking glory for myself; but there is one who seeks it, and he is the judge. I tell you the truth, if anyone keeps my word, he will never see death."
>
> At this the Jews exclaimed, "Now we know that you are demon-possessed! Abraham died and so did the prophets, yet you say that if anyone keeps your word, he will never taste death. Are you greater than our father Abraham? He died, and so did the prophets. Who do you think you are?"
>
> Jesus replied, "If I glorify myself, my glory means nothing. My Father, whom you claim as your God, is the one who glorifies me. Though you do not know him, I know him. If I said I did not, I would be a liar like you, but I do know him and keep his word. Your father Abraham rejoiced at the thought of seeing my day; he saw it and was glad."
>
> "You are not yet fifty years old," the Jews said to him, "and you have seen Abraham!"
>
> "I tell you the truth," Jesus answered, "before Abraham was born, I am!" At this, they picked up stones to stone him, but Jesus hid himself, slipping away from the temple grounds.

Galatians indicates one way Abraham "saw" Christ's day. "He believed God, and it was credited to him as righteousness" (Gal. 3:6). Paul went on to explain that those of us who have the faith of Abraham are blessed and justified as he was.

Through Abraham's harrowing experience in Genesis 22 when God spared Isaac's life through a sacrificial offering, God preached the gospel in advance to Abraham! Now meditate on the power-packed claim of Christ in John 8:58: "'I tell you the truth,' Jesus answered, 'before Abraham was born, I am!'"

Jesus' original hearers reacted so violently because they knew exactly what Christ was implying. They wanted to stone Him for blasphemy because they understood the association of His reference to God's introduction to Moses in Exodus 3:12–15. In verse 15 God told Moses, "Say to the Israelites, 'The LORD, the God of your fathers—the God of Abraham, the God of Isaac and the God of Jacob—has sent me to you.' This is my name forever, the name by which I am to be remembered from generation to generation." God introduced Himself once and forever as the great I AM.

God stated one of His primary points to Moses in verse 12: "I will be with you." This great I AM WHO I AM (v. 14), the completely self-sufficient, self-existent God of all creation, introduced Himself by this title in context with the promise to be with man. He did not need them. Rather, they needed Him, and He came in response to that need.

Later in this chapter we will develop the concept further. For now, you can safely conclude that the Jews listening to Christ in John 8 knew exactly what Christ meant by His "I am!" statement. He was identifying Himself as God. Dear ones, we must consider His claims as well. Either Jesus came as the incarnate God, or He is a liar. He cannot be anything in between. You and I say we believe Christ's words to be truth, and if we do, He is worthy of our most profound worship and "followship."

Before we conclude this point, we must take notice of John 18:6. After Judas betrayed Jesus in the garden of Gethsemane, the gathered mob of priests and soldiers asked Jesus' identity. Christ responded, "I am he," and the entire troop fell backward to the ground.

I believe the reason they collapsed before the Son of God is intimated in the original language where the Greek word for *he* is conspicuously missing. The Interlinear Bible even translates Christ's words like this: "Then when He said to them, I AM, they departed into the rear and fell to the ground" (The Interlinear Bible, p. 837).

You see, the rest of us could say, "I am . . . ," and it would mean nothing more than a common identification. When Christ says the words *I am,* they are falling from the lips of Him who is the Great I AM!

2. The word *the* is included in each title. If you go back and read each of the seven "I am" titles in John, you will find in every case Jesus said, "I am *the*" rather than "I am *a*."

The issue may seem elementary scholastically, but nothing could be more profound theologically. For just a moment forget everyone else in the body of Christ and just think about your own approach to Jesus Christ. Is He *a* light to you, or *the* Light? Is He *a* way for you to follow—perhaps here and there in life—or is He *the* way you want to go? Is He *a* means to the afterlife in your opinion? In other words, deep down inside do you think that several world religions probably offer a viable way to life after death and Jesus is but one of them? Or is He *the* resurrection and *the* life? Be as honest as possible in your response to the following question: Beloved, is Christ an *a* among several other possibilities in this life to you or is He your *THE*?

3. Each of Christ's seven "I Am" statements in John's Gospel is relational! If you look again at all seven titles but look for how each title is associated with people, you will discover a blessing:

- John 6:35—He who comes to the Bread of Life will never go hungry.
- John 8:12—She who follows the Light of the world will never walk in darkness.
- John 10:7–9—Whoever enters through the Gate to the Sheep will be saved.
- John 10:11–14—He who belongs to the Good Shepherd receives protection and is known by the Shepherd.
- John 11:25—She who believes in the Resurrection and the Life will live, even though she dies.
- John 14:6—Whoever follows the Way and the Truth and the Life comes to the Father.
- John 15:1, 5—He who remains in the True Vine will bear much fruit.

Christ is many things. He is truly the Great I AM. He is the Savior of the world. He fulfills numerous titles in the Word of God, but I believe the spiritual implication of the seven "I am" sayings in the broad approach of John's Gospel is this: Jesus Christ is everything we need. Every one of these titles is for us! Remember, He is the self-sufficient One! He came to be what we need. And not just what we need, but what we desire most in all of life. The I AM came to be with us. I could weep with joy!

We will never have a challenge He can't empower us to meet. We will never have a need He can't fill. We will never have an earthly desire He can't exceed. When we allow Christ to be all He is to us, we find wholeness. One piece at a time. Every time you discover the reality of Christ fulfilling another realm of your needs and longings, His name is written on a different part of you, and you are that much closer to wholeness.

Do you see, dear one, that Christ is everything? Oh, the blessed simplicity of the pursuit and love of Jesus! "One thing have I desired . . . , that will I seek after"! (Ps. 27:4 KJV). In our harried times, isn't the thought of becoming a "one thing" person refreshing and freeing? In one Savior we discover all things! As the apostle Paul said in 2 Corinthians 11:3, we must never allow Satan to corrupt us from the simplicity that is in Christ. Our Jesus is everything. That will never change no matter how man casts his vote.

Part 6

LIFE MORE ABUNDANTLY

I can hardly believe we have arrived at the midpoint of our present journey together. Let's recommit to see this path to its final destination and allow God to accomplish everything He purposed when we turned the first page.

I commit to you this moment that I will not slack off in my pursuit of God, my research, or my enthusiasm. I hope you'll commit not to allow the enemy to distract or discourage you from finishing. Lord, You began a good work in us. You have nothing less in mind for each of us than inconceivable riches in Christ Jesus. We don't want to miss them! Empower us to complete what we've started and reap every reward You graciously desire to grant us for seeking You (Heb. 11:6). Give us ears to hear and eyes to see! In the glorious name of Jesus, Amen.

Chapter 26

MORE OF THE HOLY SPIRIT

But the Counselor, the Holy Spirit, whom the Father will send in my
name, will teach you all things and will remind you of everything
I have said to you. (John 14:26)

The concepts of *more* and *abundance* are tucked like priceless treasures in John's Gospel. One of our first goals was to highlight what John seemed to want us to know most. Again, our point is not that John's Gospel is superior to the synoptics but that it is distinct. It also appears last in order, suggesting that God may have intended it to be like the grand finale at the conclusion of a spectacular fireworks display. The Light of the world!

Without exception, John's Gospel equips us with more information about the Holy Spirit than any of the synoptics. The Holy Spirit is the focus of our study in this chapter. I wish somehow I could write the next statement in neon lights upon this page to catch the eye of every reader: *The Holy Spirit is the key to everything in the life of the believer in Christ!* Read that statement out loud! I have testified many times to my defeated Christian life through my teenage years and early twenties, even though I rarely missed a church service or activity. I take full responsibility for my own defeat because I could have read for myself what the churches I attended at those times did not teach me.

I received many wonderful treasures from the churches of my youth, but I did not learn two of the most vital keys to a victorious life: how to have an ongoing, vibrant relationship with God through His Word and how to be filled with the power and life of the Holy Spirit. Both of these are vital concepts that the enemy does everything he can to make us miss.

The Word and the Holy Spirit are by far his biggest threats. I don't think John would mind if his contemporary, Paul, launched our study today with an explanation.

First Corinthians 2:9–14 explains why the Holy Spirit is so vital in a relationship with God through His Word:

> As it is written:
> "No eye has seen,
>   no ear has heard,
> no mind has conceived
>   what God has prepared for those who love him"—
> but God has revealed it to us by his Spirit.
>
>   The Spirit searches all things, even the deep things of God. For who among men knows the thoughts of a man except the man's spirit within him? In the same way no one knows the thoughts of God except the Spirit of God. We have not received the spirit of the world but the Spirit who is from God, that we may understand what God has freely given us. This is what we speak, not in words taught us by human wisdom but in words taught by the Spirit, expressing spiritual truths in spiritual words. The man without the Spirit does not accept the things that come from the Spirit of God, for they are foolishness to him, and he cannot understand them, because they are spiritually discerned.

Beloved, I hope you didn't miss that your own personal "1 Corinthians 2:9" is at stake in whether or not you start reaping the benefits the Holy Spirit came to bring you. Now we'll let John tell us what many of those benefits and activities are. John's primary truths on the Holy Spirit are compacted in chapters 14 and 16 of his Gospel.

One of the most revolutionary truths Christ told His disciples is in John 14:17. He told them that the Spirit of Truth at that time was living with them but would soon be in them. Think about the repercussions of that promise. What difference could the Spirit of God make living *in* a person as opposed to *with* a person?

Beloved, that very difference turned a band of fumbling fleshly followers into sticks of spiritual dynamite that exploded victoriously on the world scene in the Book of Acts. The difference is enormous! Impossible to overestimate!

Jesus told how this dispensation of the Holy Spirit would begin: "I tell you the truth: It is for your good that I am going away. Unless I go away, the Counselor will not come to you; but if I go, I will send him to you" (John 16:7).

The fulfillment of Christ's critical promise to His disciples came to them in John 20:21–22. The resurrected Jesus breathed on the disciples and told them to "receive the Holy Spirit." He then filled them in a far more powerful expression at Pentecost in Acts 2:1–4. These glorious events unleashed a new revolutionary economy of the Holy Spirit for the "Church Age" and onward until the return of Christ.

The Holy Spirit now indwells every person who receives Christ as his or her personal Savior (Rom. 8:9). Oh, that we would absorb the magnitude of that spiritual revolution! Dear believer in Christ, the Spirit of the living God—the Spirit of Jesus Christ Himself, the Spirit of Truth—dwells inside of you! Have we heard these concepts so long that we've grown calloused to them?

Luke 11:13 suggests that no greater gift exists for God to give His children than the Holy Spirit. Jesus said, "If you then, though you are evil, know how to give good gifts to your children, how much more will your Father in heaven give the Holy Spirit to those who ask him!" Not only does God give the spirit, John 3:34 tells us that He "gives the Spirit without limit."

Oh, I hope you are getting this. I am about to hop out of my chair. I can barely type! You and I need nothing on this earth like more of the Holy Spirit. Do we need to love an unlovely person? Do we need extra patience? Could we use a little peace in the midst of chaos? Do we need to show an extra measure of kindness? Could anyone stand a little more faithfulness to God? Could anyone use a strong dose of self-discipline? How about a heaping soulful of joy? Take a look at Galatians 5:22–23. They all come with the fullness of the Holy Spirit! You see, we don't just need more patience. We need more of the Holy Spirit filling us and anointing us!

Now before anybody starts writing me letters, let me go on to explain. I realize the Holy Spirit is a person. When He comes into a believer's life at salvation, He moves in personally. We believers have the Spirit, but the infinite Spirit of God continues to pour Himself into our lives. Any given day I may enjoy a greater portion of His Spirit than I did the day before. He continues to pour out more of His Spirit from on high.

Does anyone need deep insight from God's Word? An added measure of understanding? Anyone need the eyes of her heart enlightened to know the hope of her calling? Does anyone want to fulfill God's eternal purposes for her life and think with the mind of Christ instead of the misleading mind of mortal flesh? All of these come with "more" of the Holy Spirit! (see 1 Cor. 2).

Child of God, don't just absorb this truth! Get up and celebrate it! God gives the Spirit without measure! He has all that you need. Or more properly stated, He *is* all that you need. Our fulfillment and greatest joy are in the flooding of the Holy Spirit of God in our lives. He is how we understand God's Word and will for our lives!

Here's a good one: Could anyone use a sharper memory? Beloved, I could! Take a look at John 14:26. "The Counselor, the Holy Spirit, whom the Father will send in my name, will teach you all things and will remind you of everything I have said to you."

The Holy Spirit is the blessed Reminder. Have you ever noticed we have a very sharp memory about destructive things but a far duller memory over instructive things? We need more of the Holy Spirit! Recently I had to memorize lines for a Christmas pageant at our church. I had never done anything like that, and I was a nervous wreck. Because I knew John 14:26, instead of just asking God to help me with my lines, I asked Him to fill me with more of His Holy Spirit so the blessed Reminder would manifest Himself to me—and He did! He is your key to memorizing Scripture or retaining anything biblical. Take Him up on it!

What do you need most from the Holy Spirit? Are you actively praying for more of Him toward that end? Luke 11:13 implies that if we want the Holy Spirit to invade more and more of our lives, God wants us to ask Him for it! You see, the person of the Holy Spirit dwells in each of us who has trusted Christ as Savior (Eph. 1:14). We have each been sealed

(Eph. 1:13), and He will remain with us forever (compare John 14:16 and Heb. 13:5); but according to our level of cooperation, we can either quench the Holy Spirit within us or we can be utterly filled and anointed by Him. The difference defines whether we live in victory or defeat.

Since I began to learn what God made available to me through His Holy Spirit and what He is not only willing but eager to do for me, the level of supernatural power in my life in comparison has skyrocketed. I want the same for you! I am so jealous with a godly jealousy for you that I can hardly stand it!

Beloved, every one of these Bible studies as well as any book or message of value God has given me has come directly from the power of the Holy Spirit! I know better than anyone else that I am incapable of any such thing. Years ago I came face-to-face with my own self-destructive humanity, surrendered my life to be crucified with Christ, and determined to live henceforth through the resurrection power of the Holy Spirit. I certainly don't always live my days filled with the Holy Spirit, but the rule (with obvious exceptions) has become the daily pursuit of the Spirit-filled, Christ-empowered life. The difference is night and day.

Do I ask for more and more of God's Holy Spirit? You bet I do! He gives Him without measure! The beauty of His endless supply is that my portion does not take an ounce away from yours!

Now here's a word of warning. Don't confuse asking for more of the Holy Spirit with asking for more manifestations of the Holy Spirit. James 4:2–3 gives us two reasons why we don't receive: We fail to ask, and we ask with wrong motives.

We may not have experienced the fullness of God's presence and empowerment in our lives because we haven't asked. However, sometimes we ask with wrong motives or what the King James Version calls asking "amiss, that ye may consume it upon your lusts." We can have wrong motives for asking for more of the Holy Spirit. Here are a few of my own examples of wrong motives.

- If I want more of the Holy Spirit so that people will be impressed with me or so that I will feel powerful, then my motives are self-glorifying and dishonoring to God.

- If I desire a manifestation of the Holy Spirit as proof that God exists, then my motive is to prove (test) God rather than glorify God.

A right motive for asking for more of the Holy Spirit is that God be glorified in you and me through our effective and abundant Spirit-filled lives. Matthew coined it best: "Let your light shine before men, that they may see your good deeds and praise your Father in heaven" (5:16).

Remember what we learned from John Piper in our lesson on Christian hedonism? God is most glorified in us when we are most satisfied in Him. Our soul's satisfaction for God's glorification is a wonderful motive for requesting more of the Holy Spirit. After learning many lessons the hard way, I want more and more of His Spirit because I want more and more of Him! Yes, the flooding of the Holy Spirit will manifest in all sorts of ways, but God and His glorification are our purest motives, not the manifestations themselves.

I am convinced that the essence of abundant life is simply put: an abundance of God in our lives. I don't just want to do the church thing. I want to experience God every day of my mortal life! And walk with Him as surely and vividly as I could walk with flesh and bone. I want to see His glory that the prophet Isaiah said fills the earth. I don't just want to be saved from destruction, as thankful as I am for the deliverance. I want to bask in the favor of His pure presence. I want God . . . and a lot of Him! I think you do, too. Then let's start asking for Him, dear one. Every day of our lives. More of Your Spirit, Lord. More of Your Spirit!

Chapter 27

MORE FRUIT

This is to my Father's glory, that you bear much fruit, showing
yourselves to be my disciples. (John 15:8)

$\mathcal{I}$ am so overwhelmed by all the Word has to say to us next that I am nearly paralyzed. I feel like I've won a shopping spree and can have anything I can fit in my basket, but I want so much of what I see that I don't know where to start. Beloved, what we've won in Christ is so far beyond human thinking that if we don't learn to think with the mind of Christ through the power of the Spirit, we'll miss it!

Unlike a woman who has won a basket full of goodies, we are never meant to pick and choose only what suits our fancy. Nor are we limited to one basket. God has chosen what He wants for us—treasures without measure—and all the baskets you could fit in your front yard can't contain them.

We'll do our shopping from John 15:1–17. If it's familiar to you, approach every phrase as if you've never seen it before. Remember that the chapter breaks and verse numbering in the Bible came much later than the inspiration of the Scriptures themselves. They are a huge help to us, but keep in mind that each chapter is wisely considered in context with the Scriptures preceding and following it.

The last statement Christ made in John 14 was, "Come now; let us leave" (v. 31). Christ and His followers had just eaten the Passover meal—the one we refer to as the Last Supper. Obviously the teaching that followed occurred en route. The next piece of geographical information is tucked in

John 18:1. "When he had finished praying, Jesus left with his disciples and crossed the Kidron Valley. On the other side there was an olive grove, and he and his disciples went into it."

John 15 begins with Jesus teaching about Himself as the True Vine. Quite possibly Christ's teaching on the vine took place as He and His disciples walked through a vineyard on their way to the olive grove. I want you to set yourself in the scene. You are a follower of Christ. A chosen disciple in this generation.

Jesus cast three sets of players in this vineyard scene. He is the first. Jesus is the true vine. His Father is the gardener. You are a branch. The declared purpose of the Father's care is for the branch to bear fruit.

What I'm about to say is not to your pastor, your teacher, your mentor, your hero in the faith, your best friend at church, or anyone else. It's to you. Beloved, the God of all the universe has ordained that your precious life bear much fruit. Do you hear what I'm saying? Are you taking it personally? This is about God, Christ, and you. Their eyes are on you this very moment. Hear them speak these words into your spirit loud and clear: We want you to bear *much* fruit.

For several chapters we've been talking about *more*. Now we're going to talk about *much*. I will repeat it as many times as I must. God hasn't appointed you to mediocrity but to a life of profound harvest. I weep for the body of Christ I love so dearly because I am overwhelmed with Paul's godly jealousy (2 Cor. 11:2) that each of you receives, savors, and celebrates what your God has for you.

I am sick of the enemy's subtle scheme to convince the masses in the body of Christ that only a few lives in each generation are truly significant. Your life was set apart for significance! Get up right this second, look in the nearest mirror, and say it out loud to that image in front of you. And while you're at it, say, "God has chosen you, and He wants to be glorified by you bearing *much* fruit."

I'm not saying another word until you go to that mirror. My friend, sometimes what you and I need is a good fussing at. We are not yet fully believing God! If we were, we'd be so astounded and delighted in Him and living so far beyond ourselves that we wouldn't be able to contain our joy.

We somehow continue to entertain those things that hold us back from immensely productive lives.

I hope we clear a few of those obstacles out of the way through the course of our study, but I'd like to address one right away. Many think that the sins of their pasts have exempted them from tremendously fruit-bearing lives. First, if that were true, I assure you I would not be writing to you right now. Second, if we haven't repented and allowed God to restore us and then redeem our failures, we will tragically fulfill some of our own self-destructive prophecies. God is not the one holding us back from much fruit after failure. In tandem with the devil, we are the ones. God's primary concern is that He is glorified. Few unmistakable evidences glorify Him more than powerfully restored lives that humbly and authentically proclaim His faithfulness to the death.

The Father is so adamant that we bear much fruit, He has extended practically inconceivable offers to us. As I share them with you, pardon my excitement as I dangle a few happy participles. He offers to us:

A love we can live in. When will we get through our heads how loved we are? Take a look at perhaps the most astounding verse in this entire segment of Scripture: "As the Father has loved me, so have I loved you" (John 15:9). Try to grasp this truth as tightly as you can: Christ Jesus loves you like the Father loves Him. He loves you like His only begotten—as if you were the only one!

Christ follows His statement with a command in the same verse: "Now remain in my love." I love the King James word for "remain"— *abide.* The term means exactly what it implies: dwell in His love, remain in it, tarry in it, soak in it. For heaven's sake, live in it! How do we do such a thing?

Let me paraphrase what I think Christ is saying in this passage. Please put your name in the blanks:

> My love for you, _____, is perfect, divine, and lavish beyond your imagination and far beyond your soul's cavernous needs. In fact, I love you like My Father loves Me, and I am the only begotten Son and the uncontested apple of His eye.

_____, My love for you is as constant as an ever-surging fountain, but you don't always sense it because you move in and out of the awareness of My presence. My desire is for you to pitch your mobile home so intimately close to Me that you are never outside the keen awareness of My extravagant love.

Why is a constant awareness of God's love for us so vital in a profusely fruit-bearing life? One reason is that the last thing Satan wants is for our lives to bear much fruit. He will do everything he can to discourage us, accuse us, and try to condemn us. Even the most steadfast among God's servants make mistakes and foolish decisions of some kind along the way. None is worthy to serve the Holy God of all creation. We will always give Satan plenty of ammunition to discourage us. If we don't literally camp in the love of Christ, we will talk ourselves out of untold fruit by dwelling on our own unworthiness. Accept the fact that we are unworthy and we're lavishly loved by a God of redemptive grace. Next notice another great offer. God provides:

A source we can draw from. Among the kinds of things that hold us back from immensely fruit-bearing lives, you might include "a lack of talent or ability." Conspicuously missing in this unparalleled dissertation on lives bearing much fruit is any reference whatsoever to ability. The one requirement for a profusely fruit-bearing life is that we abide in Christ like a branch remains physically attached to the vine. Apart from Him we can do nothing (John 15:5). Christ is telling us that all we have to do is embed ourselves in Him, let the power source flow, and He'll do the work through us. That's the secret!

Picture the attachment between the vine and the branch. One of the most important elements of the branch is that it remains open to the flow of the vine's life. If the branch were simply wound around the vine tightly, it would still die without producing any fruit. The branch must be attached to the vine with an openness to receive its fluid. Do you see the parallel? So often we have our own agendas about how we want to serve God. We spend untold energy and never produce lavish and God-glorifying fruit. We have to be open to the power flow and the purposed work the Vine wants to accomplish.

Often we fall into the trap of making up our own minds about how we want to serve Christ based on human reasoning and personal preferences. Trying to force our own ministries is such a frustrating waste of time. We end up taking on the pained, fretful demeanor of a woman trying her hardest to birth a very big baby.

I spent the first half of my adult life trying my hardest to make something—anything—work for God. After all, He had called me! Nothing worked . . . until I gave up in exhaustion and failure and let Him work. We can't force fruit. We can only abide in the Vine. If we're going to produce much fruit, we've got to be open to the life, agenda, and timing of the Vine.

A Gardener we can depend on. You've heard of personal trainers. Our Gardener is so determined for fruitful lives to bear even more fruit, He commits Himself as their personal pruner! Notice verse 2: "He cuts off every branch in me that bears no fruit, while every branch that does bear fruit he prunes so that it will be even more fruitful." I believe this verse suggests that God works all the harder on the child that is producing fruit so she or he will produce even more.

If you are a true follower of Jesus Christ, I bet you sometimes feel like God is picking on you. Have you ever exclaimed in exasperation, "God never lets me get away with anything"? Have you ever noticed that God seems particularly jealous with you? That He extracts from your life mindless and meaningless activities that He seems to "put up with" in other believers' lives? That, dear one, is because you have proved to be a cooperative fruit-bearing child and He knows He has a prime branch through whom He can be all the more glorified.

Do you see the progression suggested in verses 2 and 5? God desires for those who bear fruit to bear more fruit and those who bear more fruit to bear much fruit! As nervous as the thought may make us, God can be trusted with a pair of shears in His hand.

The following exercise is strictly for your benefit and between you and God. Don't let Satan use it to condemn you. To the best of your biblical understanding, based on an abiding sense of God's presence and pleasure as opposed to numbers and notoriety, where do you think you may presently be on a scale from no apparent fruit, to some fruit, then more fruit, and finally to much fruit?

If you've made it past "no apparent fruit," what did your personal pruner do to take you to the next level? The pickier we let Him be with us, the more productive He will be through us. Beloved, when all is said and done and we are living in heaven, all that will matter is whether or not our lives glorified God. Let's let Him prune to His heart's content. Let's surrender to a life that will matter, as my family would say, more than a hill of beans when we've drawn our last breath.

Joy we can revel in. The fact of the matter is that we have been called to lives of obedience. Yes, the grace of God covers our sins as we trust in Christ's finished work on the cross. But we will not bear much fruit without obedience to our Father's will. In fact, according to John 15:10, if we don't walk closely to Him in obedience, we will never draw near enough to abide in His love. He loves us no matter what we do, but we will not be able to pitch our spiritual tents in His presence when we're disobedient. Does all this sound like a life of just serving and sacrificing?

Then you'd better read John 15:11 again. Jesus said, "I have told you this so that my joy may be in you and that your joy may be complete." What an amazing thought! God is sovereign and could have rigged the plan to serve Him only. He could have demanded our obedience and service—or else. He didn't. Our heavenly Father is the giver of all good gifts (James 1:17). God longs to bless us with abundant life and joy. And not just any joy—Christ's joy! Perfect, full, magnetic, and contagious!

The joy of Jesus comes to the believer only one way: transfusion. Like an intravenous drip from Vine to branch! God doesn't just have *more* for you. He has *much*. Much love. Much fruit. Much joy. And the God of the universe derives much glory from one measly mortal. Who can beat a deal like that?

Chapter 28

MORE REVELATION

*Whoever has my commands and obeys them, he is the one who loves
me. He who loves me will be loved by my Father, and I too will
love him and show myself to him. (John 14:21)*

$\mathcal{W}$hat fun I've had studying the concepts of *more* and *abundance* with
you through John's Gospel! My spiritual life—particularly my prayer life—
has already been marked by what we've discovered. Next we have the
opportunity to study yet another Scripture in John with such zenith implications that I am relying on God to help me do any justice to the topic.
We already touched on this segment of Scripture, but I purposely saved our
considerations of it for now.

The passage is John 14:19–25. Jesus told the disciples in verse 21,
"Whoever has my commands and obeys them, he is the one who loves me.
He who loves me will be loved by my Father, and I too will love him and
show myself to him." We're going to focus on the words *show myself* and
try to determine what Christ meant. The original word *emphanizo* means
"to make apparent, cause to be seen, to show . . . of a person, to manifest
oneself meaning to let oneself be intimately known and understood."[1]

A comparison between several translations of the Bible can be very
helpful when trying to understand a term or concept. Read the following
renderings of the phrase "show myself to him" (14:21 NIV) in the translations noted:

- The King James Version: "will manifest myself to him."
- The New American Standard Version: "will disclose Myself to him."
- The Amplified Bible: "will show (reveal, manifest) Myself to him.

[I will let Myself be clearly seen by him and make Myself real to him.]"
- The Contemporary English Version: "show you what I am like."
- The Message: "make myself plain to him."

In Christ's response to Judas's question, He clearly states that this particular "disclosure," "manifestation," or "making plain" would not occur in heaven but on earth. "We will come to him and make our home with him" (v. 23). This statement is in perfect context and beautiful contrast with Christ's promise in John 14:2–3. Christ promised that one day He'd come to take His followers back to be with Him. The assumption is that they (and we) would dwell in the many rooms Christ is preparing. Not coincidentally, the plural word *monai* translated "rooms" in John 14:1 is used in its singular form *monen* in "home" (14:23). Based on the use of these terms, I believe this is what Christ was saying to them:

> I am going to leave you so that I can prepare rooms for you where you will one day dwell and indeed make yourself at home where I live in heaven. Until then, I have built a room in each of you where I can make Myself at home with you. This way I am at home with you in Spirit until you are at home with Me in heaven.

Christ is making heavenly rooms for us while making earthly room in us. Glory to God! During this period of time when Christ and His Father would come to their obedient followers, Christ's promise is that He would also manifest or disclose Himself to them (John 14:21). Certainly Christ would reveal Himself to them at the resurrection (v. 19), and then they would experience a glorious manifestation of His making Himself at home with them at Pentecost. But I believe John 14:21 implies spiritual revelation as well.

R. C. H. Lenski offers this explanation of the wording in John 14:21. "The future tenses refer to the day of Pentecost and thereafter. This appears especially in the last verb; for the appearances during the forty days were only preliminary manifestations to be followed by his constant presence, help, and blessing in the spirit (v. 18)."[2]

As we have seen previously, God and Christ reveal themselves in several different ways. First and foremost, they reveal themselves through the Bible. Scripture is our only totally reliable source of revelation because it is certain rather than experientially subjective. Scripture is also clear, however, that God reveals dimensions of Himself and His glory to us through other sources. Romans 1:20; Psalm 19:1; and Acts 14:17 all point to the display of God's power and glory through creation.

God has never revealed Himself to me in flames of fire from within a bush like He did to Moses in Exodus 3:2; nor have I ever seen chariots of fire like Elisha; but I have often beheld God's glory through nature. My soul is as drawn to a certain chain of mountains in the Northwest as a river is drawn to the sea. At least several times a year I feel the wooing of God to come and meet Him there. I confer with Him every day at home, but occasionally our souls crave a display of His glory that can best be seen against a less common backdrop, don't they?

A few months ago I stayed by myself in a small place in the national park overlooking "my" mountains. Every night when I got into bed, I reminded myself that I had come for rest as well as inspiration. I'd try to talk myself into sleeping past dawn, but I never could. I rose every morning long before light, threw on a heavy coat, and drove to find a front-row seat to behold the sunrise. I rolled down my window to hear the mighty beasts of the field bugle their presence. In perfect covenant consistency, every morning God caused the rays of sunlight to baptize the tips of the mountain—then I watched until He bathed the valley as well. I was so overcome by the majesty such awesomeness suggested that I thought my heart would leap from my chest. At such a moment, Habakkuk 3:3–4 invaded my thoughts: "His glory covered the heavens / and his praise filled the earth. / His splendor was like the sunrise; / rays flashed from his hand, / where his power was hidden."

God's Word suggests He can reveal Himself in numerous ways, but His ultimate revelation to man was through His very own Son, Jesus. He came to show us God in an embraceable, visible form. I believe a very important part of Christ's promise in John 14:21 is that after His departure, He would continue to reveal, manifest, or make Himself known to His followers here until they were there. Now that His Spirit has come and His Word is complete, I believe they (the Holy Spirit and the Word) are the primary means by which Jesus discloses Himself to His followers.

Having built what I pray is a solid theological foundation for Christ's continued revelation to His followers, let's celebrate the enormous ramifications toward our lives.

Notice that John 14:21 places some restrictions on its promises: "Whoever has my commands and obeys them, he is the one who loves me. He who loves me will be loved by my Father, and I too will love him and show myself to him."

First let's immediately defuse any upset over Christ's statement, "He who loves me will be loved by my Father." Doesn't John 3:16 tell us that God so loves the world? Absolutely! First John 4:19 also tells us that we love because He first loved us! John 14:21 is not suggesting God's love for us is conditional and responsive to our love for Him. I believe the phrase is best interpreted by a deeper understanding of the nature of God's love.

Romans 5:8 tells us that "God demonstrates his own love for us in this: While we were still sinners, Christ died for us." One of the most significant qualities found in God's brand of love is that it is demonstrative. Christ directed His followers to love as He loved them. I believe John 14:21 is implying that the more we obey and love God, the more vividly we may see, experience, and enjoy demonstrations of His love.

Mind you, Romans 5:8 says His most profound demonstration of love was while we were still sinners, but like His disciples we are often unable to recognize the demonstration until we obey the wooing of the Spirit in repentance and sprout the firstfruits of love. Like you, I have always been loved by God, but I have been more aware of the demonstrations of His love or what we might call His favor when I've been loving and obedient—especially through painful circumstances. I've lived an illustration that might help:

God brought a darling young woman into my life who had been through untold turmoil. Abused and misused, she didn't trust anyone. She needed love as badly as anyone I had ever known, but she was terribly suspicious and hard to show love. God kept insisting that I show her the love of Jesus. One day I said to Him, "Lord, I'm trying to be obedient, but she is just like trying to hug a porcupine!" Over the months and years, God turned my beloved porcupine into a puppy. I loved her throughout our relationship, but the softer and more loving she became, the more love I was able to show her. On a much greater scale, I believe the principle applies to God's demonstration of love to us.

What about you? Are you more like a porcupine or a puppy in terms of receiving the demonstrative love of God (whether via His Word, His Spirit bearing witness in your inner being, or His demonstration through a human vessel)? I am convinced John 14:21 suggests that the more we obey and love Christ Jesus, the more He will disclose Himself to us. These manifestations or ways He makes Himself known and understood are seen with the eyes of the Spirit within us. Isaiah 6:3 tells us the earth is full of His glory.

Beloved, I don't believe I'm stretching the text when I say the glory of our Lord Jesus surrounds us constantly. We are perpetually surrounded by means through which He could show us His worth, His providence, and His presence. We don't want to miss them! Think of the examples all around us. I'll share a few:

- Christ sometimes discloses His forgiving nature by empowering someone to forgive us for something that seems unforgivable.
- Sometimes Christ manifests His activity in our lives so strongly through a Bible teacher or a preacher that we feel like we're the only ones in the audience and they've read our mail.
- Often we read a portion of Scripture, and suddenly our eyes are open to an astounding, transforming understanding of Christ.
- Many of us have attended a dying loved one who knows Christ, and He manifested His presence in our midst in such a way that we were overwhelmed by His care and comfort.
- Christ sometimes makes His nearness and omniscience known by working through a detail no one else knew anything about.
- Sometimes an impending disaster is suddenly averted, and we're covered by chills as we sense Him as our Deliverer.
- Very simply, sometimes as we are engaged in worship, we sense His powerful presence and sweet pleasure.

I've experienced each one of these, but I want to see more. I want Jesus Christ to manifest Himself to me! I want to know Him on this earth as well as a mortal can know Him. Don't you? Then let's pray toward that end!

At this point in our journey, I am persuaded that the truth God inspired the apostle John to pen in John 14:21 became the apostle's virtual philosophy and approach to life. We have already concluded that John forsook ambition for affection. Love became his absolute center. As we continue our journey, we also will discover that he was a man who pursued obedience even when no one was watching.

With his whole being, John lived the divine conditions of John 14:21. Years down the road, is it any wonder our immortal Savior and Lord handpicked him when He determined to deliver the incomparable Book of Revelation? How fitting. John himself represents the ultimate human example of his own penmanship.

Chapter 29

MORE INTERACTION
WITH WOMEN

Just then his disciples returned and were surprised to find
him talking with a woman. (John 4:27)

S ome of Jesus' followers are still surprised to find Him talking with women. This chapter is an unapologetic apologetic supporting the biblical fact that Jesus Christ talks to women. And highly esteems them. Before we go a single step further, please hear me say that the furthest thing from my mind is disrespecting men or downplaying their biblical roles in leadership. I have never been and will never be a male basher.

I was raised with two brothers and two sisters and tend to get along with men as easily as women (though understandably differently). I have a good, solid marriage with a man I deeply love and treat with respect. I am delighted to say that I have very healthy, respectful relationships with my brothers in Christ and very rarely have been in conflict with any. I believe strongly in the biblical roles designed for men and women and am convinced our churches are rarely stronger than the men of our churches. Ladies, our men are key! I do not want women to take men's places. I just want to see women take their own places.

Occasionally someone asks me if I wish I could have a church of my own and be a pastor. My answer? "Are you out of your mind?" Frankly, I like passing the proverbial buck to my pastor and my husband. If women realized how directly God holds men responsible for so much, we'd pray unceasingly for them. I treasure the memory of a service one night at my church when the men were called to kneel at the altar and the women formed a shield around them and cried out in intercession in their behalf. Our hearts were bound together with a unity that could only accompany a fresh realization of distinct but equal purpose.

Hear me clearly: I am pro-men. And (not but) I am also pro-women. What may come as a news flash to some is that these pros are not exclusive. The biblical roles and responsibilities of men and women differ sometimes to complement and complete each other. Our places in the heart of God, however, are the same. I am very comfortable in my womanhood in the body of Christ, but not every woman is. Sometimes a spiritual inferiority complex stems from having been exposed to steady doses of inaccurate representations of Christ and His Word.

Not long ago someone handed me the book *When Life and Beliefs Collide* by Carolyn Curtis James, and I began to read it without knowing anything about the subject matter. The author explained that God had birthed the entire concept of the book from an unsettling statement a seminary professor made to her years earlier. "With more than a hint of mischief in his eyes, he said, 'You know, there have never been any great women theologians.'"[1] He had no idea how God used him to propel her to study the Word of God and prove him wrong! Like the disciples, he might have been surprised to find that Jesus talks to women.

My purpose today is not so much to prove the tie between women in the Bible and theology as to prove an unmistakable tie between several women in the Bible and Christ. Ties, I might add, from which Christ knitted some very deep theology. Yes, Jesus speaks to women who listen. Always has. Always will. Anyone who wants to believe Christ didn't have profound encounters with women might want to skip the Gospel of John. Let me again be clear that the New Testament bulges with encounters and relationships between Christ and men. We're not taking away one iota from those. Our goal, however, is to study His interaction with women. Once again, John's Gospel supplies more detailed accounts abundant in meaning.

Each of the following segments record a time when Jesus had an important encounter with a woman. Before you become frustrated with such varied selections of Scripture, keep in mind that we want to draw conclusions based on all the snapshots rather than staring intently at one picture.

John 4:1–39 introduces us to the woman from Sychar. You probably know her by the label "the woman at the well," but do you realize she was the first person to whom Jesus declared His messiahship? Jesus sent the disciples on to town to buy food. The woman came to the well in the middle of the day to avoid those who would look down on her. She was surprised because Jesus treated her with respect. He led their conversation from His request for a drink to His gift to her of Living Water. The woman then became an evangelist as she returned to Sychar to proclaim: "Come, see a man who told me everything I ever did. Could this be the Christ?" (John 4:29).

John 8:1–11 tells of another dramatic encounter between Christ and a woman. This time the Pharisees and teachers of the law were out to get Jesus. Their method was to grab a woman who was taken in the act of adultery and bring her before the Lord. There they demanded that Jesus judge her, but He refused to play their game. He knelt and drew on the ground until their consciences began to accuse them. When the crowd melted away, Christ asked the woman, "Where are they? Has no one condemned you?" When she replied, "No one, sir," Jesus responded, "Then neither do I condemn you. Go now and leave your life of sin" (vv. 10–11).

John 11:17–44 provides us with our next glimpse of Jesus and women. This time He deals with the sisters of Lazarus, Martha and Mary. Jesus waited while Lazarus lay dying. Then Christ came when his friend had been buried three days. In this instance we see Jesus deal with the two sisters as individuals.

Martha went to meet Jesus with combined words of reproach and hope. "If you had been here, my brother would not have died. But I know that even now God will give you whatever you ask" (vv. 21–22). Jesus calmly accepted her words and revealed Himself to her in a fresh way. "I am the resurrection and the life. He who believes in me will live, even though he dies; and whoever lives and believes in me will never die" (vv. 25–26).

Mary met Jesus differently. She also stated her belief that Jesus could have healed her brother, but she fell at His feet weeping. In this case Jesus "was deeply moved in spirit and troubled" (v. 33). He asked where they had laid Lazarus, and Christ wept. Then to the joy of both sisters He called Lazarus from the grave.

John 12:1–8 continues the story of Martha and, particularly, Mary. Six days before the Passover when Jesus would die, the sisters gave a dinner in Jesus' honor. Overcome by her love for Jesus, and I suspect, both motivated by a premonition of what was to come and driven by the Spirit, Mary poured perfume on Jesus' feet and wiped them with her hair. In this incredible moment two voices spoke.

Judas Iscariot declared the gesture an extravagant waste of what could have gone to the poor. Jesus declared Mary's action sacred in anointing Him for His burial. Matthew 26:13 wraps up this scene best with Jesus' words: "I tell you the truth, wherever this gospel is preached throughout the world, what she has done will also be told, in memory of her." Our very words at this moment continue the fulfillment of His promise.

Have we seen that Jesus made time for, talked to, honored, and treated women with dignity? What passage could possibly compare with these words from the cross: "When Jesus saw his mother there, and the disciple whom he loved standing nearby, he said to his mother, 'Dear woman, here is your son,' and to the disciple, 'Here is your mother.' From that time on, this disciple took her into his home" (John 19:26–27).

I will, however, point you to a last passage. John 20:1–18 tells how Mary Magdalene first saw the empty tomb on resurrection morning. She rushed to tell Peter and John, but after they had come and gone, she lingered there. Though she had seen two angels, the truth of the risen Christ had not penetrated her grief-stricken heart. As she turned from the tomb, she saw a man. "Thinking he was the gardener, she said, 'Sir, if you have carried him away, tell me where you have put him, and I will get him'" (v. 15).

Jesus responded to her tenderly, "Mary." When she recognized Him, He said: "Do not hold on to me, for I have not yet returned to the Father. Go instead to my brothers and tell them, 'I am returning to my Father and your Father, to my God and your God'" (v. 17).

Based on these segments, three things about Christ astound me and make me fall even more in love with Him:

1. Jesus was not ashamed to be seen with a woman. At first glance this point may not seem like a big deal, but how many of us have dated someone or even married someone who seemed ashamed at times to be seen with us? Beloved, Jesus Christ isn't ashamed to be seen with you. In fact, He wants nothing more! He's also not ashamed to talk to you. I meet so many women who are timid about sharing what they've gleaned in Bible study that week because they don't have much education and they're "probably wrong." Listen here, young lady, the One who spoke the worlds into being has chosen you for a bride! Study His Word like someone being spoken of and spoken to! He wants your life to radiate proof that He's been talking to you. He's proud of you!

Not long ago a woman approached me whose husband shoots sporting clays in the same group as my husband. She said, "I thought you'd be touched to know that my husband said, 'Keith Moore sure loves his wife. You can hear it in the way he talks about her.'" If only we could hear Jesus talking behind our backs! We'd know He loves us so.

2. Though very much a man, Jesus understood the needs of a woman. I despise that ridiculous feminist "theology" that tries to make a woman out of God or at least make Him feminine so we can feel like we have an advocate—"someone who understands." Beloved, Christ understands us better than we do! Of course, He has a decided advantage over every other man. He wove us together in our mother's womb. Still, I'm relieved to know that I am never too needy for Christ—particularly when I'm feeling a tad high maintenance. Did you notice how personal He got in almost every scenario? He was totally unafraid of intimacy then—and He still is.

In each of the encounters we reviewed, did you notice? Not once did Jesus leave a single one of those women without acting on behalf of her deep need?

In every case, He looked beyond the woman's actions and into her heart. He's looking into yours at this very moment and knows what you need even more than you do. Jesus even knows what motivates you to do the things that you do. All that He requires to meet our needs is that we allow Him to draw near to us; talk to us; change us.

3. Without exception, Jesus honored women and gave them dignity. Do you see a single hint of second-class treatment? In any stretch of the imagination, can you make a woman-hater out of Jesus? Not on your life. A woman-ignorer? No way. How about a womanizer? The mere thought is absurd. Jesus is stunningly personal, intensely intimate, and completely proper. He replaces each woman's shame with dignity. He brings resurrection life to her loss. And, dear one, He appoints and approves her good works. No, Mary of Bethany wasn't called to preach, but Christ said her story would be preached throughout the world. Mary Magdalene? She was the very first to spread the good news! The adulterous woman? Surely she got her life together. Maybe even married a fine man and had a family. After all, that's what happened to Rahab, who appears in the genealogy of Jesus. And Martha? Personally, I think she invented air freshener.

Chapter 30

MORE ABOUT HIS FATHER

Jesus said to them, "My Father is always at his work to this
very day, and I, too, am working." (John 5:17)

*O*ne of the first passionate words out of a toddler's mouth is, "Mine!"
I'm not even sure this word has to be taught. I don't know many moms and
dads who stomp their feet exclaiming, "Mine!" No one will argue where
two-year-olds get "No!" but where in the world do they get "Mine"? I'd like
to suggest that possessiveness is one of the most intrinsic elements embedded in the human psyche. No one has to learn a "my" orientation. It's intertwined in every stitch of our DNA.

In our culture a large part of what we call maturity is gaining some
kind of respectable control over our "my" orientation, and rightly so. The
inmost desire to have something we can call our own, however, does not
make man bad or even selfish. In fact, I think it's fundamental to our per-
sonhood; but as usual our flesh natures etch their doctrines from basic
human rights wigged out of control.

God created us with a need to know something belongs to us. From
the time we are toddlers, we begin testing what is ours by process of elimination. Everything is "mine" until we learn from our parents what doesn't
belong to us and what can be taken from us. "No, child, that's not yours,
but here's this blanket. It is yours." In fact, perhaps we could say that maturity is not so much disregarding our "my" orientation as learning how to
appropriately recognize and handle what is and isn't ours.

I don't know about you, but I need to know that a few things really do
belong to me. I might tell you to drop by *my* house this afternoon, but even

THE BELOVED DISCIPLE

after eighteen years, that stack of bricks really belongs to the bank. For most of us, so do our cars. And speaking of banks, the bank account I call mine could disappear in some unforeseen financial disaster tomorrow and so could yours. When we really consider the facts, each of us can call very few things in life "mine." Like the toddler, we also often learn by the process of elimination. I have insisted a few things were mine that God has found very creative ways to show me otherwise.

I am convinced that a certain need to possess is so innate in all of us that if we could truly not call anything our own, our souls would deflate with hopelessness and meaninglessness. Please hear this: ours is not a God who refuses us the right to possess anything. He's simply protective enough of our hearts not to encourage a death grip on things we cannot keep. He's not holding out on us. He's not dangling carrots in front of our noses then popping us in the mouth when we lunge to bite the bait. Contrary to much public opinion, God is not playing some kind of sick "I-created-you-to-want-but-will-not-let-you-have" game with us. Quite the contrary, the Author of Life will only encourage us to call "mine" what is most excellent. Most exquisite. To those who receive, God gives Himself.

God called the psalmist David a man after His own heart. Here are a few ways he freely exercised his "my" orientation in Psalm 18:1–2:

> I love you, O LORD, my strength.
> The LORD is my rock, my fortress and my deliverer;
> my God is my rock, in whom I take refuge.
> He is my shield and the horn of my salvation,
> my stronghold.

Life abounds with boundaries and No Trespassing signs. Part of the human condition means that to live in any semblance of order, we confront a never-ending influx of "no's." In the midst of so much we cannot have, God says to His children, "Forsake lesser things and have as much as you want of . . . Me." Remember, John 3:34 says God gives His Spirit without measure. While God is the owner and possessor of all things, He freely invites us to be as possessive over Him as we desire. He is my God. And your God. He's the only thing we can share lavishly without ever decreasing our own supply.

When Christ came to this planet, He forsook many of His intrinsic divine rights in order to accomplish His earthly goals. Philippians 2:7 says he "made himself nothing, / taking the very nature of a servant, / being made in human likeness." John 1:3–4 tells us "through him all things were made; without him nothing was made that has been made. In him was life, and that life was the light of men." Yet Christ didn't walk around saying, "Hey, bud, do you see that dirt you're walking on? Who do you think made that?"

To our knowledge, Christ didn't sit with the disciples in the moonlight and tout His ownership over the heavens by giving them all the proper names of the stars. In alphabetical order. When we consider that Jesus Christ came to earth as the fullness of the Godhead bodily, He actually showed amazing restraint in exercising His divine rights. Matthew 26:53–54 offers one example. As the mob was arresting Him, He told Peter to put away his sword. "Do you think I cannot call on my Father, and he will at once put at my disposal more than twelve legions of angels? But how then would the Scriptures be fulfilled that say it must happen in this way?"

Did you notice the ultimate reason Jesus exercised restraint over His divine rights in this scene? He determined that the Scriptures must be fulfilled.

Christ exercised such restraint for another reason—because He had nothing to prove to Himself. John 13:3 says, "Jesus knew that the Father had put all things under his power, and that he had come from God and was returning to God." He knew.

Jesus made a point of fully exercising one right, however, to the constant chagrin of the Jews. That right became the apex of the argument recorded in John 5:18: "For this reason the Jews tried all the harder to kill him; not only was he breaking the Sabbath, but he was even calling God his own Father, making himself equal with God."

John 10 contains another example of the same dynamic. In verse 30 Jesus said, "I and the Father are one." The next verse tells us, "Again the Jews picked up stones to stone him." Jesus freely claimed His Sonship to the Father. None of the comparative statistics between Gospels is more staggering than the number of references to God as Father. Approximately

110 times out of 248 references to God as Father in the New Testament occur in the Gospel of John. No other New Testament book comes close.

Never lose sight of the fact that relationship came to mean everything to the apostle John. From now on, when you think about John, immediately associate him with the one so wholly convinced of Jesus' love. In turn John had much to say not only about reciprocal love but love for one another. We will see the concept only swell over the remaining chapters of our study. I don't believe we're off base in assuming that the priority of relationship with Christ is exactly what fitted him to receive the great Revelation.

To John identity came from association. He very likely absorbed this philosophy from tagging along with Jesus.

Look at the following Scriptures from the Gospel of John. Notice how each underscores identification by association:

- "For I have come down from heaven not to do my will but to do the will of him who sent me" (John 6:38).
- "Jesus answered: 'Don't you know me, Philip, even after I have been among you such a long time? Anyone who has seen me has seen the Father. How can you say, "Show us the Father"?'" (John 14:9).
- "You heard me say, 'I am going away and I am coming back to you.' If you loved me, you would be glad that I am going to the Father, for the Father is greater than I" (John 14:28).
- "But the world must learn that I love the Father and that I do exactly what my Father has commanded me" (John 14:31).
- "As the Father has loved me, so have I loved you. Now remain in my love" (John 15:9).
- "When the Counselor comes, whom I will send to you from the Father, the Spirit of truth who goes out from the Father, he will testify about me" (John 15:26).
- "All that belongs to the Father is mine. That is why I said the Spirit will take from what is mine and make it known to you" (John 16:15).
- "But a time is coming, and has come, when you will be scattered, each to his own home. You will leave me all alone. Yet I am not alone, for my Father is with me" (John 16:32).

Christ knew His constant references to God as His Father incited the Jews riotously, yet He was so insistent, He had to make a point. Through His actions and expressions, Christ seemed to say, I've set aside My crown, My position, My glory, and soon I'll set aside My life for all of you. Hear me well: I will not lay down my Sonship. God is My Father. Deal with it.

The Son of Man had no place to call His own. He had no wife. He had no children. He had no riches though the diamond and gold mines of the world belonged to Him. He laid claim to nothing. He laid aside everything to condescend to earth and wrap Himself in our injured flesh. Taking on our humanity, He also took on our most intrinsic need. In all the loss and sacrifice, He needed something He could call "Mine." "I and My Father are one" (John 10:30 KJV). Christ came to earth with nothing but His Father, and He was nonnegotiable.

The revolutionary message Christ told Mary Magdalene to extend to His disciples (past and present) can only be grasped in context with Jesus' magnificent obsession with His Father throughout the book. Let the words fall fresh on your heart. "Jesus said, 'Do not hold on to me, for I have not yet returned to the Father. Go instead to my brothers and tell them, "I am returning to my Father and your Father, to my God and your God"'" (John 20:17). Do you feel the impact of those words?

Now behold how the following verses echo Christ's glorious announcement.

> For you did not receive a spirit that makes you a slave again to fear, but you received the Spirit of sonship. And by him we cry, "Abba, Father." (Rom. 8:15)

> But when the time had fully come, God sent his Son, born of a woman, born under law, to redeem those under law, that we might receive the full rights of sons. Because you are sons, God sent the Spirit of his Son into our hearts, the Spirit who calls out, "Abba, Father." (Gal. 4:4–6)

Dear child of God, if you and I were as unrelenting in exercising our rights of sonship (or daughtership), our lives would be transformed. Satan would never be able to dislodge us from God's plan and blessing. You see,

Christ had to make the decision to lay aside many rights, but because He retained the most important one of all, His right of Sonship, Satan could not win. Christ led many sons to glory and got to once again pick up every right He laid aside.

As those who have received Christ's Spirit of Sonship, the same is true for us. Times may arrive when God asks us to lay down the right to be acknowledged in a situation. Or the right to give our opinion or take up for ourselves. The right to a promotion we think we deserve. The right to leave a spouse even though we might have biblical grounds. The right to withhold fellowship when the other person has earned our distance. The right to be shown as the one who was right in a situation. The right to our dignity in earthly matters. The right to our basic human rights.

But let this truth be engraved on your heart: You will never be required to lay aside your rights of sonship nor must you ever fall to Satan's temptation to weaken your position. As long as you exercise your rights of sonship, constantly reminding yourself (and your enemy) who God is and who you are, Satan will never be able to defeat you or thwart any part of God's plan for your life. Any loss or other right God permits or persuades you to lay aside is temporary. You will ultimately receive a hundredfold in return.

Hold your position, beloved! Never let anything or anyone talk you out of exercising your rights of sonship! The very reason Satan targets us is because we are the sons (or daughters) of God. He is defeated when we refuse to back off from our positional rights. The last thing he wants to hear from you is, "I am a born-again, justified child of God, and I exercise my right to rebuke you! You, devil, are defeated. You can't take me from my Father nor my Father from me." So, say it!

No matter what you may lose or lay aside, you can call the Father of life "Mine!" As His child, you have 24/7 direct access. God will never turn a deaf ear to you or look the other way when you are treated unjustly. You aren't left to "hope" He hears you, loves you, or realizes what's going on. Know it, Sister. Never view your situation in any other context than God as your Father and you as His child.

Are you trying to hold on to all sorts of rights that are completely secondary, yet not exercising the most important right you have?

Part 7

LETTERS FROM THE HEART

Now we are ready to consider the epistles penned by John under the inspiration of the Holy Spirit. We will gain insight into the fires that fueled his passion. We'll discover a man who could express great depth in few words. (I could use a couple of lessons, don't you think?) I hope John's terms of endearment will bless you. Somehow he had a way of approaching his recipients as "little children" without talking down to them. Reap the wisdom of age as you consider the letters of the apostle John. You will undoubtedly recognize the ideas he prioritized most as he matured.

Chapter 31

KOINONIA

We proclaim to you what we have seen and heard, so that you also
may have fellowship with us. And our fellowship is with the Father
and with his Son, Jesus Christ. (1 John 1:3)

*Y*ears passed. John's beard grayed. The skin once leathered by the sun's
reflection off the Sea of Galilee bore the deeper creases of age. His voice
rasped the telltale signs of a fiery evangelist. The calluses on his feet became
thick with age and country miles. The wrinkles around his eyes folded
and unfolded like an accordion as he laughed and mused. While some
scholars believe that John's Gospel and his letters were written within just
years of one another, few argue that the epistles slipped from the pen of
anything other than an aging man. Most believe 1 John was written around
A.D. 85–90.[1]

John had celebrated many Passover meals since the time he leaned his
head against the Savior's strong shoulder. So much had happened since that
night. He'd never get the picture of Christ's torn frame out of his mind, but
neither would he forget his double take of the resurrected Lord. The last
time John saw those feet, they were dangling in midair off the tip of the
Mount of Olives. Just as quickly, clouds covered them like a cotton blanket. The fire of the Holy Spirit fell . . . then the blaze of persecution seared.
One by one the other apostles met their martyrdom. People changed and
landmarks vanished. Just as Christ had prophesied, Herod's Temple, one of
the wonders of the ancient world, was destroyed in A.D. 70.

The winds of the Spirit whisked John from all that was familiar to the
city of Ephesus. Decades separated him from those early days of water

193

turned to wine and fishes turned to feasts. For most of us age means sketchy memories and vague details. Not John. He recorded his clear memories in indelible words: "That which was from the beginning, which we have heard, which we have seen with our eyes, which we have looked at and our hands have touched—this we proclaim concerning the Word of life. The life appeared; we have seen it and testify to it, and we proclaim to you the eternal life, which was with the Father and has appeared to us" (1 John 1:1–2).

John didn't climb gradually to a pinnacle in his writings. He started at one. His letters seem to open with the mouth of a crescendo as if he had waited until he was about to explode to write it all down. I'm not sure the Holy Spirit as much fell on John as leaped.

Again and again I love to remind believers that our faith is based on fact. Beloved, decades had passed. Each of the disciples had hoped Jesus would return before they died; yet even with the promise yet to come, not one of them wavered! You would think John's certainty might have waned or weakened with time and distance but listen to his unrelenting witness! He said the reason he kept preaching was "so that you also may have fellowship with us. And our fellowship is with the Father and with his Son, Jesus Christ" (1 John 1:3).

The Greek word for "fellowship" is *koinonia*. The Amplified Bible illustrates: "What we have seen and [ourselves] heard, we are also telling you, so that you too may realize and enjoy fellowship as partners and partakers with us. And [this] fellowship that we have [which is the distinguishing mark of Christians] is with the Father and with His Son Jesus Christ (the Messiah)" (1 John 1:3).

Both concepts of partnership and partaking are wrapped up in the wonderful word *koinonia*. My husband is a partner in business, but his partnership can as easily translate into deficit as profit. If the company doesn't do well, he loses. If the company surpluses, he gains. As partner, he always partakes of the work but not necessarily the profit. As those in fellowship with God the Father and His Son, Jesus Christ, our partnership in the kingdom never translates into a deficit. The kingdom of God only operates in surplus—inconceivable riches and more than we could ask or imagine!

Dear partner, do you more actively partake in the works involved in partnership or the profits involved in partnership? You and I can be saved to the bone and yet blend in perfectly in our workplaces and neighborhoods. Goodness knows, carnal and ineffective Christianity are rampant. I can say that without condemnation because I've practiced both. Our fellowship with the very presence of God is the only thing that sets us visibly apart.

I love verse 4. At this point in John's life, he began to sound a lot like his Teacher. "We write this to make our joy complete." Sounds a lot like the words of Jesus in John 15:11, doesn't it? "I have told you this so that my joy may be in you and that your joy may be complete."

I'm experiencing one of those times when I want to stand up to type. In fact, I believe I will. Based on our previous discussions of John 15 and John 17, do you grasp that Jesus so thoroughly enjoyed His relationship with His Father and with His followers that He wanted everyone else to enjoy it too? Perhaps the most distinguishing mark of a true partaker of the riches of God and Christ is that the partners cannot hoard the treasures. They want everyone else to enjoy them too. Authentic partners and partakers of *koinonia* simply cannot be selfish. Their joy is only complete as others share in it.

Beloved, my *koinonia* with the Father and Son is light-years from the apostle John's, but I do know what he's talking about. In fact, it's my fever and my total passion. I so thoroughly love and enjoy seeking and finding the living, breathing Son of God that I cannot stand for others to miss the joy. That many have diluted the dance of true *koinonia* to the ritual footsteps of stale religion drives me crazy! He's so thrilling and adventurous that I can't keep Him to myself. I want others to fellowship with me as I fellowship with Him! Do you hear 1 John 1:3–4? That's what I believe John was trying to say. From receiving many letters along the way, I believe many of you feel the exact same way.

The next verses in 1 John 1 describe some of the reasons why this *koinonia* is so precious to me. In verse 5, John wrote, "God is light; in him there is no darkness at all." I can hardly wait to tell you what that statement means to me.

Dear one, I've seen such a dark side of life. I have seen darkness in people of light. I then nearly despaired of life as I faced the dark side of my own self. We can run from the reminders of the dark side of this world, but we cannot hide, for we find them in ourselves. If we stick our heads out of our shells at all, the newspapers and magazines are full of reminders. In the time it takes you to complete this day's study, a father has been murdered, a woman has been raped, and a child has been abused. At times I read specific accounts and feel as if I can hardly bear to stay on this planet another minute. Only knowing God has not forsaken this world and that He is light and in Him is *no* darkness at all keeps us hoping and believing.

God has no dark side. Hear that! Absorb it to your marrow! No matter how many theological questions remain unanswered to you, of this you can be sure: God has no dark side at all! You see, that's why He can purify all of us no matter how dark our sides have been. He is utterly, perfectly pure. Oh, don't you just want to stop right now and tell Him how much you love Him? Do you see that His total lack of darkness is also why you can trust Him? He is incapable of having an impure motive where you are concerned.

The safety I find in Christ and the pure "blast" He is to me make me desperately want to stay in fellowship with Him. Don't you?

First John 1:9 tells us the secrets to sharing a life of fellowshipping with Christ and walking in the light. "If we confess our sins . . ." The basic Greek word for "confession" is *homologeo,* which is derived from two other words. *Homou* means "at the same place or time, together."[2] *Lego* means "to say."[3]

In essence, confession is agreeing with God about our sins. The portion of the definition that holds the primary key to remaining in *koinonia* is the expediency of "the same place or time." I have confessed and turned from some sins in my life that profoundly interrupted *koinonia.* Why? Because I waited too long to agree with God about them and turn. I still found forgiveness, but *koinonia* was broken through the delay. As God began to teach me to walk more victoriously, I learned to often respond to the conviction of the Holy Spirit at the "same place or time," thereby never leaving the circle of fellowship or the path of "light."

You see, some of us think fellowship with God can only be retained during our "perfect" moments. I want you to see how 1 John 1:8 refutes that philosophy. "If we claim to be without sin, we deceive ourselves and the truth is not in us."

You might ask, "How can a person sin grievously and still remain in fellowship?" Please understand, all sin is equal in its demand for grace, but not all sin is equal in its ramifications (see Ps. 19:13). A person who commits robbery, adultery, or vicious slander departed *koinonia* when he or she refused to agree with God over the sin involved in the thought processes leading up to the physical follow-through. Think of *koinonia* like a circle representing the place of fellowship. We don't just walk in and out of that circle every time a flash of critical thinking bolts through our minds. I don't even think we leave that circle if a sudden greedy, proud, or lustful thought goes through our minds.

If we're in *koinonia* with God, the conviction of the Holy Spirit will come at that place and time and tell us those thoughts or initial reactions aren't suitable for the saints of God. We never depart *koinonia* if we respond with something like: *Yes, Lord, You are absolutely right. That's not how I want to think. I do not desire to entertain those kinds of destructive thoughts. Forgive me and help me to have thoughts that are honoring to You and unharmful to me.* Confession without delay not only helps keep us in *koinonia;* it is part of our *koinonia!*

I have had many conversations with people who can't imagine being that honest and "out front" with God over their thought lives. If we don't learn to get honest with God over our thought lives, we will never allow Him to teach us new ways to think. If we never develop renewed minds, consistent victory and glorious *koinonia* will tragically elude us. Dear one, God already knows your thought life! Our conviction is telling us not only that He knows but that He wants to apply His grace to the problem and correct it. By agreeing with God, we bring our thoughts or initial actions straight from our minds or mouths into the light! But I'd rather keep them hidden in the dark; I'm too humiliated, some might say.

We're not keeping anything hidden in the dark from God. Psalm 139:11–12 tells us that darkness can't hide us because God sees in darkness as if it were bright day. The only thing we accomplish when we leave our sins in the dark is opening a door for the enemy to tempt us to the next level. Ultimately Satan's goal is that we heap sin upon sin. Our joy and protection is right in the circle of *koinonia* light!

Here's one catch: We can respond to conviction and agree with God expediently over our sin and still inadvertently exit the circle of *koinonia*. How? By refusing to accept and believe God's forgiveness and our fresh purification. You see, agreeing with God over our forgiven state is just as important as agreeing with God over our sin! If Satan can't tempt us to hide our sin and refuse to confess, he'll tempt us not to accept our forgiven and purified state. If we persist in feeling badly, we will think destructively and then ultimately act it. Don't let the devil get away with that! *Koinonia* is your right in Jesus Christ! Make His joy complete.

Chapter 32

A LOVE LETTER

How great is the love the Father has lavished on us, that we should be called children of God! And that is what we are! (1 John 3:1)

$\mathscr{I}$ can hardly type for wanting to rub my hands together and say, "Hot dog! Let's get to the love!" (Aren't I scholarly?) One of the most important transitions we've seen in our study of the life of the apostle John is his abandonment of ambition for affection. If we get any one-liner out of this Bible study, let that be it! But let us go further than the issue of ambition and abandon any number of dead works for affection.

Ambition may not be your issue, although I am convinced we can possess it without even realizing it. Secretly and subconsciously wanting to make a name for oneself—all the while rationalizing that God can share the glory, too—is frighteningly common in the body of Christ. We either glorify God or ourselves, never both. Somewhere along the way, the apostle John chose God alone, engaging heart, soul, mind, and strength.

The beauty of choosing to glorify God alone and to pursue a love for Him beyond all else is that every other thing of authentic value comes in the package. Remember Matthew 6:33? "Seek first his kingdom and his righteousness, and all these things will be given to you as well."

One of our greatest needs as we try to live sanely in our tornadic culture is simplicity. God offers us the privilege of surrendering ourselves to the only "one thing" that ensures everything else of great value. You can't beat a deal like that! We see a perfect example of this concept in the apostle John. As the "disciple Jesus loved," John chose to believe and fully receive the love of Christ above all other things. What was the result? Just

199

as Solomon asked for wisdom and became the wisest man in history, John prioritized love and became a flooding wellspring of affection. When God esteems our prayers, we get what we asked and far more.

I wish we had the time and space to study all five chapters of 1 John. Remember, our purpose in studying John's writings is to glean insight into the man himself and to learn what he seemed to want us to know most. We don't have to be scholars to quickly ascertain that John's entire focus in his first epistle was relationship. In our previous chapter, we targeted *koinonia*. For the remainder of our focus on 1 John, we'll cut straight to the heart and study his favorite subject: love. First we'll hear John's heartbeat on God's love *for* us. Next chapter we'll hear from John concerning God's love *through* us.

I originally learned 1 John 3:1 in the King James Version: "Behold, what manner of love the Father has bestowed upon us"! Keep in mind that all the major Bible translations still trace back to the Greek for accuracy. By "behold" I think the apostle John was saying, "Can't you see it? Don't you perceive it? The love of God surrounds us with evidences! Just look!" The original word for "manner" speaks of "disposition, character, quality"[1]

If we asked God to help us more accurately grasp the true disposition, character, and exquisite quality of His love for us, our lives would dramatically change! Because John chose to prioritize love, God opened his eyes to behold it and his soul to perceive it. Paul discovered something similar and prayed for all of us to do likewise. His prayer thrills me that we might "know this love that surpasses knowledge" (Eph. 3:19). I think Paul wanted us to experience God's love to the full measure of our capacity through the Spirit of God within us, then try to comprehend that its true measure and nature are far beyond that very experience. Just a taste. Just a glimpse. We are invited to know a love that is beyond human knowledge.

Beloved, God's love for you exceeds all reason. I'm not talking about your pastor, your Bible study leaders, or anyone else you greatly admire in the church. I'm talking about you. First John 4:16 says, "And so we know and rely on the love God has for us." The word for *know* in this verse is the same one Paul employed in Ephesians 3:19. You see, we can't define God's love, but we can behold it, experience it, and rely on it. Is 1 John 4:16

a reality for you? Have you come to experience and rely on God's love for you? His love for you and me is an absolute reality, but we can be so emotionally unhealthy that we refuse to experience it and absorb it into our hearts and minds.

The NIV translates 1 John 3:19–20 powerfully: "This then is how we know that we belong to the truth, and how we set our hearts at rest in his presence whenever our hearts condemn us. For God is greater than our hearts, and he knows everything." Ironically, many people are resistant to God because they imagine Him to be very condemning. In reality humans are far more condemning and often emotionally dangerous. I am intrigued by a statement about Christ recorded in John 2:24: "Jesus would not entrust himself to them, for he knew all men."

I can almost imagine Christ saying to humanity, "I am perplexed with all your talk about whether or not you can trust Me. Actually, your heart can be at complete rest in My presence. My love is perfectly healthy. The greater risk is in My entrusting Myself to you." You see, our unhealthy hearts not only condemn us; they condemn others. I have seen marriages destroyed because one spouse refused to accept the reality of the other spouse's love for him or her. Our hearts sometimes even condemn God as we decide for ourselves that He can't be trusted and that He doesn't really love us unconditionally. Our natural hearts are very deceitful and destructive on their own. We may have a condemning heart without ever facing it.

Picture a house that has been condemned by the city government. Imagine the sign posted on the door: "This property condemned." Is that your heart? Is it in shambles? Beyond proper living conditions? Are broken pieces of glass scattered all over it? Has it not only been endangered but become dangerous? As most of us know, hurt people hurt people.

My heart used to resemble a condemned property. Oh, I kept a fresh coat of paint over it so no one would know, but I knew the wreck it was on the inside. I even turned the sign over on the other side and wrote, "Fun person who has it all together . . . as long as you keep your distance and don't look closely." I wish we could sit down over a cup of French roast coffee and you could tell me what your sign might have said.

Some of us may think our hearts aren't unhealthy because we assume they all look alike. Nothing could be further from the truth. Unhealthy hearts come in all shapes and sizes. Some are cold. Others are indiscriminate. Some have thick walls around them. Some have no remaining boundaries at all. Some are forthright and angry. Others are passive and self-disparaging. Some are completely detached. Others are so attached that the object smothers.

I have had the privilege of getting to know many believers over the course of this ministry. Based on what I've seen, I am convinced that few people possess a virtually whole heart who have not pursued it deliberately in Christ. We don't have to be raised in severely dysfunctional homes to develop unhealthy hearts. All we have to do is expose ourselves to life. Life can be heartless and mean. Purely and simply, life hurts. We can't check ourselves out of life, however. Instead, God hopes that we'll turn to Him to heal us from the ravages of natural life and make us healthy ambassadors of abundant life in an unhealthy world.

Let me suggest two sure signs of an ailing heart: (1) You're convinced that nothing in life is reliable. Code name: Jaded. (2) You keep trying to convince yourself you can rely on something that has proved unreliable over and over again. Code name: Denial.

In case you have a heart like the one I had, please know that God can heal your heart no matter what got it in such a condition. First John 3:20 tells us that God is greater than our hearts! And He knows everything! Even the thing we secretly believe makes us unlovable . . . and unloving. Knowing all things, God loves us lavishly. Perfectly. Unfailingly. If He can heal my shattered, self-destructive heart, He can heal anyone's.

Perhaps you've allowed the enemy to hang a "condemned" sign on your heart, and you've almost given up on authentic love. Perhaps he's even talked you into becoming a cynic. Beloved, Satan is a liar! He knows if you and I take this thing about God's love seriously, we might become a John or a Paul in our generations. Oh, let's glorify God, spite the devil, and do it! It's not too late. Take your pulse. If your heart is still beating, it's worth healing! Here's the catch, however: God's method of healing a condemning heart is to love it to death . . . then create in us a new heart. A healthier heart. A heart filled with faith instead of fear. His perfect love is the only thing that will drive out that fear of ours.

Please allow me to ask you a very personal question. At this season of your life, deep down in your heart, what things are you most afraid of?

Fears are fillers. Mind fillers. Heart fillers. Soul fillers. The enemy fuels them because they leave virtually no space for the filling of the Spirit and the welcomed flood of divine love. Second Timothy 1:7 (KJV) tells us that God has not given us the spirit of fear but of power, and of love, and of sound mind. Does that tell you why Satan would want to do anything possible to supply us with fillers other than the Holy Spirit?

Satan neither wants us to know who we could be nor what we could do. Lives full of God's power, love, and soundness of mind are a terrible threat to the kingdom of hell. After all he's done to me and to so many others, I want to be a threat. Don't you? How do we begin? By allowing God's perfect love to start driving out our destructive fears and condemning natures like an eighteen-wheeler plowing through a cornfield!

Wholeness begins by deliberately and daily receiving the lavish, unreasonable, unfailing love of God all the way into our marrow. When life is too foggy to see the evidences of His love around us, behold it in His Word, dear one! Know it until you feel it.

Chapter 33

LOVING THROUGH US

If anyone says, "I love God," yet hates his brother, he is a liar.
For anyone who does not love his brother, whom he has seen,
cannot love God, whom he has not seen. (1 John 4:20)

$\mathcal{I}$ am convinced that virtually everything in an individual believer's life hinges on his or her deliberate belief and active acceptance of the lavish, unconditional love of God. I'm not sure we can be reminded too often of God's absolute priorities for our lives. No matter how different our personalities, gifts, styles of worship, or denominations, God's chief priority for every single one of us is that we love Him with everything in us (Mark 12:30). Like two chambers in one heart, the lifeblood of His first priority cannot flow apart from the second: that we love others as ourselves (Mark 12:31). What does the fulfillment of God's unparalleled priorities for us have to do with deliberately believing and actively accepting His lavish, unconditional love? Everything! First John 4:19 says, "We love because he first loved us."

One of the biggest hang-ups many believers have in loving God and others lavishly is a distrust or unwilling acceptance of the immutable fact of God's love! Everything begins there. How can we get on with loving God and loving others? We can consider all God has said and done to prove His love through His Word and His Son. Then we can confess the sin of unbelief and choose to act upon what God has said and done regardless of the ebb and flow of our emotions. If we would but practice this daily, how life would change!

Let's take a look at a few things John has to say about loving others in his first letter. I urge you to read the passages from your Bible. Here are my summary statements for several key passages about love.

- In 1 John 3:11–15 John posed two options. We can either love one another, with the probable result that the world will hate us, or we can be murderers like Cain. The litmus test for whether we have passed from death to life is whether we love our brothers.
- Then in 1 John 3:16–22 the aged apostle tells us how we know what love is: "Jesus Christ laid down his life for us. And we ought to lay down our lives for our brothers" (v. 16). He says if we hoard our wealth and don't care for others, we show that we lack the love of God. We already saw the connection that Jesus' power is greater than our hearts. I'd suggest that when we get busy allowing Jesus to love through us, we've made a great step toward also allowing Him to overcome our self-condemnation.
- First John 4:7–12 extends the teaching of love. Not only does love come from God, but "everyone who loves has been born of God and knows God." The only reason we can even know love is because He "loved us and sent his Son as an atoning sacrifice for our sins." The greatest manifestation of God this side of heaven appears as we love one another.
- First John 4:16–21 makes the connection between God and love so closely that "God is love. Whoever lives in love lives in God, and God in him." As we become like Jesus, love matures. It provides our confidence facing the day of judgment, and it drives out fear. But love must be practical. We can't say we love God and hate others. "Whoever loves God must also love his brother."
- First John 5:1–5 ties love to believing and overcoming. If we believe Jesus is the Messiah, we can't help loving the Father and the Son. The natural result becomes loving obedience. When we obey Him in love, the result becomes an overcoming life. So we begin with God's reasons to love, and if we stay with the Father, victory results through faith.

Admit it. Loving is a mammoth challenge. Because we cannot see Him, loving God can be even more challenging. Developing what St. John of the Cross called an "answering love" requires the active participation of faith and the willingness to learn to "live by the Spirit" (Gal. 5:16), no matter how awkward the process.

Let me assure you based on my personal experience, God is so patient! He simply wants to see that our heart's desire is to follow hard after Him even if the process isn't pretty. How in the world is a person with two broken legs spiritually and emotionally supposed to walk pretty? Take it from me on this one. Just keep taking another step in His direction no matter how ugly—and if you fall, fall forward and not back. Eventually and miraculously along the way, He will heal those legs. That's a big part of what will make loving Him so irresistible.

Somehow I don't find loving God quite as challenging as loving a few others I've known. I fear they'd say the same thing. Allow me to say that "Oh, brother!" is a common figure of speech for frustration for good reason. Our most serious challenges are usually not with circumstances. They're with people.

My younger daughter called from college recently on a rampage about someone she "just cannot stand." She is a God-seeking young woman with a fiery passion for His Word, but she agrees with most of us who feel we could serve others more successfully if others weren't so—otherly! I reminded her of a difficult relational challenge she'd had the year before. Then I "consoled" her with the assurance that she'd have another next year . . . and the next. Why? Because loving people we find difficult is so important to God. Just about the time we get one challenging relationship under the Spirit's control, God will supply another.

Have you found this principle to be true? How many people would you estimate you've been very challenged to love in the last five years? I just have a suspicion born of experience. I bet some of those relationships have become some of the dearest in your life.

When I began this chapter, I intended to use the phrase "loving difficult people," but under the direction of the Holy Spirit, I changed the description to "loving people we find difficult." As hard as this suggestion may be on our egos, just because we find someone difficult to love doesn't make him or her a difficult person.

The difficult person in my challenging relationship may be me! I'll never forget when someone who had just completed *Breaking Free* told me that I was her stronghold! Another who just completed *Jesus the One*

206

and Only told me she could hardly stand the way I taught, but she toughed it out, received a blessing, and likes me better now. Sometimes two people just don't make an easy mix. What a perfect combination for the practice of agape!

That we exercise and strengthen weak muscles of what I'll call "otherly affection" is paramount to God. If I may be simplistic, it's why we're still here. So what's a believer to do with all the challenges to love people we find difficult? Forget faking it. The first sentence of Romans 12:9 says: "Love must be sincere."

You and I are called to the real thing. God already knew that commanding us to love others sincerely would force the issue of heart change in those who truly desire to obey and please Him.

While loving others God places in our paths will never cease to be challenging, the key is learning to draw from the resource of God's own *agapao* rather than our own small and selfish supply of natural *phileo* or fondness. *Agapao* is many things we imagine as love, but two primary elements set it apart.

Agapao begins with the will. It is volitional love. In other words, the beginning of true love is the willful decision to agree with God about that person and choose to love. Secondly, when Scripture makes a distinction between *agapao* and *phileo, agapao* love is based on best interest while *phileo* love is based on common interests.

Both kinds of love are biblical and wonderful expressions in the body of Christ, but *phileo* love often originates through preference and taste as in a naturally developed friendship or sisterly relationship. Based on my limited biblical understanding, *agapao* tends to be the more "expensive" love because the element of sacrifice is part of its nature. God's directive in places like Luke 6:27 to love our enemies involves *agapao*. It's simply harder and necessitates will over emotion.

Earlier I pointed out that the key is to draw from the resource of God's own *agapao*. First John 4:7 tells us love comes from God and not from our own determination. His will is involved in choosing to receive and exercise God's love, not our own. Romans 5:5 displays the concept beautifully. It says, "God has poured out his love into our hearts by the Holy Spirit, whom he has given us." The first quality of the fruit of the Spirit in Galatians 5:22 is love.

God's chief goal is to deepen each of our relationships with Him. He knows that if we don't see our need for Him, we will never understand how sufficient and wonderful He is. Therefore, He continually challenges us to live beyond our natural abilities. God knows that challenges like loving someone we find difficult will place the obedient in the position to come to Him constantly for a fresh supply of His love. We have to pour out our own toxic and preferential affections so our hearts can be filled with His affections. As we ask for our cups to overflow with *agapao,* the liquid, living love of God will not only surge through our own hearts; it will splash on anyone nearby. Glory!

So did John practice what he preached? I thought you'd never ask! Did you hear the gush of affection in John's constant endearments?

The original word for children is *teknion,* meaning "a little child." The seriousness of the subject matter tells you John didn't write to young children. He was an older man by this time, and his flock was as dear to him as flesh and blood. Jerome, one of the early church fathers (approximately A.D. 340–420), "tells the story that John lived to an advanced age in Ephesus. So feeble was he that only with difficulty could his Christian disciples carry him to the church building. He could hardly speak, but when he did he said the same words: 'Little children, love one another.' Eventually his disciples grew weary of hearing the same phrase, so they asked him why he always spoke it. 'It is the Lord's command,' he replied, 'and if this alone be done, it is enough.'"[1]

My favorite account from the early church fathers concerning John was preserved by Clement. It begins with the statement, "Listen to a story which is not a story but a true tradition of John the Apostle preserved in memory." While visiting a new bishop and his congregation in Smyrna, John "saw a young man of strong body, beautiful appearance, and warm heart. 'I commend this man,' [John] said, 'to you with all diligence in the face of the church, and with Christ as my witness.'" John returned to Ephesus and, as promised, the bishop took the young man under his wing and baptized him. Time passed and the bishop "relaxed his great care and watchfulness. . . . But some idle and dissolute youths, familiar with evil, corrupted him in his premature freedom." Before long, the young man gave himself entirely to a life of sin, committed crimes, and even renounced his salvation. Eventually John was summoned back to Smyrna and asked for a report of the young man. Somewhat taken aback, the bishop answered, "He has died."

John inquired, "How and with what death?" When the bishop described the young man's abandoned faith as death, John replied, "Well, it was a fine guardian whom I left for the soul of our brother. But let me have a horse, and someone to show me the way." (Sounds a bit like the old Son of Thunder, doesn't it?) When the elderly John found the young man, he started to flee. John called out to him, "Why do you run away from me, child, your own father, unarmed and old? Pity me, child, do not fear me! You have still hope of life. I will account to Christ for you. If it must be, I will willingly suffer your death, as the Lord suffered for us; for your life, I will give my own. Stay, believe; Christ sent me." (These were figures of speech meaning that John would give his life to see the young man return to Christ. John knew better than anyone that only Christ could ransom a man's life.)

The young man wept bitterly, embraced the old man, and pleaded for forgiveness. The account says that John led the young man back and "baptized him a second time in his tears. . . . He brought him to the church, he prayed with many supplications, he joined with him in the struggle of continuous fasting, he worked on his mind by various addresses and did not leave him, so they say, until he restored him to the church, and thus gave a great example of true repentance and a great testimony of regeneration, the trophy of a visible resurrection."[2]

Yes, John practiced what he preached. I wonder how many fewer castaways might leave our pews empty if we practiced what he preached?

Chapter 34

LOVE IN THE TRUTH

The elder, to the chosen lady and her children, whom I love in the truth—
and not I only, but also all who know the truth. (2 John 1:1)

I'm having a bad day. A really bad day. I can either lose a writing day over it or write about it. I inherited a strong work ethic from my father, Major Dad, so brace yourself. I'm having that kind of day when I may do something rash like eat nothing but sweets. And I may go back and see if that woman who told me to have a nice day is still in the elevator. If she is, I'm going to push all the buttons at the same time and see if I can get her stuck between floors for a minute—then when the door opens, I might just say something mature like, "Same to you and more of it!"

This day takes my husband by surprise every year. He's not accustomed to my beginning a day bawling out loud. Then when he says, "Please don't cry," I reply (loudly), "I'll cry if I want to. And I want to!" He even called to check on me when he was halfway to work. He knows I'll be OK. This happens every year. I don't plan it. It just happens. I have a bad case of anniversary grief.

The silly thing is, the day isn't the anniversary of anything tragic. It was one of the sweetest days of my whole life: the day our son of seven years came to live with us. The day on the calendar need be of no importance to anyone but Keith and me. And God. He knows. My head was so full of dreams that night. I had never seen a more beautiful little boy. He looked so much like Keith. But tiny. Almost fragile. He played with Keith's plastic fishing worms while I planned his whole future in my head. He would be my man-child. The one I always wanted. One day his wife would say,

"I hope he loves me someday as much as he loves you." And I would think, *He won't. Not really.*

I just feel fussy today. I really like the song "Trading My Sorrows," but I have absolutely no intention of trading them today. For now, this pain in my heart is all I have left. Although I'm aware of the loss every other day, I rarely give it permission to shift to the gear of full-throttled pain. Today's the day. So for now, it's my party, and I'll cry if I want to.

For reasons known to God, the dreams spun in my head that first night were not to be. The whole situation has been hard to understand and impossible to explain. God, however, has gone out of His way to clearly state that we are not to interfere. We were on temporary assignment, and He'll let us know if and when He has further need for us. Period.

Every other day of the year, I can look at my life through a telescope and sit in utter amazement. God has fulfilled dreams I couldn't have had sense enough to dream. He has done the unimaginable. He delivered me from a life of recycling defeat and deeply embedded bitterness. He saved my marriage. Had anyone told me twenty-five years ago that I'd still be wild about my husband a quarter century later and have two young adult daughters who are crazy about Jesus, I might have thought they were dreaming. Not to mention God's scandalous love to allow such a former pit-dweller like me to serve someone like you. Oh, He has been indescribably gracious to me . . . just as He has to you.

On hard days we just need to pull back the lens a touch and look at the wider picture. But on those microscope days when we determine to slap the most upsetting thing we can think about on a slide and stare at it for hours, we throw a pity party and resent any loved one who refuses to come.

Do you have microscope days? And if so, what do you tend to focus on during a microscope day?

Let me warn you, Satan will rarely refuse to attend a good pity party. I appreciate the way Psalm 18:17–18 exposes the opportunism of an enemy. Of God David wrote, "He rescued me from my powerful enemy, / from my foes, who were too strong for me. / They confronted me in the day of my disaster, / but the LORD was my support." Don't think for a moment that Satan won't confront you on the day of your disaster—

whatever that may be. Sometimes we give him credit for having a heart and respecting when something should be off limits. After all, fair fighters don't hit a person when she's down.

Satan is not a fair fighter. He confronts us on our worst days and approaches us with his specialty: lies. You can't imagine the lies he tries to tell me on my microscope day. Lies like: "You didn't love him well enough." "You failed him." "You failed God." "If you had just tried this . . . or that." "If you had waited a little longer." Other times he tries a different approach. "Never take that kind of risk again." "Taking someone into your heart like that isn't worth it. You will always get hurt." "Love will fail you. Here's your old hammer, and I even saved the nails. Rebuild that fortress around your heart. Don't let anybody hurt you again."

Just about the time I want to default back to my old coldness, the Spirit of God within me whispers warm breath upon my cooling heart: "My little child, love comes from God . . . whoever does not love does not know God because God is love."

Be still my soul. Set your heart at rest in His presence. Let not your heart condemn you, . . . for God is greater than your heart, and He knows everything.

Let's stay with our microscope one moment longer as we consider the letter called 2 John. My favorite words in this brief letter are "love in the truth." Truth breeds trust. We also considered that trust is often developed more deeply through truth than even love.

Many of us have been loved by unhealthy people who proved deceptive in other ways. We were left injured and confused. Incidentally, if we didn't let God heal us, we likely became unhealthy people ourselves who continued the process. Unhealthiness is contagious, and deceived people deceive people.

Truth sets us free. God, the great I AM, is the totality of wholeness, completeness, and self-existence. He is both truth and love! While Satan approaches us with hate and lies, we can be "loved in the truth" by God and those His Spirit fills. Our God will only tell us the truth, and one of His chief truths is that loving is always worth doing.

I feel much better. Sometimes I just have to talk it out. I'm ready to put up my microscope and go back to my bifocals because 2 John also has a few other things to say. I love trying to figure out a good mystery, and this small piece suggests a marvelous one.

The letter bears an address "to the chosen lady and her children, whom I love in the truth" (v. 1). Scholars admit that 2 John may very well have been written to an actual woman and her children. Many, however, believe that the address was more likely metaphoric to hide the identity of New Testament believers in a time of fierce persecution. If the letter fell into the wrong hands, no one could be singled out. The letter may well have been written to a church.

Ephesians 5:25–27 compares the love of a husband for his wife to the love of Christ for the church. In that passage the Word gives the church the metaphorical female gender. John's reference translated in the NIV "to the chosen lady" could certainly have spiritual implications.

In 2 John 1 we see another possible hint in John's proclamation of love for "the chosen lady and her children . . . and not I only, but also all who know the truth." What individual would be loved by "all who know the truth"? Yet all who know the truth love the church (as the corporate body) and "her" children (or individual believers).

John's reference to "we" in 2 John 5 may suggest an additional hint. In the exhortation to love one another, he wrote, "I am not writing you a new command but one we have had from the beginning." Also, don't miss the exclusion of any mention of the father of the children. None of these suggestions on its own may lend strong support to "the chosen lady" constituting a metaphor for the church but, considered together, make me inclined to lean toward a corporate intention.

After calling the chosen lady and her children to walk in love, John gives them a warning. "Watch out that you do not lose what you have worked for, but that you may be rewarded fully" (v. 8). No sooner does God reveal truth than Satan goes on the warpath with lies. Deception is his specialty, and his obvious goal is to get us to believe the lies. Therefore, they can't be blatant or we'd recognize them.

Notice John said nothing about these false teachers refuting all doctrine concerning Christianity. Some of the false teachers in John's day did not refute that Jesus was divine. They simply said He wasn't man as well as God. John focused on this exact false teaching in his first letter: "Every spirit that acknowledges that Jesus Christ has come in the flesh is from God, but every spirit that does not acknowledge Jesus is not from God" (1 John 4:2–3).

The issue of Christ coming in the flesh is so vital because we "enter the Most Holy Place by the blood of Jesus, by a new and living way opened for us through the curtain, that is, his body" (Heb. 10:19–20). Satan is ever trying to undermine the issue of salvation. Think about this with me.

God created man in His image. John 4:24 says, "God is spirit." You and I were created in three parts: body, soul, and spirit. I believe the "spirit" part of us is that which is created most pointedly in God's image. The *spirit*—when distinguished in Scripture from the *soul*—is the part of each human being that has the capacity to know and have a relationship with God. Our Maker literally equipped us with an inner longing to find Him.

First Corinthians 6:17 says that "he who unites himself with the Lord is one with him in spirit." When we receive Jesus as our Savior, our spirit or the part of us with the capacity to know God unites with the Holy Spirit, and they become one.

Because I am a believer in Christ, when I refer to the spirit within me, I am talking about the Holy Spirit. Satan wants to do anything he can to keep people blinded to the truth and lost. He knows all of us are created with a longing for God that we often confuse with a longing for anything "spiritual."

The good news of Jesus Christ was running rampant all over the Middle Eastern part of the world in John's day and heading north, south, east, and west. Jesus was a hot topic of conversation. Once Satan established that he couldn't squelch spiritual hunger or stop the talk about Christ, he determined to supply a new story that made best use of both. He suggested through false teachers that Christ indeed came but not in the flesh. Therefore, the spiritually hungry could still have a belief system involving God but remain, as my relatives would say, as lost as a goose. Why? Because our access to God is through the torn flesh of Jesus Christ. To deny the incarnation is to deny the one and only means of salvation.

I imagine you know someone at work or elsewhere that may be very "spiritual" but doesn't believe in the incarnate death of Christ as the means to salvation. Do you see what Satan has done? He has tried to feed their need for the spiritual and still keep them blind to the truth. Clever and terribly destructive, isn't he?

Don't judge them. Pray like mad for them! Pray for the veil to be removed and the torn veil of Jesus' flesh to be made clear! Pray as well for those who teach such false doctrines.

John warned "the chosen lady" not to take any such teacher into her house. In those days, of course, most gatherings of believers met in what we now call house churches. In many countries they still do. Though John's directive is certainly important for any individual believer, you can imagine how vital it is for an entire church gathering. Traveling teachers were very common. I think John was saying, "Don't even consider giving anyone who teaches such false doctrine freedom to speak in your gatherings!"

Recently I spoke in a denominational church I haven't often had the privilege to serve. The pastor stood in the back of the sanctuary and listened to every word I taught. Someone asked me if I was bothered by his presence. I assured them I had nothing but respect for a pastor who watched over his flock so carefully. I also was quite relieved when I passed his test!

Pastors aren't just the shepherds of the men of the church. I have met pastors who I could tell were totally unconcerned about what their women were studying or to whom they were listening. Some of them think we're all just sipping tea and talking girl talk. I find myself thinking, *Mister, with all due respect, if your women catch a fire of false doctrine, they can burn down your whole church! Watch who you take into your "house"! Watch me, for heaven's sake! Watch all of us!* Many would never knowingly teach deception or distortion, but all are dreadfully human.

Well, well, well. In his second letter John certainly said volumes in so few words. If only I could do the same. One of the things I like best about him is his balance. "Love one another!" And while you're at it, "Test the spirits!" Now that's a fine teacher.

Chapter 35

BODY AND SOUL

*Dear friend, I pray that you may enjoy good health and that all may go
well with you, even as your soul is getting along well. (3 John 2)*

$\mathcal{W}$e conclude our brief look at John's letters with 3 John. While you and
I may still have much we'd like to explore in these rich epistles, I believe we
have met our goals. We've peeked further into the heart of John and centered on the elements I believe he wanted us to explore most: *koinonia*,
love, and truth.

I enjoyed the mysterious elements involved in trying to identify "the
chosen lady and her children" in our previous letter. In contrast, John's
third letter leaves no doubt that he addressed it to a specific individual. In
fact, John drops several names in this one-chapter letter. Gaius appears as
John's dear friend. Diotrephes loved to be first and excluded others.
Demetrius bears a good name so that not only others but even the truth
speaks well of him.

Imagine being named in a letter that turned out to be inspired
Scripture for all the world to see! Whether in commendation or criticism,
having your name immortalized in Scripture is a heavy thought! When
I see a portion of Scripture with brief testimonials, I almost shiver. After all,
if just one sentence were written about each of our lives in Scripture, what
do you suppose it would be? What would we want it to be?

A number of times in my life, I would have been anywhere from devastated to humiliated over what might have been written in a one-sentence
statement about my life. I love knowing that as long as we're kicking and
breathing, we can change our testimonies. God hasn't put a period at the

216

end of our sentences yet, but that tiny little dot doesn't take long to jot. We may think we're only mid-sentence when we're not.

Attending as many funerals as I do is a constant reminder to me. Let's not put off working toward what we hope God's testimonial for our lives will state. As the writer of Hebrews said, "Today, if you hear his voice, / do not harden your hearts / as you did in the rebellion" (3:15).

I love the insight we're gaining into the lifestyle and practices of the apostle John. We're getting to see him engaged with people—which I believe was his specialty. As we determined in the previous chapter, nothing is more refreshing than a Christian leader who practices what he preaches. Obviously you can see that John also had people in his life who were difficult to love. Poor Diotrephes. You'd think with a name like that, he wouldn't have wanted to be first. Can you imagine such a one-sentence testimonial? "Beth loved to be first and didn't like to have anything to do with the common folks." Egads! The hair on the back of my neck is standing up!

Notice John didn't say the man was lost. He was obviously a member of the church. Though his actions weren't loving, he could easily have been a Christian. If gossip and divisiveness are unquestionable signs of "lostness," the few folks that go to heaven are liable to have considerable elbow room. Thank goodness we won't have hard feelings and conflict in glory. Otherwise, I could almost imagine Diotrephes saying to John, "Did you have to go and write it down? Why couldn't you have just gossiped like I did?"

Gaius, on the other hand, was obviously easy for John to love. I don't prefer the NIV rendering of John's term of endearment for Gaius. The original word translated "my dear friend" is *agapeto*, meaning "beloved." Gaius wasn't only John's dear friend. He was John's dearly loved friend. The Gaius to whom John's third letter is addressed could very likely have been the one by the same name mentioned several other times in Scripture.

A companion of Paul named Gaius suffered at the hands of the mob in Ephesus (see Acts 19:28–31). When we went to Greece and Turkey on the Beloved Disciple tour, we stood in the very amphitheater where the riot took place. This same Gaius appears again in Acts 20:4–5, where he traveled ahead of Paul. Paul says in 1 Corinthians 1:13–15 that he baptized a man named Gaius.

The fact that Paul's Gaius and John's Gaius can both be traced to ministries in and around Ephesus strongly suggests the same individual. If so, I love to imagine the conversations that took place between them. John was old. Gaius couldn't have been young. Don't you know John and Gaius had a great time talking about Paul? What a character he was! Surely John and Gaius must have shared some good laughs about him.

You'll laugh when I tell you I'm sitting here with a lump in my throat. You see, I love these guys! I've spent months and months getting to know Paul and now John from the pages of Scripture. They were real men with real relationships. They agreed and disagreed just as all of us do. Imagine all of them knowing, loving, appreciating, and getting aggravated with one another. The stuff of real life. Every time Jesus Christ touches the hard hearts of human beings, a divine drop of rain hits the carnal sod of earth, and it is refreshed.

Refreshed. What a wonderful word! It just happens to be a word I'd like to target for the remainder of our chapter. I hope you didn't miss John's desire for Gaius to be as healthy in body as he was in soul. The Amplified Bible says, "Beloved, I pray that you may prosper in every way and [that your body] may keep well, even as [I know] your soul keeps well and prospers" (3 John 2).

My beloveds, you and I need to do what we can to watch after our health! Certainly our spiritual health is paramount, but while we're on this earth, the Spirit of God dwelling in each redeemed person is linked explicitly to our physical bodies. God created man as one entity made up of three parts: body, soul, and spirit.

In 1 Thessalonians 5:23 Paul penned a prayer we should all echo. "May your whole spirit, soul and body be kept blameless at the coming of our Lord Jesus Christ." Most believers instinctively know that the health of their souls and spirits are vitally important, but notice Paul's plea that we would allow God to sanctify us through and through, meaning our entire soul, spirit, and body.

God has taught me serious lessons about the impact my physical body has on both my soul and my spirit. Think about the soul for a moment. If my body is completely exhausted, my soul is deeply affected and over time can absorb the physical weariness and translate it into depression or feelings of hopelessness. If we eat poorly, we can fuel anxiety and fear. Most of us know that stress is linked to heart problems, high blood pressure, and many digestive problems. As long as our souls and spirits are imprisoned in these physical bodies, they are greatly affected by their condition.

You and I live stressful lives. I've heard many of your testimonies, and I am astounded at some of your challenges. Some of you work all day then tend a sick loved one all night. Others of you hold down several jobs as you try to keep your children in college. I often hear from young mothers who have three or four children under five years old. Now that's stress! I can't even imagine some of your challenges. I never dreamed I would have the challenges I face today. I am so grateful and humbled by God's present calling on my life to minister to women, but I will not kid you. It is work! Yes, God does most of it all by Himself, but the little He requires from me is everything I've got!

Paul described the participation of labor between a believer and God in Colossians 1:29: "To this end I labor, struggling with all his energy, which so powerfully works in me." My dear colaborer, you and I can't effectively fulfill our callings if we don't watch after our health. Our bodies are temples of the Holy Spirit. Each of us faces a life beyond our natural capabilities. My calendar is overwhelming, and I take each scheduled date very seriously. If I end up with a virus and can't make a conference that was scheduled a year earlier, I am devastated. If I'm going to be faithful to you, I've got to cooperate with God and do my part.

I take a handful of vitamins every day then pray to stay well. At times when I get sick, I either know my schedule is out of control again, Satan is on the warpath, or God is checking me out of the loop for a while. All of us deal with illness, but I think God's expectation is for us to do everything reasonable to avoid poor health. Meanwhile, we've got to keep our heads on straight about our motivation. Satan simply wants us in bondage. He loves the bondage of poor health, but he also delights in the yoke of excessive, compulsive fretting over the physical body. Ecclesiastes' directive to avoid all extremes speaks volumes to me about this subject (Eccles. 7:18).

Scripture also frequently prescribes rest for the weary faithful (see Ps. 127:2; Matt. 11:28; Mark 6:30–32).

Beloved, I am convinced one of our severest needs is pure rest. Not only sleep, but refreshment and recreation. Recently God spoke to me about capturing what He and I are calling "Sabbath moments." Like many of yours, my schedule right now is particularly tough, and I see no time in the near future for a number of days off. God spoke to my heart one Saturday morning while I was preparing for Sunday school: "My child, in between more intense rests, I want to teach you to take Sabbath moments." I wasn't certain what He meant. Just that morning God confirmed His desire for me to drive all the way to the other side of Houston to the medical center to visit a patient with brain cancer. I was very thankful for the privilege of visiting this patient, but I knew in advance it would be tough emotionally and far from restful.

I fought the traffic across Houston, then visited with my new friend and her husband while choking back the tears. They have two young sons, and unless God performs a miracle, their mother will go home to be with the Lord before they are grown. I got in my car and prayed. I pulled out of the parking garage, fighting the tears. A few blocks later as if on autopilot, I turned my steering wheel straight into the parking lot of the Houston Zoo!

Christ seemed to say, "Let's go play." And that we did. I hadn't been to the zoo in years. I heard about all the improvements, but I never expected the ultimate: Starbucks coffee! (OK, so I don't have all my health issues down pat.) Can you imagine watching a baby koala take a nap in a tree on a rare cold day in Houston with a Starbucks grande cappuccino in your hand? Now that's a Sabbath moment! God and I had a blast.

A few weeks later I kidnapped my hardworking staff for a few hours to go play a practical joke on another staff member who was running an errand. We hid in the store and had her paged to our department where we—grown Christian women—were hiding in the clothes rounders. We rolled all over the carpet with laughter at the look on her face. After we made complete fools of ourselves, one of the salesladies walked up to me and said, "Don't I know you from somewhere?" We went to pieces. And then we went back to work . . . the better for it, I might add.

Sabbath moments! We live in a hard world. If you have guts enough not to disconnect and hide from the overwhelming needs out there, you need some Sabbath moments to help you keep your head on straight. Start taking them!

"Beloved, I wish above all things that thou mayest prosper and be in health, even as thy soul prospereth" (3 John 2 KJV).

I wouldst wish for thou to goeth and concludest by thinking of thine own example of a Sabbath moment. If thou canst remember one, get thy rest-rebellious self out of thy workplace before thou collapseth.

Part 8

AMONG THE
LAMPSTANDS

Next we take a turn with the apostle John that he couldn't have expected. We can be quite sure he never sketched Patmos on his personal itinerary. I wonder what the old man felt as he was shipped like a criminal from his loved ones in Ephesus to a remote, unfriendly island in the Aegean Sea. He had no idea what awaited him. God's ways are so peculiar at times. The greatest privilege of John's life waited for him in the gravest circumstances. Have you ever noticed how Christ suddenly seems to reveal Himself to us in the places that seem most remote? Our brief overview of the study of Revelation will remind us afresh that Jesus will never send us anywhere He will not meet us.

Chapter 36

BANISHED TO PATMOS

I, John, your brother and companion in the suffering and kingdom and
patient endurance that are ours in Jesus, was on the island of Patmos because
of the word of God and the testimony of Jesus. (Revelation 1:9)

$\mathcal{I}$ am both sobered and elated over the present stage in our study. For the remainder of our journey together, we will join John in exile on the island of Patmos in the Aegean. Don't bother packing your swimsuit. This six-mile-wide, ten-mile-long island is not exactly paradise. In John's day its rocky, barren terrain attracted the eye of the Romans as a perfect place to banish criminals. Under the rule of the Roman emperor Domitian (A.D. 81–96), Christianity was a criminal offense, and the apostle John had a fierce case of it.

We don't know the detailed reason for John's confinement on the island. The only absolutes we have are those explained by John himself in Revelation 1:9. He was there "because of the word of God and the testimony of Jesus." Beloved, if we must suffer, I can't think of a greater reason.

I am curious why John, an undeniable Son of Thunder, was exiled rather than killed under the authority of Roman rule like the other apostles. Scholars agree we can assume he was harshly treated even at his age and forced into hard labor in the mines and quarries on the island. I still wonder why the Romans bothered since they publicly and inhumanely took the lives of so many other Christians. Ultimately, God wasn't finished with John's work on earth, and no one was taking him without his Father's permission. I wonder if the traditional teaching of the early church fathers is accurate—that the Romans tried to kill him . . . and couldn't.

Many scholars through the centuries have believed that John journeyed to Rome for at least a brief stay. Tertullian, often called the "father of Latin theology," lived during the generation closely following that of the apostles (A.D. 150–225). In a work called *On Prescription against Heretics,* Tertullian made a stunning claim: "The apostle John was first plunged, unhurt, into boiling oil, and then remitted to his island exile!"[1]

Very few scholars question the reliability of the early traditions held about Peter's death on a cross to which Tertullian referred. Yes, he endured a passion like his Lord's; yet because he felt unworthy to die in exactly the same manner, early tradition says that Peter requested he be crucified upside down. Likewise, I've never read a commentary that cited reason to question the traditional information that Paul was beheaded like John the Baptist. We are, therefore, left to wonder whether the account of Tertullian regarding John the apostle was simply fiction.

I certainly don't know if the account regarding John's plunge into boiling oil is reliable, but if you ask me if such an event is possible, I could only answer yes! In Acts 12, God wasn't ready for Peter's work on earth to end, so He loosed his chains and caused him to walk right out of the prison. I can't even count the times the apostle Paul narrowly escaped death. I seem to recall a trio in the Old Testament who experienced fire without even the smell of smoke (see Dan. 3). Beloved, don't let the modern church make you cynical. Ours is a God of wonders, and don't you forget it! Never let the words of Jeremiah 32:17 only be a popular chorus. "Ah, Sovereign LORD, you have made the heavens and the earth by your great power and outstretched arm. Nothing is too hard for you."

If Tertullian's account has any accuracy, the Romans may have tried to take John's life and in their foiled efforts banished him to exile on Patmos. His charge may have been failing to die when told.

Though a number of chronological orders are proposed for John's stays outside Jerusalem and Judea, I lean toward the following proposition: John lived and ministered in Ephesus first. At some point he made a trip to Rome where he fell into persecution, then he was banished to Patmos where most scholars believe he remained for about eighteen months.

Though I used to believe differently, I am now most convinced by the commentators and early teachers who said he returned to the city of Ephesus where he spent the time until his death.

With these thoughts in mind, perhaps in pencil rather than permanent marker, let's read our introduction to the mysterious and wonderful Book of Revelation. Keep in mind that our approach to the last book of the Bible will be general and not primarily a study of eschatology, or last things. We will search Revelation for insights into the apostle John himself and for the facts and concepts he most wanted us to know.

The Book of Revelation is unique in its inspired promise of blessing to those who read it, hear it, and take it to heart (1:3). Please read Revelation 1:1–10.

> The revelation of Jesus Christ, which God gave him to show his servants what must soon take place. He made it known by sending his angel to his servant John, who testifies to everything he saw—that is, the word of God and the testimony of Jesus Christ. Blessed is the one who reads the words of this prophecy, and blessed are those who hear it and take to heart what is written in it, because the time is near.
> John,
> To the seven churches in the province of Asia:
> Grace and peace to you from him who is, and who was, and who is to come, and from the seven spirits before his throne, and from Jesus Christ, who is the faithful witness, the firstborn from the dead, and the ruler of the kings of the earth.
> To him who loves us and has freed us from our sins by his blood, and has made us to be a kingdom and priests to serve his God and Father—to him be glory and power for ever and ever! Amen.
> Look, he is coming with the clouds,
>   and every eye will see him,
> even those who pierced him;
>   and all the peoples of the earth will mourn because of him.
> So shall it be! Amen.
> "I am the Alpha and the Omega," says the Lord God, "who is, and who was, and who is to come, the Almighty."

> I, John, your brother and companion in the suffering and kingdom and patient endurance that are ours in Jesus, was on the island of Patmos because of the word of God and the testimony of Jesus. On the Lord's Day I was in the Spirit, and I heard behind me a loud voice like a trumpet.

Even though our approach to the Book of Revelation will not include verse-by-verse exposition, I believe we can expect a measure of blessing as a direct result of our study. I'm going to be looking for mine, and I hope you will look for yours, too. The most profound revelation in Revelation is the revealing of Jesus Christ Himself, not only in visions but in authority.

The word *revelation* meaning "unveiling" is translated from the Greek word *apokalupsis*. Thrown onto a boat transferring criminals, John had no idea what God would unveil to him upon the island of Patmos. Imagine John's frail, aging frame as he held on tight while the sea vessel tossed its long way across the Aegean.

John probably pushed his gray hair out of his face to look at the few other prisoners sharing his destination. Don't picture a bonding experience. No one would likely carry him through a small group of worshipers while he said, "Dear children, love one another." Exile was intended not only for overwork and overexposure to elements; it was purposed for crazing isolation. The tactic would be wasted on John just as it can be wasted on us when Satan tries to force us into isolation.

John most likely would have preferred death. His long life may have frustrated him. If forced to remain on earth, exile from ministry and isolation from those he loved was certainly not the way he envisioned spending his senior years. I can't imagine at one point or another in the labors forced upon him that John didn't slip on the jagged, rocky surfaces and rip his thinning skin like paper. He had no bedding for his aching body at the end of a day. I also can't imagine that he thought, *Finally! A little peace and quiet for writing a new book!* He couldn't have expected to meet Jesus on that island as he did. Beloved one, how many testimonies do we need to hear before we accept that sometimes the places and seasons we expect Jesus least, we find Him most? And oddly, sometimes the places we expect Him most, we find Him least.

Revelation 1:7 says, "Look, he is coming with the clouds, / and every eye will see him." When Christ returns to this groaning soil in His glorious splendor, every eye will see Him. Until then, He sometimes comes with clouds. God's glory is so inconceivably brilliant to the human eye that He often shrouds His presence in a cloud (see Exod. 16:10; 24:15–16; Lev. 16:2; 1 Kings 8:10; Luke 9:34).

One day the clouds will roll back like a scroll and Christ will stand before us revealed. He has much to disclose to us in the meantime, and we'll be greatly helped when we accept that clouds are not signs of His absence. Indeed, within them we most often find His presence. In the July 29 entry of *My Utmost for His Highest,* Oswald Chambers wrote figuratively of clouds:

> In the Bible clouds are always associated with God. Clouds are the sorrows, sufferings, or providential circumstances, within or without our personal lives, which actually seem to contradict the sovereignty of God. Yet it is through these very clouds that the Spirit of God is teaching us how to walk by faith. If there were never any clouds in our lives, we would have no faith. "The clouds are the dust of His feet" (Nahum 1:3). They are a sign that God is there. . . . Through every cloud He brings our way, He wants us to unlearn something. His purpose in using the cloud is to simplify our beliefs until our relationship with Him is exactly like that of a child—a relationship simply between God and our own souls, and where other people are but shadows. . . . Until we can come face-to-face with the deepest, darkest fact of life without damaging our view of God's character, we do not yet know Him.[2]

Is your life covered in dark clouds right now? Or perhaps the clouds aren't dark. They are simply obscuring clarity and tempting you to be confused by your circumstances. I've been on Patmos when the clouds that settled on the island obscured what might otherwise have been a beautiful view. I wonder if the clouds covered the island as Domitian thought he left John to the island's harsh volcanic mercy? I wonder how the old apostle "viewed" his circumstances? I wonder if he ever imagined getting off that island? Or what he'd see while he was there?

John had a critical decision to make while exiled on the unkind island. Would he relax his walk with God at the very least and at most resist? After all, no one from his church or ministry was watching. Would he lie down and die? Goodness knows he was weary. Or would John the Beloved love Christ all the more and seek Him with his whole heart amid the rock and wasteland? His answer rises like a fresh morning tide baptizing the jagged shore: "On the Lord's Day I was in the Spirit" (1:10). And there He was: the Alpha and Omega. The first and last Word on every life. Every trial. Every exile.

> When darkness seems to hide His face, I rest on His unchanging grace;
> In every high and stormy gale, my anchor holds within the veil.
> On Christ, the solid Rock, I stand. All other ground is sinking sand. (Edward Mote, 1834)

Chapter 37

TO THE CHURCH
IN EPHESUS

Yet I hold this against you: You have forsaken your first love. (Revelation 2:4)

$\mathcal{W}$ithout exception in every book or letter he wrote, John was adamant that we know Jesus Christ Himself. The letter begins with a salutation followed by a majestic vision of Christ. Drawing images from Daniel and Ezekiel, John described the resurrected Lord in terms of unmistakable power.

In Revelation 1:19 Christ supplied a basic three-part outline for the entire book. He said, "Write, therefore, what you have seen, what is now and what will take place later." I believe the vision of Christ and His introduction as recorded in 1:12–20 may have constituted "what you have seen." Christ's specific address to each of the seven churches in Revelation 2 and 3 may have constituted "what is now."

All seven of the cities were locations where believers in Christ lived and practiced their faith at the time of John's exile. Years ago I learned a good rule of thumb that I've tried to keep before me in study: when plain sense makes common sense, seek no other sense. Through the ages various interpreters have sought to make the churches symbolic, but what we can know for certain is that they were actual believers and real churches. The order of scriptural presentation is actually geographic in Revelation 2 and 3. All seven cities were located in Asia Minor, and their orders in Scripture suggest a very practical route a messenger might take if he began a journey in Ephesus and traveled on to the other six cities.

231

Much of the future prophecy in the Book of Revelation is beyond chapter 4; therefore, the remainder of the message is considered by many scholars to fall under the third category: "what will take place later." To the chagrin of many, we cannot dogmatically interpret most of the symbolism in Revelation. Christ did, however, identify the mystery of the seven stars and the seven lampstands. "The seven stars are the angels of the seven churches, and the seven lampstands are the seven churches" (Rev. 1:20).

Scholars disagree over the exact interpretation of the "angels" of the seven churches. Some believe the angels are literal celestial beings assigned to each church. Since the basic meaning of the word is "messenger," however, others think the messenger is a man and perhaps the pastor or overseer at each church. Thankfully, the message is the same no matter who Christ deemed messenger. We will spend much of our focused time in Revelation on the messages to the seven churches. The fact that God included the communication in Holy Writ tells us they have something to say to us. In fact, Christ Himself pointed out their relevance to others as He drew all seven letters to a close with a broad invitation.

Christ's invitation is first recorded in Revelation 2:7: "He who has an ear, let him hear what the Spirit says to the churches." Now, feel the side of your head. Do you feel an ear? Try either side, for you only need one: "He who has an ear. . . ." If you have one, Jesus would like you to hear what the Spirit says to the churches. I have one, too, so I'm in with you. The reason is obvious. We of His church today have much to learn from the successes, failures, victories, and defeats of the early churches. The generations may be far removed, but our basic nature and the truth of Scripture remain consistent.

Actually, Christ had more in mind than talking to people who had at least one physical ear on the sides of their heads. I certainly had ears throughout my young years, but I'm not sure how well I used them to listen to God. For the most part my ears were important hair accessories. Will I put my hair behind both ears today? One ear? Or shall I let my hair hang over both ears? I was so deep. The messages to the seven churches are for people with a little more depth than that. Christ's broad invitation was more like this: What I've said to them will speak volumes to anyone who really wants to hear and respond.

The prophetic portions of Revelation are going to occur just as God wills according to His kingdom calendar. Our thorough study of them may increase our knowledge and understanding of future events, but their personal application in our daily lives is a little more challenging. On the other hand, Christ's messages to the seven churches could be applied by the Holy Spirit to change us and indeed affect the condition of Christ's church today. So let's each grab an ear and hear!

The first message appears in Revelation 2:1–7. The letters contain several repeated elements that I want you to identify from the very beginning. Pinpoint these where they appear in each letter. Here are the common components in Christ's messages to the churches. (An asterisk [*] marks the components that don't appear in all seven letters.)

- *Identification.* Christ identified Himself in a specific way using some element of the first vision in Revelation 1:12–18.
- *Commendation.* Christ issued a commendation* based on intimate acquaintance. While not every letter contains a commendation, all seven include the phrase "I know your. . . ." I practically shudder every time my eyes settle on the Scripture that tells us Christ "walks among the seven golden lampstands" (2:1). We already know that the lampstands are the seven churches. The verb tense suggests a continuous action.

  As surely as Christ "walked" among the churches and knew them intimately in the first century, He walks among our churches today. We would be tragically amiss to think Christ is uninvolved and unmoved by the conditions, activities, and inner workings of His present churches. He walks among us. Nothing is more important to Christ in any generation than the health of His church since it is the vehicle through which He purposes to reach the lost and minister to the hurting.
- *Rebuke.* Based on His intimate knowledge, Christ issued a rebuke.*
- *Exhortation.* Christ issued an exhortation of some kind. He instructs each church to do something specific.

- *Encouragement.* Christ issued an encouragement to overcome. Celebrate the fact that no condition was utterly irreversible! In each case, the church (made up of individual believers) is invited to overcome, but we also must be aware that time is of the essence!

Using the elements common to each letter to the churches, let's see what Christ had to say to the church at Ephesus.

Identification. Note what Christ pinpoints about Himself to the church in Ephesus: "These are the words of him who holds the seven stars in his right hand and walks among the seven golden lampstands" (Rev. 2:1). The description corresponds with verse 12 of chapter 1.

Commendation. Based on His intimate knowledge of the church of Ephesus, Christ strongly commended them in verses 2 and 3: "I know your deeds, your hard work and your perseverance. I know that you cannot tolerate wicked men, that you have tested those who claim to be apostles but are not, and have found them false. You have persevered and have endured hardships for my name, and have not grown weary."

Rebuke. "Yet I hold this against you: You have forsaken your first love" (2:4). Remember the apostle John was most involved in the church at Ephesus. Knowing what we've learned about him, how do you think he responded internally when he heard this particular rebuke concerning his dear ones in Ephesus? He was the pastor who had sought to teach them to love the Lord Christ. Did he feel a sense of failure or reproof?

Exhortation. In verse 5, Christ said, "Remember the height from which you have fallen! Repent and do the things you did at first. If you do not repent, I will come to you and remove your lampstand from its place." Note a detail about the warning. Christ told the church in Ephesus that if they did not repent and do the things they "did at first," He would come to them and remove their lampstand from its place. The terminology doesn't mean they would lose their place in heaven. We lose our lampstand when we lose a vibrant position of godly influence on earth. In other words, we lose our light in the world.

Keep in mind that a church is no stronger than its people. A church isn't bricks and mortar. It's the people of God. I've been in a church God confronted with the sins of division and cynicism. Though individuals repented and did not lose the light of godly influence, the church as a whole refused to "go face to the ground," as I call it, in corporate repentance. For an excruciating season, she completely lost her place of viable influence in the community. Her sins were serious, but they were not hopeless! Read on. . . .

Encouragement. "To him who overcomes, I will give the right to eat from the tree of life, which is in the paradise of God" (2:7). The sins of the church at Ephesus weren't hopeless either. Nor are ours! Let's repent, though, so we can overcome!

I can't help but camp out a while on the rebuke to the church at Ephesus. I don't want us to miss its great relevance to the modern church. You noticed that the church in Ephesus received tremendously noble commendations from Christ and yet she had somehow let go of the most important thing of all: her sacred romance with Jesus Christ. We've seen in John's ministry the unparalleled priority of love. You and I can work hard, persevere through extreme difficulty, not tolerate wicked men, and accurately discern false teachers but yet forsake our first love.

Ironically, many believers don't view an absence of love for Jesus Christ as sin. They view it simply as something they lack. This misunderstanding may be part of the holdup. If God's absolute priority for all followers of Christ is love—for Him first and others second—then the absence of such love is sin. I pound this point but not to condemn. Remember, it's not an irreversible condition! I pound the point so that we can do what we must to get on with the business of loving! God says, "Repent!" I'm not sure we'll be able to welcome the resource of love and His means of shedding it abroad in our hearts until we do.

Repent means turn. I believe God told them and is telling us to turn from whatever has taken the place of our sacred romance with Christ and pour our lives back into the first things. Keep in mind that with the "first things" rightly established, all other things of value come to us as well. The church in Ephesus very likely allowed their spiritual busyness and all their stalwart religiosity to displace the law of love. Since everything else hinges on the laws of love (Matt. 22:40), over time all things of eternal value would have crumbled in Ephesus. Surely this exhortation speaks to each of us in one way or another.

Somehow in my previous studies of this letter, I have overlooked the original meaning of a critical word in the phrase "forsaken your first love." I am astonished to find that the original word for "forsaken" is the same word often translated "forgive" in the New Testament. The word *aphiemi* means "to send forth, send away, let go from oneself."[1] The word is used in the phrase describing Christ's physical death when He "gave up the spirit" in Matthew 27:50. The New Testament uses *aphiemi* in many contexts and simply means giving up or letting go of something. The word is translated "forgive" both times in the familiar words of Matthew 6:12 (KJV): "Forgive us our debts, as we forgive our debtors."

I could easily sit right here and sob. The thought occurs to me how often we forsake our first love—our indescribably glorious sacred romance—because we refuse to forsake our grudges and grievances. How many times has Christ watched those He loves give up intimacy with Him in order to hang on to unforgiveness? Please allow me to say this with much compassion as one who has been there: We cannot hang on to our sacred romance with Jesus Christ and also our bitterness. We will release one to hang on to the other.

Today, precious one, release the one that is nothing but bondage. Life is too short. The room unforgiveness is taking up in your life is cheating you of the very thing you were born (again) to experience. Send it forth! Not into oblivion, but into the hands of the faithful and sovereign Judge of the earth. Grab the neck of Jesus Christ and hang on to Him instead with every breath and every ounce of strength you have. Pray to love Him more than you pray for blessing, health, or ministry. Unless our lampstands are lit with the torch of sacred love, they are nothing but artificial lights. Fluorescent, maybe. But sooner or later, the bulb burns out.

Chapter 38

TO THE CHURCH
IN SMYRNA

*Be faithful, even to the point of death, and I will give
you the crown of life. (Revelation 2:10b)*

$\mathcal{N}$ext we focus on the second of seven messages to churches in Asia
Minor. Smyrna (modern Izmar) was an exceptionally beautiful city about
forty miles due north of Ephesus. The people of Smyrna placed a high pre-
mium on learning. Science and medicine flourished, contributing to great
wealth in the metropolis during the early New Testament era in which John
received the revelation. With this landscape picture of Smyrna in mind,
let's look at the specifics of the message to Smyrna. You'll note the same
common elements we saw in the message to Ephesus, with a couple of different twists.

Identification. "These are the words of him who is the First and the
Last, who died and came to life again" (2:8).

Commendation. "I know your afflictions and your poverty—yet you
are rich! I know the slander of those who say they are Jews and are not, but
are a synagogue of Satan" (2:9).

Rebuke. Unlike Ephesus, Christ offered no rebuke to this church.

Exhortation. "Do not be afraid of what you are about to suffer. I tell
you, the devil will put some of you in prison to test you, and you will suffer persecution for ten days. Be faithful, even to the point of death, and
I will give you the crown of life" (2:10).

Encouragement. "He who overcomes will not be hurt at all by the second death" (v. 11).

Now let's consider some thoughts about these elements of the message. We won't always be able to link Christ's specific self-identification to something noteworthy about the recipient, but we are probably wise to assume a link existed. In the letter to the believers in Smyrna, Christ identified Himself as the "First and the Last." Almost every book and commentary I studied mentioned the ancient inscription on the coins in first-century Smyrna: "First in Asia in Beauty and Size."[1]

As Christ addressed His letter to humble believers surrounded by arrogant pagans, He essentially declared, "I am the First in Asia, Africa, and everywhere else. In fact, I spoke them into existence. What's more, I am also Last. I am the inescapable One, the Judge of the Living and the Dead, and I have come to commend you."

Smyrna stands out among the churches as one of two that received no rebuke. As Christ walked beside this lampstand, He found no fault in her. Impressively, she didn't pass her tests because her exams were easy. To the contrary, no other church is characterized by greater depths of suffering. Christ didn't mince words when He described her afflictions and poverty. Christians were despised and terribly mistreated in Smyrna primarily because no other city in Asia Minor held more allegiance to Rome.

"As early as 195 B.C., Smyrna foresaw the rising power of Rome and built a temple for pagan Roman worship. In 23 B.C., Smyrna was given the honor of building a temple to the Emperor Tiberius because of its faithfulness to Rome. Thus, the city became a center for the cult of emperor worship—a fanatical 'religion'"[2] The obsessive allegiance of the people of Smyrna became deadly for Christians under the rule of emperors like Nero (A.D. 54–68) and Domitian (A.D. 81–96). Anything the emperor reviled, the people of Smyrna reviled. For these two emperors and others that followed, Christians were on the top of the hate list.

"I know . . . your poverty." Surrounded by wealth, those known to be Christians were persecuted in many ways, not the least of which was economically. Decent jobs were often refused to them, and many merchants withheld goods from them. Against the sparkling backdrop of opulence and affluence, the Christians in Smyrna were invited to take their poverty personally. In *Voice of the Martyrs*,[3] you can read current bone-chilling accounts of Christians forced to live in horrendous poverty in parts of the world because of their faith. A single mouth never goes unfed without God's notice. No government or people group gets away with a lack of compassion or outright oppression. God feels so strongly about the poor that I believe He is fully capable of withholding blessing from cities and nations that neglect or oppress them.

Christ commented about the slander of those who falsely claimed to be Jews but instead were a synagogue of Satan. This fact may imply that the Jews in Smyrna identified the Christians to the government and greatly heightened the persecution against them.

Imagine God's derision for a people who not only look the other way but actively enforce poverty and affliction. They had no idea the King of the earth walked through the perfectly paved streets of their fair city checking on those who called themselves by His name. The people of Smyrna took great pride in the beauty of their city. I found the following quote out of *Bible Illustrator* quite ironic: "The hills and the sea added to the picturesque quality of the city. The city itself nestled under the hill Pagos, which made an ideal acropolis. This beauty was marred, however, by a drainage problem in the lower city which resulted in the silting up of the harbor and an accumulation of unpleasant odors."[4]

Try as they might to build the most impressive city in Asia, they just couldn't do anything about that putrid smell. Don't think for a moment that their unrelenting persecution of innocent people didn't rise up to the nostrils of God. Interestingly, the name *Smyrna* means "myrrh."[5] The ancient extract by the same name was used in Scripture for anointing oil, perfume, purification, and embalming. Myrrh was among the gifts offered by the Magi to Jesus. Nothing but stench ascended to the heavens from the arrogantly pristine, highly educated, and wealthy of Smyrna. From the hidden slums, however, rose a fragrant incense of great expense. No perfume is more costly and more aromatic to God than the faithfulness of believers who are suffering.

A few nights ago I served on a team with a pastor whose son will soon die of a malignant brain tumor unless God intervenes miraculously. I stood not far from him during praise and worship. This precious father did not deny his immense pain. His tears fell unashamedly, but all the while his worship rose just as unashamedly. I can hardly hold back my own tears as I picture his face. Many of us felt the favor of God over our interdenominational prayer gathering that night. Somehow, I believe in the midst of much praise, a fragrance of greater price and exceeding sweetness ascended to the throne from one grieving servant of God.

How are people like my pastor/friend and the believers in Smyrna able to be faithful through such terrible suffering? As resistant as we are to absorb it, 1 Peter 1:7 indicates one primary reason: "These have come so that your faith—of greater worth than gold, which perishes even though refined by fire—may be proved genuine and may result in praise, glory and honor when Jesus Christ is revealed."

Those who are faithful in the midst of immense suffering somehow allowed their fiery trials to purify them rather than destroy them. If we've never suffered like some of the saints we know or have read about, we tend to indict ourselves with failure before our trials ever come. We must remember that God grants us grace and mercy according to our need. No, I do not have the strength or character to be faithful under such heart-shattering conditions, but when my time comes the Holy Spirit will impart a power and grace I've never experienced. The challenge is whether or not to accept it.

The tragedy is that in our pride and anger we sometimes refuse the grace of God during our times of suffering. The believers in Smyrna did not refuse the grace. They inhaled it like air because they were desperate. As much as the church in Smyrna had suffered, Christ warned them of more to come. He wanted them to be aware, but He did not want them to be afraid. I believe much of the Book of Revelation was written to believers for the same purpose.

Mind you, imprisonment and death awaited some of those among the fragrant church of Smyrna. We don't know what Christ meant by the time segment of "ten days." Some scholars believe it was literal. Others think it represented ten years. Still others assume it is a figure of speech for a segment of time known only to God. Whatever the length of trial, Christ called the church of Smyrna to be faithful unto death. His self-identification as the one who died and came to life again reminded them of the absolute assurance of resurrection life. He also promised to reward them with a *stephanos* or victor's crown. They would not be touched by "the second death," a term for the final judgment for all unbelievers.

Father, how desperately we, Your children, need the renewing of our minds! In our human ways of thinking, overcoming a life-threatening situation always means staying alive!

We inhale the sweet fragrance of the church of Smyrna to learn another option under the heading of overcoming. Sometimes Jesus defines overcoming not as living well but dying well. In other words, dying with faith and spiritual dignity. Beloved, dying is the one thing each of us is going to do unless we're the chosen generation to "meet Him in the air" without tasting death (1 Thess. 4:17).

At least one of the saints in Smyrna to which Christ addressed His letter left us a profound and wonderful example of an overcoming death. His name was Polycarp. He studied directly under the apostle John's tutelage and was alive at the time the Revelation was penned. He became the bishop of the church in Smyrna and served the generation that followed John's heavenly departure. Foxe's *Book of Martyrs* shares the following account of Polycarp's trial and martyrdom.

> He was, however, carried before the proconsul, condemned, . . . The proconsul then urged him, saying, "Swear, and I will release thee;—reproach Christ." Polycarp answered, "Eighty and six years have I served Him, and He has done me no wrong. How then can I blaspheme my King who has saved me?" At the stake to which he was only tied, not nailed as usual, as he assured them he should stand immovable.[6]

Polycarp's persecutors tried to fight fire with fire, but they failed. His faithfulness to the death only heightened the flames of godly passion, carrying the costly fragrance of myrrh past the jeers of the crowd to the throne room of God. He had overcome. Perhaps crucifixion is the only slow death with pain exceeding the fires of a stake. As long as those moments must have been, nothing could have prepared Polycarp for the sight he beheld when death gave way to life and faith gave way to sight. The only Jesus he had ever seen was in the face and heart of John the Beloved. That day the old bishop of Smyrna saw the One he loved and had served for eighty and six years. Face-to-face. With a victor's crown in His hand.

When I get to heaven and meet him, I'm going to try to remember to ask Polycarp if he thought his suffering was worth it. Oh, I already know the answer, . . . but I want to see his expression.

Chapter 39

TO THE CHURCH
IN PERGAMUM

*To him who overcomes, I will give some of the hidden manna. I will
also give him a white stone with a new name written on it, known
only to him who receives it. (Revelation 2:17)*

$\mathcal{N}$ext we travel farthest north in the cluster of the seven churches to the
city of Pergamum. About sixty-five miles above Smyrna, Pergamum was
the administrative capital city of Asia until the close of the first century and
the legal center for the district. You may still have Smyrna pictured in your
mind. Imagine a city with exceeding grandeur as we make our way through
the city gate of Pergamum. I was stunned by the pictures of the ornate
ruins. Not only did the city boast imposing gymnasiums, theaters, and
government facilities; its 200,000-volume library was second only to the
library in Alexandria.

When word of the plans for such a library circulated, an Egyptian
importer of papyrus was so offended by the thought of a rival that he
stopped Pergamum's shipments. The deficit forced the development of
parchment, which is the Greek word *pergemene,* from Pergamum.[1] We
have more to learn about the architecture and personality of Pergamum,
but let's go straight to Scripture to pour the concrete.

Identification. "These are the words of him who has the sharp, double-
edged sword" (2:12).

Commendation. "I know where you live—where Satan has his throne.
Yet you remain true to my name. You did not renounce your faith in me,

even in the days of Antipas, my faithful witness, who was put to death in your city—where Satan lives" (2:13).

Rebuke. "Nevertheless, I have a few things against you: You have people there who hold to the teaching of Balaam, who taught Balak to entice the Israelites to sin by eating food sacrificed to idols and by committing sexual immorality. Likewise you also have those who hold to the teaching of the Nicolaitans" (2:14–15).

Exhortation. "Repent therefore! Otherwise, I will soon come to you and will fight against them with the sword of my mouth" (2:16).

Encouragement. "He who has an ear, let him hear what the Spirit says to the churches. To him who overcomes, I will give some of the hidden manna. I will also give him a white stone with a new name written on it, known only to him who receives it" (2:17).

Christ identified Himself to the church of Pergamum as Him who has the sharp, double-edged sword. The word picture could mean many things in Scripture. One primary purpose of a double-edged sword is to divide. As Christ "walked among" the people of this lampstand, He obviously found those who were true to His ways and those who were not. Likewise, as He walks among our lampstands today, Christ sees us as individuals who together comprise a church. The faithfulness or rebelliousness of any given individual never gets swept up or "grayed" in the corporate whole. How I wish at times it did!

In defense of the young church in Pergamum, we can only imagine what kind of warfare they experienced. Christ referred to the city as the place "where Satan has his throne." Since Satan is not omnipresent, Christ's claim is hair-raising. We can't be certain what He meant, but historical evidence from the first century tells us Pergamum was the uncontested center of pagan worship in Asia Minor. Keep in mind that Satan's primary goal is to keep people blinded to truth while providing something that momentarily seems to assuage their spiritual hunger. Pergamum delivered. Christ spoke about the church in Pergamum remaining true to His name. Goodness knows, inhabitants had plenty of names to choose from. Within its walls were temples to Dionysus, Athena, Asclepius, and Demeter; three temples to the emperor cult; and a huge altar to Zeus.

Although the philosophy of the city seemed to be "pick a god, any god," two primary religions exceeded all others in Pergamum: the worship of Dionysus, considered god of the royal kings (symbolized by the bull), and the worship of Asclepius, called "the savior god of healing" (symbolized by the snake). Does that second title make your skin crawl like it does mine? I know the Savior God of Healing, and I assure you it isn't the snake. God heals in many ways, but He alone is Jehovah Rapha.

I'm reminded of God's words in Hosea 11:3. The prophet said of Israel, "They did not realize it was I who healed them." All healing is meant to reveal the Healer. Satan will do anything he can to block the connection. The first psalm I memorized was Psalm 103. I still love it. It urges us to praise the Lord and not to forget His benefits. When given the opportunity, Satan gladly supplies a counterfeit "savior" providing a dandy benefit package. Any world religion or brand of humanism will do.

Since man was created to seek God's benefits, Satan works most effectively if he is able to offer alternatives. For instance, he's sly to suggest other ways for people to unload their guilt. One workable way is to convince them they haven't sinned. He also needs to address health issues. Worship of the body works nicely as a preoccupation. He has all sorts of means of providing counterfeit "redemption."

Not long ago I received a letter from a loved one with whom I shared my testimony about the transforming power of God's Word. He, a practicing Buddhist, wrote me his own testimony about how life had improved since he changed his "karma." My heart broke over the inevitable disillusionment of self-worship. At some point surely a self-worshiper looks in the mirror and says, "If I am as good as God gets, life stinks." What about love and compassion? Counterfeits can be sold or manufactured on any corner. And the renewal of youth? One of the hottest moneymakers in the world economy. Keeping people preoccupied is big business to the devil.

Though surrounded by counterfeits, Christ's commendation tells us many believers in Pergamum remained true and did not renounce their faith even when Antipas was put to death. Several sources say that Antipas was publicly roasted in a bowl-like vessel. Others claim we have no dependable information on him. Perhaps all we have for certain is the meaning of his name, "against all."[2] Sometimes I travel to countries all by myself. One was particularly dangerous, and the thought occurred to me that I could find myself in trouble without a single local ally. The odds of one-against-all can be overwhelming.

We don't have to cross an ocean to feel those kinds of odds. All some of us have to do is go to work. Or go home! At times when we realize we're "against all" in a given environment, we are wise to ask God to confirm whether or not we are right. Sometimes I've been out on a limb when God confirmed that I wasn't even in the right tree!

On the other hand, if God confirms our positions, we are challenged to gracefully accept them as opportunities to display His glory. Romans 8:31 becomes our watchword: If God is for us, who can be against us? The day Antipas died, God was for him. Like Polycarp, Antipas stood against all and he overcame. You and I are going to learn something vital from our study of Revelation: death doesn't always mean defeat.

Not every member of the church in Pergamum was a faithful witness like Antipas. Christ rebuked an undesignated number for holding to the teachings of Balaam and the Nicolaitans. If Christ commanded the repentance of the whole church, the number had to be significant. Although God esteems repentance of the faithful on behalf of the unfaithful, He doesn't require it from people who haven't sinned. Look back at His commendation to the church of Ephesus in Revelation 2:2. I suspect the church in Pergamum may have tolerated "wicked men" and false apostles more than the church of Ephesus.

We can't dogmatically identify the teaching of the Nicolaitans, but they are closely associated with the teachings of Balaam. The account of Balaam and Balak is found in Numbers 22–24. In a nutshell, Balak, the king of Moab, greatly feared the Israelites as they settled in the promised land. He hired Balaam the soothsayer to curse Israel, but he blessed them instead. Balaam did, however, instruct Balak how to defeat the Israelites. He told Balak to seduce them into idolatry through the harlotry of the Moabite women. Based on all I've read, I believe the basic concept of Balaam's teachings is this: If you can't curse them, try to seduce them!

The whole idea makes my blood boil. You see, Satan is waging war on our generation with Balaam's weapon (see 1 Tim. 4:1). Satan can't curse us because we are blessed (Eph. 1:3) children of God, covered by the blood of the Lamb. If the devil can't curse us, then how can he defeat us? He can try to seduce us! How does seduction differ from temptation? All seduction is temptation, but not all temptation is seduction. Many temptations are obvious. The aim of seduction is to catch the prey off guard. That's why Satan's best henchmen (or women) are often insiders rather than outsiders. Some in the church of Pergamum were enticed into sin by others among them. Whether or not the seducers were truly saved is unclear. Either way, Christ expected the church to jump to action.

If the seducers were true believers, they needed to be confronted properly and restored when repentant. Some may wonder how believers could be used by Satan to seduce. Beloved, seduced people seduce people. If the devil's scheme is not exposed and the chain is not broken, it perpetuates. Without a doubt, some of Satan's most effective seducers can be within the church. We must develop discernment and guard our hearts jealously without becoming fearful and suspicious. Authentic godliness rather than religiousness is our best defense against seduction.

Christ's letter to the church in Pergamum must have hit hard, but the tenderness and encouragement of the conclusion spared their hearts.

Christ promised two things to those who overcame: hidden manna and a white stone. The hidden manna contrasts beautifully with the food sacrificed to idols. Jesus Christ was the Bread of Life sacrificed on the altar before the one true God. Now His Spirit falls like manna from heaven to all who hunger. Jewish tradition holds that the ark with the pot of manna in it was hidden by order of King Josiah and will be revealed once again during the earthly reign of the Messiah.

The most probable meaning of the white stone in verse 17 is remarkable. In an ancient courtroom, jurors voting to condemn the accused would cast their vote by tossing a black stone or pebble. In contrast, jurors voting to acquit the condemned would cast their vote by tossing a white stone or pebble. Scripture actually records this ancient practice, but our English translations don't portray it. In the course of sharing his testimony,

Paul said he "cast a vote against" the Christians (Acts 26:10). The original wording is *katenegka psephon.* The Greek word *katenegka* means "to deposit or cast." The Greek word *psephon* means "pebble or stone," and is only used in Acts 26:10 and Revelation 2:17.[3] Paul formerly deposited or cast his pebble to vote against the saints.

If we're on target, the terminology Christ used was perfectly fitting for Pergamum. Do you remember one of the first facts we learned about the city? It was the legal center in the district. How I praise God that the Judge of all the earth pitches a white stone to acquit us—not because we're innocent but because Someone already served our sentence. And the new name on the stone? It could be Christ's, but I also think we each have an overcoming name not unlike Abram had Abraham, Simon had Peter, and Saul had Paul.

I'll be honest with you. I'll be glad to leave Pergamum. I learned plenty from the annals of their famous library, but I'm not crazy about the food. I'm also petrified of seducers. But the manna and the stone? Those were worth the trip. See you in Thyatira!

Chapter 40

TO THE CHURCH IN THYATIRA

Nevertheless, I have this against you: You tolerate that woman Jezebel,
who calls herself a prophetess. (Revelation 2:20)

$\mathcal{L}$et's take the inland route and travel about forty-five miles east of Pergamum to the city of Thyatira. Few ruins can be explored today because the modern city of Akhisar in Turkey stands atop its ancient history. Perhaps we're better off. She has a shady past. We'll learn as much as we need to know and be thankful God spared us further details. As we walk through the ancient city gates today, we won't find the splendor and opulence we witnessed in Smyrna and Pergamum. Thyatira was not known for her beauty. She was known for her commerce. We read her story in Revelation 2:18–29. Here are the highlights:

Identification. "These are the words of the Son of God, whose eyes are like blazing fire and whose feet are like burnished bronze" (2:18).

Commendation. "I know your deeds, and your love and faith, your service and perseverance, and that you are now doing more than you did at first" (2:19).

Rebuke. "Nevertheless, I have this against you: You tolerate that woman Jezebel, who calls herself a prophetess. By her teaching she misleads my servants into sexual immorality and the eating of food sacrificed unto idols" (2:20).

Exhortation. "Only hold on to what you have until I come" (v. 25).

Encouragement. "To him who overcomes and does my will to the end, I will give authority over the nations—

'He will rule them with an iron scepter;
    he will dash them to pieces like pottery'—

just as I have received authority from my Father. I will also give him
    the morning star" (vv. 26–28).

Thyatira found her significance in two identities, both of which Christ intimates in His letter. During the Greek epoch the city originally was an important military headquarters. Thyatira unfortunately suffered under one conqueror after another but never stopped thinking of herself as a power. Her military legacy continued under Roman rule, but she evolved into one of the most thriving commercial centers in all of Asia. Her city walls bulged with wool and linen workers, dyers, leather workers, potters, tanners, bakers, slave dealers, and bronze smiths.

Many scholars believe Christ described Himself with blazing fire and burnished bronze because inhabitants of Thyatira took such pride in their metal works. Thyatira's dual identity was captured in a commemorative coin struck by the Roman government in her honor. The coin depicted "a metalworker seated at an anvil hammering out a helmet in the presence of the goddess Athena, who stands ready to receive it."[1] A metalworker representing commerce, a helmet representing military government, and a goddess representing feminine influence. Don't forget those three inscriptions. They tell the story of Thyatira.

The New Testament mentions the ancient city of Thyatira one other time. Not coincidentally, the two references fit together as contrasting puzzle pieces inviting us to reflect on the best and worst of womanhood. This lesson is one in which this female author will act on the right she reserves to completely single out women. A brother is welcome to observe, but it's not for him, ladies. This one's entirely for us.

Acts 16:13–15 tells about Lydia, the businesswoman who became the first named convert in Europe. Lydia was from Thyatira. I love the words of verse 14: "The Lord opened her heart to respond to Paul's message." Then her entire household followed Christ.

Scripture associates Thyatira with two different women: Lydia and Jezebel. Some scholars interpret Jezebel as a reference to a false doctrine, a type of demonic spirit, or a behavioral concept. Others believe she was a flesh-and-blood woman who played havoc in the church at Thyatira. I am strongly inclined to agree with the latter, but I am also thoroughly convinced she is representative of a kind of woman none of us want to be. "Nevertheless, I have this against you: You tolerate that woman Jezebel, who calls herself a prophetess. By her teaching she misleads my servants into sexual immorality and the eating of food sacrificed to idols. I have given her time to repent of her immorality, but she is unwilling" (Rev. 2:20–21).

Jezebel could have been the woman's actual name, but Christ was far more likely drawing the parallel between the woman in Thyatira and the brazen wife of King Ahab. The account of the "original" Jezebel can be found in bits and pieces from 1 Kings 16 to 1 Kings 21. She came from Sidon, a commercial city not unlike Thyatira, known for idolatry and licentiousness. She married Ahab, a king of Israel, and moved to Jezreel. The city served the one true God, but she determined to turn it into a center of Baal worship. The wicked, idolatrous queen soon became the power behind the throne. Obedient to her wishes, Ahab erected a sanctuary for Baal and supported hundreds of pagan prophets.[2] She massacred the prophets of the Lord when they opposed her. Many of those who escaped her hid in caves. Elijah became and remained a thorn in her flesh. He was a man who witnessed inconceivable wonders of God, defeating her prophets as God sent fire from heaven. Yet Jezebel wielded such power and intimidation that when she threatened Elijah, he ran for his life and for a time fell into deep depression.

After Ahab died in battle, Jezebel retained her control for the next ten years through her sons Ahaziah and Joram. After their bloody deaths, the servants threw Jezebel from a window just as Elijah had predicted. Her body was trampled by horses and eaten by dogs (2 Kings 9:33–35). A gruesome death, indeed, but had we seen her factual story in a movie, her demise would have been the moment when the audience cheered.

Fast-forward to the New Testament and a woman who bears her predecessor's name. The ancient city of Thyatira tells the story of women and power. It's a story we may not want to hear but we need to hear. Surrounded by a male-centered culture, Thyatira was, in tired twentieth-century terms, "liberated." Women could be quite successful, which was—and is—admirable. Just leave it to someone to give it a bad name. Since the fabric of the ancient city was practically woven in military green, the bigger the stick one carried, the better. Authority was everything. You can even hear Christ intimate their authority issue in His promise to overcomers. "To him who overcomes and does my will to the end, I will give authority over the nations" (Rev. 2:26).

Under Roman rule, the evolution of Thyatira's commerce shifted militant authority to successful merchants. Almost every commentary I researched talked about the powerful trade guilds that ran the city like the mob. Clubs and societies, some of which were "underground," were not only social but also highly political. They were strangely "religious" because they entrenched their members in all sorts of idolatrous practices. Much pressure for membership existed, and refusal automatically tagged you an enemy.

The networking between these trade clubs and societies was more like a web. They came with offers a citizen wasn't wise to refuse. Not only did unethical deals and practices prevail, sexual immorality was rampant. Somehow, extramarital sexual expression got twisted up in their concept of liberation. Of course, nothing provokes more bondage than sexual immorality, but Satan is ever the liar, isn't he?

The Revelation 2 Jezebel was a very powerful woman in Thyatira. Likely up to her elbows in secret guilds and society climbs, she did everything she could to infiltrate the church with them. Lydia was also a powerful woman in Thyatira. Together they provide a lesson on abuse versus wise use of authority. Let's perform a character sketch of Jezebel and invite Lydia to hold up a lamp of contrast in her counterpart's insidious darkness.

You and I live in a culture in which women can be very successful and hold many authoritative positions. Many women have strong gifts and rise to the top in various professions. That's wonderful—as long as they know what to do with position. Unless we are women actively submitted to the true liberation of Christ's authority, we can be terrifying. If God has gifted us professionally, we want to be Lydias. The following characteristics describing Jezebel will help shed light on any shred of her character living in us.

1. Jezebel assumed places of authority God did not assign her. "You tolerate that woman Jezebel, who calls herself a prophetess" (v. 20). Before you jump to the conclusion that her infraction was assuming a role that could belong only to men, note the Scriptures below and the association between women and the gift of prophecy.

- "There was also a prophetess, Anna, the daughter of Phanuel, of the tribe of Asher. She was very old; she had lived with her husband seven years after her marriage, and then was a widow until she was eighty-four. She never left the temple but worshiped night and day, fasting and praying" (Luke 2:36–37).
- "In the last days, God says, / I will pour out my Spirit on all people. / Your sons and daughters will prophesy, / your young men will see visions, / your old men will dream dreams. / Even on my servants, both men and women, / I will pour out my Spirit in those days, / and they will prophesy" (Acts 2:17–18).
- ". . . Philip the evangelist, one of the Seven. He had four unmarried daughters who prophesied" (Acts 21:8–9).

The New Testament undeniably records the viability of a woman having the God-given gift of prophecy, or what we might generalize as "speaking forth." Jezebel had no such God-given gift. She wasn't called. She was controlling! She wasn't wisely authoritative. She was bossy! Oh, that none of us—male or female—would confuse the two!

Certainly God calls women into places of leadership, but in the spirit of 1 Corinthians 11:5, I believe our heads must be covered by higher authority. I cannot express how strongly I feel about this issue. As women, we enjoy a wonderful umbrella of protection as the biblical proverbial buck stops with the men of our households and churches. If God calls a woman to assume a leadership role, I believe with all my heart she is only safe and operating in God's authentic anointing under that umbrella!

Given my past and my lack of credentials, I will never understand the sovereignty of God to appoint me to an area of leadership. At the same time, I know what He has called me to do for this season, and I'd be in direct disobedience to God if I let someone's disapproval dissuade me. I cannot describe, however, the terror that shoots through me over finding myself in an area of leadership. How anyone can have an intimate relationship with God and be arrogant and fearless in a position of authority is beyond me.

James 3:1 warns, "Not many of you should presume to be teachers, my brothers, because you know that we who teach will be judged more strictly." Why would anyone ask for stricter judgment?

Jezebel was asking for it whether or not she knew it. Please don't miss that Jezebel's most serious infraction was not her sin but her unwillingness to repent! Lydia stands in stark contrast to Jezebel as a woman of success. She was a worshiper of God—not of herself or position. She opened her heart to Paul's message rather than pull rank on him. Both professionally and spiritually, the tone of Scripture suggests she was a servant leader.

Now also notice another difference.

2. Jezebel abused her feminine gift of influence. "By her teaching she misleads my servants" (v. 20). I am convinced women have a unique God-given gift of influence. I am married to a very strong man. He no doubt wears the cowboy boots in our family. But, if I used my feminine wiles just right (or just wrong), I fear I could talk him into almost anything. I have to be very careful because he loves me and wants to please me. You see, in some ways I am his weakness.

Do you understand what I mean? Many accounts in Scripture attest to the power of a woman's influence. Eve and Sarai represent some biblical blights, but, thankfully, we can find more scriptural examples of positive womanly influence than negative. Lydia is certainly one of them. She influenced her whole household to follow Christ.

Then note another difference between the two women from Thyatira.

3. Jezebel misused her sexuality (v. 21). Sisters, I'm not sure our culture has taught us to use anything more powerfully than our sexuality. Don't think for a moment that seducing someone into fornication is the only way a woman can use her sexuality to manipulate. We can be completely clothed and in broad, public daylight and still misuse our sexuality.

I might have a sister in Christ who is horrified right this minute by our discussion of this tawdry topic. True, she may never have dreamed of using her sexuality seductively or manipulatively. Then again, this same woman may wield it like a massive weapon in her marriage.

Sexuality was given by God as a gift. Not a tool. Just because we're married doesn't mean we don't horrifically misuse our sexuality to get what we want. Routine withholding is just one example. Recently, my precious firstborn and I had a very intimate talk. I wasn't naïve enough to think she didn't know the facts of life, but I wanted to make sure she knew the etiquette of the godly marriage bed and the misuse of sexuality as a weapon. We were both a bit uncomfortable but loved each other even more and laughed all the harder in the wake of our talk. Perhaps your mother had a different kind of talk with you. Or none at all. I'm still waiting for my mother to have "the talk" with me. Sweet sister, I'm not your mother, but I am honored to be your friend. God created us to be women complete with all our gifts, contributions, and influences. But let's be women well.

Part 9

FROM A THRONE'S-EYE VIEW

Second only to the sense of Christ's presence in my life, I crave His voice. I want to hear Him speak more than I want my next breath. Christ's words are life to me even when they must hit hard to plunge to the depths He desires. As we continue our study of Christ's messages to the seven churches, we stand to learn as much from the rebukes as the commendations. Christ meant for His church to be a blazing torch in the blackness of a desperate world. When He uncovers our weaknesses, His motivation is always to uncover the light He has placed within us. After we complete the journey through the seven churches, we'll conclude with an earthly glimpse of a heavenly throne room followed by a Lamb worthy to open the sealed scroll. Let's ask God to help us discover hidden treasures in the mines of Revelation.

Chapter 41

TO THE CHURCH IN SARDIS

Wake up! Strengthen what remains and is about to die, for I have not found your deeds complete in the sight of my God. (Revelation 3:2)

*W*ith the winds of Thyatira at our backs, let's set our sights about thirty miles southeast toward the ancient city of Sardis. As we travel together, I wonder if you are as sobered as I am by Christ's meticulous attention to all who gather in His name. We, the people of His churches, carry the reputation of Christ in our cities like those holding banners in a town parade. What do our banners say about Him? Christ isn't looking for perfect churches because He knows they are comprised of imperfect people. He is looking for churches that glorify God and lift up Christ by correctly estimating their worth through worship, teaching truth, and living love.

Like you, I do not attend a flawless church. In the wake of difficult times caused by the departure of key personnel, I've watched her develop a strangely purer kind of beauty. A beauty that comes from desperation. With the loss of five ministers, we no longer had a person's name from which to draw our reputation. Days turned into months, and months turned into several years with no permanent replacements. We had to find out who we were as a church without a man's name. I believe we have. Our church stands for many things but none more strongly than missions. Though I fear we'd have some less noble graffiti scribbled elsewhere on our banner, I believe the banner of our church might read, "Take your faith to the streets and the nations."

I would not encourage you to think critically of your church, but every member is wise to take stock of the reputation of Christ his or her church carries. If the church you attend and serve carried a banner representing Christ, what positive statement would it make? Such thoughts prepare us for our visit to ancient Sardis. Our passage is Revelation 3:1–6.

Identification. "These are the words of him who holds the seven spirits of God and the seven stars" (v. 1).

Commendation. Christ delivered no commendation to this church.

Rebuke. Christ severely rebuked the church: "I know your deeds; you have a reputation of being alive, but you are dead" (v. 1).

Exhortation. "Wake up! Strengthen what remains and is about to die, for I have not found your deeds complete in the sight of my God. Remember, therefore, what you have received and heard; obey it, and repent. But if you do not wake up, I will come like a thief, and you will not know at what time I will come to you" (vv. 2–3).

Encouragement. "Yet you have a few people in Sardis who have not soiled their clothes. They will walk with me, dressed in white, for they are worthy. He who overcomes will, like them, be dressed in white. I will never blot out his name from the book of life, but will acknowledge his name before my Father and his angels" (vv. 4–5).

If we studied the seven churches of Asia Minor and seven hundred more in our cities today, we would quickly discover a disturbing fact. The personalities and moral attitudes of any given city permeate its churches unless the church works to deliberately overcome. For instance, churches in wealthy areas with upper-crust attitudes will have to overcome misguided superiority to keep from portraying the same things. Why? Because the people who comprise churches are also products of their societies. Likewise, churches in cities of deeply ingrained prejudice will carry the same banner unless they deliberately risk being different. A church can be refreshingly dissimilar to its surrounding society only through deliberately renewing their minds.

We might accurately say that the city surrounding the church of Sardis had nearly killed it. Christ had little to say in favor of this ancient church. In fact, I can think of few indictments more serious to a group of believers than these three words: "You are dead" (Rev. 3:1). Perhaps you'll be as interested as I was to learn that Sardis was best known for a necropolis called the "cemetery of the thousand hills" about seven miles from town. A city preoccupied with death, Sardis looked on a distant skyline of burial mounds. Can you imagine a city known for its cemetery?

One thing I've learned about Christ through years of studying His life is that He is a master of words. His wordplays in Scripture are fascinating, and they are concentrated in His letter to the seven churches. The church in Sardis could not have missed the parallel Christ drew concerning their renowned necropolis when He confronted their deadness. He also said, "You have a reputation of being alive" (Rev. 3:1). The KJV and the NASB both use "name" rather than "reputation"; either is a good rendering of the Greek word *onoma*. One commentator suggested that Christ might have performed a wordplay concerning the name of the present bishop of Sardis. His name Zosimus or Zotikus is associated with *zoe* in Greek, meaning "life." Whether or not Christ implied the irony of the bishop's name, He was incensed over the church's deadness.

I believe dead churches are one of the most confounding mysteries to the hosts of heaven. The ministering spirits that invisibly flood the atmosphere must look on the church then back on the radiance of Jesus Christ and wonder how anything that carries His name can be dead. Above all things, Christ is life!

I am convinced that few things mar the cause of Christ like lifeless churches. Before we all shout amen, let's keep in mind that lifeless churches are made up of lifeless Christians. Thankfully, Christ still raises the dead, but His serious warning was to wake up and respond without delay! Like an athlete who let his muscles atrophy before the end of his season, the church needed spiritual rehab—beginning by strengthening the little that remained.

What invaded the church of Sardis with such deadness? The history of this ancient city suggests three permeating contributors:

1. *The people of Sardis were fixated on death rather than life.* Where burial mounds become idols, thoughts of death overtake thoughts of life. In a previous study I received a letter from a sister in Christ who was alarmed

that I mentioned visiting the graveside of a friend. She was not unkind. She was simply surprised that anyone who believed so strongly in heaven would esteem meaningless remains by visiting a grave. Though I didn't agree with her philosophy, if I were more focused on my believing friend's death than her life, my sister would have a point.

Some might ask, "Why would *any* of us be more fixated on death than life?" We don't have to idolize burial mounds like the Sardians to focus on death more than life. Worship in its simplest essence is attentiveness. One way we can focus on death more than life is to possess a life-inhibiting fear of it. I have known people who were so scared of death they could hardly live. You might say they were worshiping burial mounds much like the Sardians—whether or not they realized it. A chronic fear of death can inhibit a believer's entire life and ministry.

My beloved grandmother was petrified of death. Perhaps she had good reason after losing three children and a husband. Having been greatly affected, my mother also had a troubling fear of death. I witnessed the adverse effects of such fears on both their lives and determined I did not want to follow suit. I have had to be very deliberate about not allowing the attitudes of my surroundings to permeate my belief system.

2. The people of Sardis relied on their past achievements. Commentator William M. Ramsay wrote, "No city of Asia at that time showed such a melancholy contrast between past splendor and present decay as Sardis."[1] Sardis was like a leading lady in a Greek tragedy who waltzed around town in riches turned to rags thinking everyone still saw her as she was thirty years ago. In essence, Christ wrote the church of Sardis to hand this self-deceived woman a mirror—just like He's handed one to me a time or ten. Christ does not hand someone a mirror to destroy, however. He hands her the mirror to wake her up!

Last year I was invited to attend some special homecoming festivities at my college alma mater. I greatly enjoyed renewing friendships and acquaintances. I was mystified and somewhat amused, if the truth be told, as I watched other people "time warp." I saw people with a death grip on the past, trying to use the same smooth lines that didn't work twenty-five years ago. Some even attempted to comb the few hairs they had left the same old way. May I simply say the '70s weren't a great time for hair. If time warping weren't so pitiful, it would be hilarious. Sardis was warped by time. She lived off her past fame, and the results were tragic. Unfortunately, the church within its walls followed suit.

I have the privilege of knowing a number of people who stand in resolute contrast to the time warp of Sardis and my old university. They held startling achievements in their pasts, but you'd never know it unless someone else told you. They are much too busy being who they are in their present. My mentor, Marge Caldwell, is one of those. She is too busy contributing in her eighties to rest on the laurels of who she was in her fifties. How I praise God for her! She reminds me of Paul's life philosophy, "Forgetting what is behind [past achievements] and straining toward what is ahead [serving Christ], I press on toward the goal to win the prize for which God has called me heavenward in Christ Jesus" (Phil. 3:13–14).

3. *The people of Sardis likely interpreted rejection as a deathblow.* Though Sardis housed an incomplete temple of Artemis, the city lost its bid to build a temple to Caesar in A.D. 26. Smyrna won the bid instead. Though the church of Sardis had nothing but disdain for pagan practices and temples, my hypothesis is that the people of the church unknowingly wore the same cloak of dejected identity as their surroundings. After all, they, too, were pagans until the gospel reached their gates—most likely under the preaching of the apostle Paul. I'd like to further hypothesize that the people of Sardis knew they needed a fresh shot of life and vitality when they bid Rome for the new temple. When they were rejected in favor of a rival city, I wonder if they took on an attitude all too common after rejection: Why should we even try? Who cares anymore? Unless good reason exists to respond otherwise, rejection can cause people to lose heart faster than almost anything else.

By any chance, have you or someone you love interpreted rejection as a deathblow? We can all too easily slip into a pattern of considering ourselves worthless due to rejection.

Perhaps the following commentary best sums up the deadness of Sardis at the time of John's vision: "Sardis was a city of peace. Not the peace won through battle, but the peace of a man whose dreams are dead and whose mind is asleep. The peace of lethargy and evasion."[2] I find that statement stunning not because it speaks so perfectly to an ancient city's decay but because it speaks to many of us today. What has happened in our lives to take the wind out of our sails? To cause us to drop arms and cease defending ourselves against our enemy? To leave works incomplete? Have we grown lethargic? What would we rather evade than face? If Christ has given us life, who has the right to impose deadness upon us with their rejection?

Christ's identity to the church in Sardis is also the key to their resurgence. Christ is the one who holds the "seven spirits of God" or the sevenfold perfect Holy Spirit. Like the day of Pentecost, life infiltrates our churches when God pours out His lavish Holy Spirit. Spirit-flooded churches are built one way: through Spirit-flooded people.

Chapter 42

TO THE CHURCH IN PHILADELPHIA

I know your deeds. See, I have placed before you an open door that no one can shut. I know that you have little strength, yet you have kept my word and have not denied my name. (Revelation 3:8)

My spiritual journal is running over with lessons learned the hard way from our travels to Pergamum, Thyatira, and Sardis, but I could use a breather, couldn't you? I think our next destination will provide one. Our travel time is briefer too. We only have about twenty-eight miles to travel southeast of Sardis to find Philadelphia, a high plateau city. About that breather: I guess I should mention that the city was built on a dangerous volcanic area. Barring an eruption, our visit should be refreshing.

Very few ruins are visible today because the modern Alasehir perches on top of them. Interestingly, the most prominent ruin is that of an ancient church dedicated to John.[1] What ruins cannot tell us, the Word of God can. We find the message to Philadelphia in Revelation 3:7–13. It follows the pattern we have seen before.

Identification. "These are the words of him who is holy and true, who holds the key of David. What he opens no one can shut, and what he shuts no one can open" (v. 7).

Commendation. "I know your deeds. See, I have placed before you an open door that no one can shut. I know that you have little strength, yet you have kept my word and have not denied my name" (v. 8).

Rebuke. Christ delivered no rebuke to this faithful church.

Exhortation. "I will make those who are of the synagogue of Satan, who claim to be Jews though they are not, but are liars—I will make them come and fall down at your feet and acknowledge that I have loved you. Since you have kept my command to endure patiently, I will also keep you from the hour of trial that is going to come upon the whole world to test those who live on the earth" (vv. 9–10).

Encouragement. "I am coming soon. Hold on to what you have, so that no one will take your crown. Him who overcomes I will make a pillar in the temple of my God. Never again will he leave it. I will write on him the name of my God and the name of the city of my God, the new Jerusalem, which is coming down out of heaven from my God; and I will also write on him my new name" (vv. 11–12).

Pergamenian King Attalus II (159–138 B.C.) established Philadelphia. The city was named for his nickname Philadelphus, meaning "brother lover" in honor of his love for his brother. I was astounded by the many times the name of the city changed. At one time it was renamed Neocaesarea (New Caesar) and another time, Flavia. Later, due to the establishment of the emperor cult in the city, it earned the title Neokoros or "temple warden." Little Athens became its nickname in the fifth century. Jesus may have referred to the ever-changing identity of the city in the verse-12 promise of a new name.

Living in a city with an ever-changing identity wasn't the only challenge the church in Philadelphia faced. Christ said, "I know that you have little strength" (Rev. 3:8). Scholars almost unanimously agree that the reference was not to spiritual strength, or Christ would not have placed the characteristic in context with such commendation. Christ never commends spiritual weakness. Rather, He views weakness as an opportunity to discover a divine strength beyond our imagination (2 Cor. 12:9–10).

Bible commentators believe Christ's reference to the "little" strength of Philadelphia's church referred to their diminutive size and small visible impact. Lower, less influential classes comprised the church of Philadelphia, yet they endured patiently (v. 10). In our numbers-oriented society, we can hardly overestimate when we see ourselves as ineffective.

I believe outright opposition can be easier to bear than the thought of futility or incompetence.

Don't think for a moment the enemy won't do everything he can to convince you that your efforts in Christ's name are in vain. Nothing is more destructive than feelings of uselessness and worthlessness. That's precisely why the enemy seeks every avenue to fuel and perpetuate them. Beloved, each of us has a God-given need to matter.

You are not self-centered and vain because you have that need; you are human. What you and I do with the need can become extremely vain and self-centered, but the need itself is sacred. Fragrant flowers don't need someone to smell them to keep blooming. Lions don't kill their prey for significance. They're simply hungry. Man alone yearns to matter. God acknowledged the need immediately following our creation and significantly before our fall into sin.

Notice how God granted purpose to humans in each of these scriptural examples.

• He gave the assignment to be fruitful, fill the earth, and have dominion over it (Gen. 1:28).

• He gave Adam the charge to care for the garden (Gen. 2:15).

• He commissioned Adam to name the animals (Gen. 2:19).

God could have created the beasts of the field naturally subservient to humans. Instead, He acknowledged our God-given need to matter by telling us to rule over them and subdue them. Furthermore, God could have made the garden of Eden self-maintaining. Instead, He appointed Adam to work it and take care of it. God could have created the animals with names, but He knew Adam could use the challenge and the satisfaction naming them would bring. In the same way Eve received a purpose that granted significance. No one else was a suitable helper to Adam.

Why is the need to matter sacred? God formed us to seek lives of purpose and, for those of us who follow His lead, find them ultimately in Him alone. Have you recognized your own need to matter?

The Father desires for each of our lives to bring forth much fruit. I desperately want you to flourish in the ministries God has for you, and I think the church of Philadelphia offers us a few pointers in the process.

First, Christ alone is judge of what matters. The small, seemingly insignificant band of believers in Philadelphia may have been blind to the fruit of their own efforts, but Christ found them beyond rebuke. I think the key word in His commendation is the description He used for how they endured: patiently. So often we are tempted to give up before the harvest comes.

Ecclesiastes 3:1 tells us "there is a time for everything, and a season for every activity under heaven." In Genesis 8:22, God promised "as long as the earth endures, / seedtime and harvest, / cold and heat, / summer and winter, / day and night / will never cease." Though far less predictable, we experience seasons spiritually as well. The church in Philadelphia had been in the seedtime season without a large harvest probably longer than they wished—yet they continued to endure patiently.

According to the parable of the sower in Luke 8:11, the seed is the Word of God. After acknowledging their little strength, Christ commended the church in Philadelphia because they kept His word and did not deny His name (Rev. 3:8). Unashamed of Christ's name against a bitter majority, they kept Christ's word, thereby faithfully planting seeds. They did not give up though the harvest seemed dreadfully distant. Remember, a landowner doesn't judge a harvest by the quantity of fruit alone. Diseased fruit means nothing but loss to him. He looks for quality.

Do you happen to be frustrated by what appears to be a small return on much effort in a ministry opportunity? Keep in mind that God not only allows long seasons of seedtime but also sometimes appoints them to enhance the quality of eventual harvest. At times He actively tests our faithfulness in smaller things to see if we can handle bigger things. I hesitate to make this point because "big" is not the goal. Christ revealed is the goal. However, if a high-volume ministry is one way God chooses to reveal His Son, those to whom He temporarily appoints them by His grace (1 Pet. 4:10) could undoubtedly describe countless appointments to small and frustrating "opportunities" along the way. In retrospect most now recognize them as crucial tests.

I can remember pouring my heart into preparing several discipleship courses when only two or three people showed up. I sensed God asking me,

"What are you going to do now? Cancel the class? Or give them no less than you would give twenty-five and finish out the semester?" I am certain those were not only precious opportunities; they were tests. I also believe He tested me to see whether I would esteem the opportunity to teach Mother's Day Out or four-year-olds in Sunday school. Both extended the profound opportunity to mark young lives for eternity, yet some would be foolish enough to deem them unimportant.

Thankfully, we obviously don't have to be a genius or particularly gifted to pass God's tests because I certainly would have failed. God is primarily looking for faithfulness to fulfill whatever duty He has placed before us. He also guards our hearts by dissuading us from feeding our egos with result-oriented service.

Only after we have learned to prioritize faithfulness rather than results are we ready for the next truth. Christ is the door opener. Revelation 3:8 tells us something critical about doors Christ opens and shuts. What He opens no person can shut.

One reason for so much frustration in ministry is our determination to open our own doors—in Jesus' name, of course. Some of our fists are bloody from beating down doors that we believe were supposed to open for ministry. When our blood, sweat, and tears produce little or nothing, we are often offended by God, whom I imagine sitting on His throne saying, "Did I tell you that was the right door? And if it were, would I not have opened it for you?" I often think of the gate of Peter's prison automatically opening for his escape because God appointed it (Acts 12). I picture God with an invisible remote control in His hand, controlling every door of opportunity on earth.

As a rule of thumb but not without exceptions, I usually conclude that if the door requires beating upon to open, it's probably not the right one. And if God has shut a door, forget trying to open it! Remember, for a true harvest to result, the Holy Spirit has to prepare the way and go before us through the door. That's how it opens! Otherwise, it's either the wrong door or the wrong time. Watch for doors that open by God's remote control, and patiently remain faithful until they do.

Because the church of Philadelphia endured patiently, Christ placed before them an open door that no one can shut. Many scholars believe that open door was for missions directed farther east to other parts of Asia. Therefore, some commentators call the church of Philadelphia the "missionary church." Scripture often uses the open-door terminology to describe a missionary opportunity. Paul wrote of "a great door for effective work" that God opened to him in 1 Corinthians 16:9.

Dear one, each of us is called to missions. As we seek to "keep" Christ's Word and stay unashamed of His name (Rev. 3:8), He will open doors of opportunity for us in His own time. If we faithfully sow seed, the harvest will one day come. Some missionaries never viewed their harvests from the fields of earth, but what better seat than heaven to get the full picture?

I want you to see two more jewels in the crown of the Philadelphians. Refresh your memory over Christ's promise to them. He said of those who persecuted the believers, "I will make them come and fall down at your feet and acknowledge that I have loved you" (v. 9).

One of the meanest tricks Satan ever plays on us is to try to convince us God doesn't love us and that we're exerting all this energy and exercising all this faith for nothing: Look at all you've done, and He doesn't even care! It's all a big joke! He used the Jews in Philadelphia to demoralize the small church, and he uses countless puppets to demoralize us. Christ promised the church in Philadelphia that one day the very people who sneered at them would acknowledge how much He loves them.

Beloved, you and I are not to be motivated by spite. At the same time, Jesus wants you to know that one day everyone will know how much He loves you. You have been unashamed of Him, and He most assuredly will prove unashamed of you.

Finally, Christ promised to make the overcomers pillars in the temple of His God. What significance this terminology had to the Philadelphians! The city was under constant threat of earthquakes. The threat was especially vivid after a devastating earthquake in A.D. 17. Decades later some historians say the church had already rebuilt their small sanctuary several times because of tremors. Often the only things left standing in a city lying in ruins are the pillars.

Hebrews 12:26–27 says God will shake both the heavens and the earth so that only that which cannot be shaken will remain. "Therefore, since we are receiving a kingdom that cannot be shaken, let us be thankful, and so worship God acceptably with reverence and awe, for our 'God is a consuming fire'" (Heb. 12:28–29).

Christ's promise to the overcomers was that they would be kept from the hour of trial that is going to come upon the whole world, and they would stand like pillars in a kingdom that can never be shaken. Why? Because they mattered and, contrary to popular opinion, they chose to believe it. So, dear one, do you. Let no one take your crown by convincing you otherwise.

Chapter 43

To the Church
in Laodicea

You say, "I am rich; I have acquired wealth and do not need
a thing." But you do not realize that you are wretched, pitiful,
poor, blind and naked. (Revelation 3:17)

$\mathcal{N}$ext we have quite a trip before us. The final stop in our tour of the
seven churches is Laodicea. We'll find the city forty-five miles southeast of
Philadelphia and about one hundred miles due east of our first stop in
Ephesus. As we walk through the gates, we will have indeed come virtually
full circle. By the way, you might want to fill up your canteen in
Philadelphia before we leave. I hear the water in Laodicea isn't worth drinking. We'll meet at Revelation 3:14–22.

Hear Christ's message to the Laodiceans:

Identification. "These are the words of the Amen, the faithful and true
witness, the ruler of God's creation" (v. 14).

Commendation. Christ offered no word of commendation to the church.

Rebuke. "I know your deeds, that you are neither cold nor hot. I wish
you were either one or the other! So, because you are lukewarm—neither
hot nor cold—I am about to spit you out of my mouth. You say, 'I am rich;
I have acquired wealth and do not need a thing.' But you do not realize that
you are wretched, pitiful, poor, blind and naked" (vv. 15–17).

Exhortation. "I counsel you to buy from me gold refined in the fire, so
you can become rich; and white clothes to wear, so you can cover your

shameful nakedness; and salve to put on your eyes, so you can see. Those whom I love I rebuke and discipline. So be earnest, and repent" (vv. 18–19).

Encouragement. "Here I am! I stand at the door and knock. If anyone hears my voice and opens the door, I will come in and eat with him, and he with me. To him who overcomes, I will give the right to sit with me on my throne, just as I overcame and sat down with my Father on his throne" (vv. 20–21).

The wordplays and inferences are so plenteous in this segment of Scripture that I am frantically asking God to help me choose what to teach and what to leave behind. I want to excavate the whole city! In one word, how would you describe Laodicea? Many adjectives could apply, but let's consider the following three:

1. The church of Laodicea was indifferent. No one could accuse Christ of a lukewarm rebuke. Center on the impassioned statements, "You are neither cold nor hot. I wish you were either one or the other!" I agree with scholars who resist the interpretation that Christ wanted the Laodiceans to be either hot or cold spiritually. Though such figures of speech are common in our era, terming someone "hot" or "cold" in the faith wasn't part of their vernacular. Furthermore, I hope we could safely conclude that Christ—who never desires for anyone to perish—would also not prefer anyone to be cold toward Him rather than lukewarm. I believe Christ meant, "For crying out loud, be of one use or the other!" We have much to learn about this distinct city that will shed light on Christ's rebuke and exhortation.

In Colossians 4 Paul spoke of Epaphras's ministry to the Laodiceans. Epaphras was probably somewhat of a circuit preacher from Colossae. He divided his time between the church in his hometown and churches in Laodicea and Hierapolis. Laodicea lay directly between the other two cities, seven miles southeast of Hierapolis and less than ten miles north of Colossae. Hierapolis was famous for therapeutic hot springs. Colossae was known for sparkling cold waters, but ruins reveal a sophisticated six-mile-long aqueduct that drew water from other sources for Laodicea.

In 1961–63 a team of French archaeologists excavated a structure called a *nymphaeum* located practically in the center of the city. The square water basin had stone columns on two sides and two semicircular fountains attached to it.[1] The ornate fountains very likely stood as beautiful center-pieces in the city square. Characteristic of Laodicea, their beauty vastly exceeded their usefulness. You see, by the time the water was piped to the city from miles away, it was neither cold nor hot.

You might easily imagine someone cupping her hands under the entic-ing waters to take a refreshing sip only to spit it out in disgust. Sound familiar? Hot water has therapeutic value, and nothing is like the refresh-ment of cold water, but lukewarm? If only I knew the Greek word for "yuck!"

Christ's vehement frustration with the church of Laodicea was that she'd be of some use! The last thing I want to tout is a works-centered faith, but we have been called to faith-centered works. Christ intends for us to be useful! Churches are meant to be viable, active forces in their communities.

In our previous chapter we talked about how each person's innate need to matter requires us to discover how our gifts and contributions can be useful. Anyone can be useful. In the spirit of Christ's exhortation to Laodicea, anyone can offer a cold glass of water to the thirsty or a hot cup of tea to the hurting. Or how about a frozen casserole? Or a warm pound cake? At times of my life, nothing has ministered to me more than those two things! Christ exhorts His bride, "Be of use to my world!" At times therapeutic. At other times refreshing. Each of us can be hot and cold.

2. The church of Laodicea was independent. If we all need to be signifi-cant, what in the world happened to the church of Laodicea? Where was their need to be useful? The Laodiceans did what many people in our cul-ture do today. They filled their gaping need to matter with possessions then gauged their usefulness by their wealth. Praise God, neither then nor now can wealth state worth. Save your breath trying to convince Laodicea, how-ever. When Christ drafted His letter to John, Laodicea was the capital of financial wizardry in Asia Minor, a marvel of prosperity. She described her-self as rich and in need of nothing (Rev. 3:17).

Mind you, Christ's letter isn't addressed to the city of Laodicea. It is addressed to the church of Laodicea. I can almost imagine the preacher glancing at the order of service during worship and saying, "Skip the offertory! After all, we're rich! We do not need a thing!" We'd die of shock at our church. I can't remember a time when we've had more money than needs. If we can't think of a thing to do with our surplus, I fear we've lost touch because the needs out there are endless.

I discovered some interesting pieces of information that help explain the audacity and laxity of the Laodicean church. In A.D. 26 the city placed a bid to the Roman senate to build a temple to the Emperor Tiberius. They were denied on the basis of inadequate resources. Their wealth so vastly increased over the next several decades that by A.D. 60 after the devastation of an earthquake, they didn't accept aid from Nero. They had plentiful resources to rebuild themselves. (Do you hear the hints of independence?) In a nutshell, they thanked Rome but assured them they "did not need a thing."

Much of Laodicea's original fortunes in the first century came from the fertile river valley that supplied lavish grazing for nice, fat sheep. The Laodiceans specialized in a tightly woven, black wool fabric that sold for a pretty penny. Behind their fortune, however, were farm animals that stank.

I grin as I recall Keith's glib comment many years ago over a sudden outburst of superiority from one of his beloved sisters. He looked over at me and said, "I wonder if now would be a good time to remind her that our family 'fortune' was made in other people's toilets?" (His father owned a plumbing company.) With much glee, Keith and I have occasionally reminded our own daughters of the same profession that butters their bread.

Money. The Laodiceans had it. They were in the lap of luxury and didn't think they had a care in the world. Little did they know that Christ was walking among their lampstands.

The last portion of Psalm 62:10 speaks a good word to the Laodiceans and us. "Though your riches increase, / do not set your heart on them." I live in a city that never expected to be known for the collapse of one of the biggest financial empires in America. We learned the sobering lesson that billions of dollars can be lost as instantly as hundreds. We cannot set our hearts securely on riches no matter how vast.

In Matthew 13:22 Christ addressed another wealth-related issue readily recognizable in Laodicea. He told of the person who received the Word then allowed "the worries of this life and the deceitfulness of wealth" to choke the fruitfulness out of it.

Beloved, wealth by itself is not the issue. We serve a God of infinite wealth who can distribute the riches of the world any way He sees fit. Our troubled world certainly needs resources in the hands of wise people.

The problem is the deceitfulness of wealth. Two of my precious friends have not been deceived by wealth. Frankly, I never knew they were wealthy until someone told me. I've served in the same church with them for several decades and have never met less pretentious, more generous people. They are constantly involved in inner-city and foreign missions.

I'm convinced their only attitude toward their resources is that of stewards over a trust. While others in their position might have locked themselves behind gates and pretended much of the world wasn't starving to death, they threw themselves right in the middle of it. The Laodicean church could have used my friends! This wealthy church somehow didn't grasp the principle in Luke 12:48: "Unto whomsoever much is given, of him shall be much required" (KJV).

3. This brings us to our final point: The Laodicean church was self-deceived. Their worth was so ingrained in their wealth that they honestly saw themselves as utterly independent. We "do not need a thing." Famous last words. Beloved, I'm not sure any of us get away with "not needing a thing" for long. Certainly the kinds and intensities of our needs differ from season to season, but I don't expect God to risk our growing an independent spirit through sustained sufficiency. Of course, I don't know this for a fact because I can't remember having one.

The older I get and the more my eyes open to the facts of life and ministry, the more my list of needs exceeds my list of wants. For instance, I need to have an active, effervescent daily relationship with Jesus Christ or I'm sunk. I need my husband's blessing. I need my coworkers. I need my church family. I need a friend I can trust. These are just a few necessities of life to me right now.

You see, one reason we readily give (through lives that matter) is because we, too, need. Taking stock of both our contributions and our needs helps guard us against self-deception. Sadly, the Laodiceans had needs, too. They just didn't recognize them.

Christ had a stunning response to the Laodicean deception. "You say, 'I am rich' . . . But you do not realize that you are wretched, pitiful, poor, blind and naked" (Rev. 3:17). One of my worst nightmares is to think I'm rich when Christ knows I'm poor and my estimation of myself is higher than His. Notice how Christ's address to Smyrna stands in stark contrast to Laodicea's: "I know your afflictions and your poverty—yet you are rich!" (Rev. 2:9).

How grateful I am that Christ had a remedy for the Laodiceans! Their self-deceived indifference had not deemed them castaways. Christ wrote the Laodiceans a three-part prescription. His first prescription was gold refined in fire. Peter gives us a clear idea of what Christ meant. Peter wrote of "your faith—of greater worth than gold" (1 Pet. 1:6–7).

Christ's second prescription to Loadicea was "white clothes to wear." The black wool fabric for which Laodicea was famous was the fashion rage all over that part of the world. He suggested they trade their fashions for purity. Ouch.

Jesus' final prescription was salve to put on their eyes. Remember my telling you the Laodiceans could boast almost anything? Not only was the city a marketing center and financial capital, it also housed a well-known medical center. Ever the marketers, they were best known for Phrygian powder that was used to make salve for eye conditions. All the while, they were blind as bats and poor as beggars. I've been both.

One thing I've learned about God is that He is faithful in every way. He is faithful to forgive, redeem, bless, and provide. He is also faithful to chastise when His child won't readily turn from sin. Yes, the Laodiceans had a prescription, but Christ had no intention of letting them wait a month of Sundays to get it filled without consequences.

My head is spinning from all we've learned through our tour of the seven churches. I wish I could hear what truths most stand out to you. I offer mine in closing: Christ has invested everything on earth in His church. He willingly fills her, frees her, purifies her, and restores her, but He never takes His eyes off of her. Lives are at stake. Church matters. Bride, make yourself ready.

Chapter 44

THE THRONE ROOM

Day and night they never stop saying:
"Holy, holy, holy
is the Lord God Almighty,
who was, and is, and is to come." (Revelation 4:8)

$\mathcal{N}$ext we get to approach the very throne of God through the vision extended to John in the fourth chapter of Revelation. If we had any idea who and what we approach when we go to the throne of grace (Heb. 4:16) through prayer and communion with God, our lives would change dramatically. I am convinced we would fall on our faces far more often, and we'd pray with far more substance and certainty.

As you and I prepare to read Revelation's description of the throne room of God, please keep in mind that John related the completely unfamiliar through the familiar. Imagine escorting an Indian who had never ventured farther than the most primitive part of the Amazon to tour state-of-the-art technology at NASA. When he returned to his fellow tribesmen, how would he describe jets or rockets? He'd probably have to begin his illustration by using birds as an example and try to stretch their imagination from there. Likewise, throughout much of Revelation, John employed known concepts to express images beyond our understanding.

Christ's revelation to John shifts dramatically as chapter 4 unfolds. In chapters 2 and 3, the earth-focused spotlight of the Spirit cut through religious appearances, revealing the best and the worst about the seven churches in Asia Minor. In Revelation 4, the spotlight swung back to the origin of all illumination as Christ summoned John heavenward in Spirit to behold the divine.

> After this I looked, and there before me was a door standing open in heaven. And the voice I had first heard speaking to me like a trumpet said, "Come up here, and I will show you what must take place after this." At once I was in the Spirit, and there before me was a throne in heaven with someone sitting on it. And the one who sat there had the appearance of jasper and carnelian. A rainbow, resembling an emerald, encircled the throne. (Rev. 4:1–3)

Heaven was awhirl with activity, yet all attention centered on an occupied throne. God jealously guarded His majestic transcendence by an absence of detailed description. John simply describes the splendor of the One seated on the throne like brilliant gems.

The jasper known to John's world can be pictured something like a diamond in ours. I wonder if John saw something like light reflecting in spectacular displays off the prisms of a diamond-like object. The carnelian stone was a bloodred form of quartz that could symbolize access to the throne the one and only way: through the shed blood of Christ. The emerald green of the encircling rainbow could easily symbolize God's eternal covenant with those who receive His life. When the scales of humanity peel away from our eyes and we behold heaven, I believe we will see colors as never before. Perhaps only the crystal sea will be clear.

"Before the throne there was what looked like a sea of glass, clear as crystal" (v. 6). Oh, how I praise God for the crystal sea! Micah asks the kind of questions that come to mind with this scene.

> Who is a God like you,
>   who pardons sin and forgives the transgression
>   of the remnant of his inheritance?
> You do not stay angry forever
>   but delight to show mercy.
> You will again have compassion on us;
>   you will tread our sins underfoot

and hurl all our iniquities into the depths of the sea.
(Mic. 7:18–19)

The throne of God is beyond anything we can imagine, yet Hebrews 4:14–16 tells us that because of our great High Priest, Jesus, we can approach it with confidence. God wants us to "receive mercy and find grace to help us in our time of need" (v. 16).

First John 1:8 tells us none is without sin but because Christ became our atoning sacrifice, we need never fear approaching God with our confessions. In the imagery of the throne room, I like to imagine God the Father catching those confessions in the palm of His mighty hand and casting them into the sea. What sea? Perhaps the one most conveniently located right in front of His throne. No matter how many confessions are made, this sea is never muddied by our sins. Rather, as God casts them into the sea, I like to imagine our sins instantly bleached into utter nonexistence, swallowed in the depths of crystal-clear waters.

Are you a deep-sea fisherman? Are you tempted by guilt, condemnation, and unbelief to dredge up old sins and agonize over them? Satan constantly volunteers to be our fishing guide and provides a handy lure to cause us to doubt God's forgiveness. How successful has he been with you?

I certainly have done some deep-sea fishing in my lifetime. What a waste of time and energy! If we're fishing in the right sea, our line will always come up bare. Anything we think we're seeing on the end of that line is a vain imagination. We won't even catch an old boot. Let's consider giving the enemy one instead.

Scripture includes several visions of God's throne room in beautiful consistency. One appears in Isaiah 6:1–5 and another in Ezekiel 1:22–28. What relief to know the throne is never depicted without Someone sitting on it! God never vacates His throne. He is never off duty. His sovereignty is never usurped. He is unceasingly praised. The three-fold acclamation of God's holiness or perfect "otherness" significantly occurs only in the visions of the throne room.

Exodus 26:33 distinguishes between the Holy Place and the Most Holy Place in the Old Testament tabernacle. The Holy Place was the room where the priests ministered before the Lord on a daily basis. It was the location of the table of shewbread, the lamps, and the altar of incense. Behind the veil was the Most Holy Place, which the high priest entered only once a year and with fear and trembling. The Presence of God dwelled between the cherubim on the atonement cover of the ark in the Most Holy Place.

The original rendering of the term *Most Holy Place* actually repeats the original word for "holy" for emphasis. The original wording for the Holy Place could be translated "the Holy" and the Most Holy Place, "the Holy Holy."

Scripture characterizes some things as *holy*, others as *holy holy*, and yet another as *holy holy holy*. I wonder if the following explanation could be plausible: the places where God's people serve and minister before their God might biblically be characterized as once holy. In other words, as saints, we are set apart in our service to Him as holy, but an even holier interaction exists. The places God agrees to meet with His people on earth through reverence and genuine worship might be characterized as twice holy. True worship is the most holy experience we can have on this earth. But one day, when our feet leave their last prints in this soil and we approach God in His glorious heavenly abode, we will stand before the three-times holy. We will join the seraphim who cry, "Holy, holy, holy is the Lord God Almighty!" The word *seraph* means "to burn." Surely the closer we come to God's true Presence, the more we will burn with passion!

Perhaps like me you often look for the distinctions or contrasting inseparabilities of the Holy Trinity. Let's discuss what part of the Godhead may be depicted on the throne in these three revelations in Isaiah, Ezekiel, and Revelation.

Before you immediately assume God the Father as the occupant of the throne or no distinction at all, please read Revelation 5:6.

> Then I saw a Lamb, looking as if it had been slain, standing in the center of the throne, encircled by the four living creatures and the elders. He had seven horns and seven eyes, which are the seven spirits of God sent out into all the earth. (Rev. 5:6)

I don't believe the revelator meant us to picture Christ standing up on a chair. Our familiarity with a throne is entirely related to a piece of furniture. Though God is most assuredly sitting in an actual seat of authority, the word *throne* seems to encompass the center from which He presides with all authority. I am very intrigued that Ezekiel's vision describes "a figure like that of a man" (1:26) upon the throne, and, according to John 12:41, Isaiah saw Jesus' glory when he beheld the vision in Isaiah 6.

Ordinarily the man-like descriptions in the Godhead are attributed by most scholars to Christ. According to comparisons of Daniel 7 and Revelation 5, both the Father and the Son inhabit the throne room. Could it be that in the Old Testament God wanted most to reveal Christ and in the New Testament Christ wanted most to reveal God? I think it's quite possible and very like each of them to shed light on the other.

Return your focus to Revelation 4. Beloved, the fixed point in John's vision is the same immutable point in the entire universe. The center of all existence is God upon His throne. John had the hair-raising, perspective-changing opportunity to do something all of us secretly wish we could do. For a little while recorded in Revelation 4 and onward, he got to see life from heaven's perspective. In his description, he implied something tremendously profound: everything else in existence is most accurately described only in its relationship to the throne of God.

Before we discuss our nearsighted vision (2 Pet. 1:9), never lose sight of the fact that God looked upon His prize creation and liked us very much. Look carefully at Revelation 4:11, which clearly states that God created us by His will.

> You are worthy, our Lord and God,
>> to receive glory and honor and power,
> for you created all things,
>> and by your will they were created
>> and have their being.

God's *thelema* ("will") is an expression or inclination of pleasure; a want or desire that pleases and creates joy.[1] In other words, He created us because it pleased Him. Our attitudes and actions don't always please Him, but creating us, loving us, and redeeming us give Him great joy.

Much of humanity's trouble stems from our naturally insatiable self-centeredness. We often see ourselves as the center of the universe and tend to describe all other components in reference to us rather than God. The human psyche almost invariably processes incoming information in relationship to its own ego. For example, if the news forecasts an economic slump, the natural hearer automatically processes what it could mean to self.

While this response is natural, in perpetual practice this self-absorption is miserable. In some ways our egocentrism is a secret lust for omnipotence. We want to be our own god and have all power.

Our first reaction might be to deny we've ever had a desire to be God, but how often do we take immediate responsibility for handling most of the problems in our midst? How often do we try changing the people we know and feeding our control addiction with the drug of manipulation? Simply put, we try to play God, and frankly, it's exhausting.

No wonder God never sleeps, nor does He slumber (Ps. 121:3)! Those of us who are redeemed are also given what 1 Corinthians 2:16 calls the "mind of Christ." Life takes on a far more accurate estimation and perspective when we learn to view it increasingly through the vantage point of the One who spoke it into existence.

Think of some of your greatest challenges. Picture them. Then go back and stamp the words "before the throne" before each of those challenges.

The heart of prayer is moving those very kinds of challenges from the insecurities and uncertainties of earth to the throne of God. Only then can they be viewed with dependable accuracy and boundless hope. Close your eyes and do your best to picture the glorious seraphim never ceasing to cry, "Holy, holy, holy!" Imagine the lightning emitting from the throne, and hear the rumblings and the thunder. Picture the elders overwhelmed by God's worthiness, casting their crowns before the throne.

I ask you the following question under my own tremendous personal conviction: Do we think God, the blessed and only Ruler, the King of kings and Lord of lords, who alone is immortal and who lives in unapproachable light, can manage our lives and our problems? Oh, beloved, fight the good fight of faith! Approach the throne of grace with confidence! Our God is huge.

Chapter 45

THE LAMB

I wept and wept because no one was found who was worthy . . .
Then I saw a Lamb. . . . (Revelation 5:4, 6)

𝒥 want to cry with John, and we haven't even begun the lesson. Oh, how I long for the day when we will sit at the feet of the true Rabboni and hear Him expound upon His own Word, just like the two on the road to Emmaus. "Beginning with Moses and all the Prophets, he explained to them what was said in all the Scriptures concerning himself" (Luke 24:27).

I cannot help but weep! If we could only grasp the perfections of Scripture, holding up the Word like a large, brilliant diamond. Only in the spray of colors cast by the prisms of the old covenant can we tilt the diamond to see the new. The Bible is a divine masterpiece, dear student! A progressive unveiling of marveling mystery and astounding consistency. Find a good seat in the auditorium. Our study takes us before a stage where the most profoundly consistent concept in Scripture is fully unveiled.

"Then I saw in the right hand of him who sat on the throne a scroll with writing on both sides and sealed with seven seals" (Rev. 5:1). We can't be certain what the scroll represents. One possibility is that it is like the one in Ezekiel's vision (Ezek. 2:9–10). That scroll contained words of lament and woe. Certainly the coming chapters announce woes, so the interpretation is plausible for the Revelation 5:1 scroll. When Christ victoriously claims the scroll, however, the eruptions of praise cause me to wonder how the scroll can be associated with woes and laments alone. I tend to think the seals themselves involve wrath, but the words within unfold something glorious.

Interpreters pose another possibility—that the scroll represented the will or testament of God concerning the completion of all things on earth and the transition to all things in heaven. The ancient Romans sealed wills or testaments with six seals. A slight variation of this view compares the scene to the Roman law of inheritance. Some scholars believe the scroll is the title deed to earth.

Though I'm curious, I am comfortable not knowing the exact identity of the scroll because, whatever it is, it is in the hands of Christ. Now concentrate on verses 2 and 3. These events may not have happened over a simple matter of seconds.

> I saw a mighty angel proclaiming in a loud voice, "Who is worthy to break the seals and open the scroll?" But no one in heaven or on earth or under the earth could open the scroll or even look inside it. (Rev. 5:2–3)

The verb tense of the Greek word for "proclaiming" may suggest the mighty angel could have repeated the question several times, scattering glances to and fro for someone who was worthy. The deafening silence left by no answers heightened the anxiety of the listener.

John tells us that he "wept and wept because no one was found who was worthy to open the scroll or look inside" (Rev. 5:4). His reaction certainly shows the importance of the scroll. By now surely you have some picture of John in your mind and affection for him in your heart. Keep in mind that the power and presence of the Holy Spirit doesn't make us feel less. The Spirit brings life. Every one of John's senses was surely quickened. His response to the sight of the throne must have been indescribable awe. When he heard the angelic proclamation, a tidal wave of grief crashed against that reverent backdrop. The word used for "weep" usually implies accompanying demonstrations of grief.

In our previous chapter, we stood transfixed with John as witnesses to the vision of the throne room of God. Something dramatic happened in the transition of the scene in chapter 5. Suddenly John was no longer watching revelation. He was part of the scene. Previously a bystander as the elders cast their crowns before the throne, he then was approached by one as he wept.

> Then one of the elders said to me, "Do not weep! See, the Lion of the tribe of Judah, the Root of David, has triumphed. He is able to open the scroll and its seven seals."
> Then I saw a Lamb, looking as if it had been slain, standing in the center of the throne, encircled by the four living creatures and the elders. He had seven horns and seven eyes, which are the seven spirits of God sent out into all the earth. (Rev. 5:5–6)

John must have expected to see a Lion, as the elder had described. Instead, he saw "a Lamb, looking as if it had been slain." The Lion of the tribe of Judah had triumphed the one and only way possible according to the plan probably written within that scroll: as a Lamb that had been slain. Simply put, the Lion triumphed by becoming the Lamb slain.

Revelation chapter 4 concludes with the hymn of the elders praising God for creation. Now in chapter 5 the hymn is addressed to the Lamb and called "a new song" (vv. 9–10). Why was the praise a new song? I wonder if the reason may be that praises like those described in Revelation 4 have been sung throughout eternity, but the word *new* is a time-related word. Words like *old* and *new* only have meaning within created time and for created beings. They have no reference in that which pertains to heaven alone.

Obviously, something glorious happened involving earth and those bound by time that releases a "new song." The song itself tells what happened.

> You are worthy to take the scroll
>   and to open its seals,
> because you were slain,
>   and with your blood you purchased men for God
>   from every tribe and language and people and nation.
> You have made them to be a kingdom and priests to serve our
>   God,
>   and they will reign on the earth. (Rev. 5:9–10)

Beloved, not only did the new song have to do with something that involved the earth, it proclaimed the one and only immutable hope of earth: the Lamb slain!

Throughout Scripture, titles given to God were inspired in perfect context with the verses in which they appear. Not coincidentally, John referred to Christ as "the Lamb" twenty-eight times in an unfolding revelation that ultimately prophesied the culmination of all things concerning humankind and the earth. The primary image of Christ in Revelation is undoubtedly Jesus as the Lamb. This title bursts forth repeatedly like fireworks in the grand finale of Holy Writ. And for good reason. No concept in the Word of God has been more consistent.

Revelation 13:8 majestically refers to Jesus as "the Lamb that was slain from the creation of the world." You see, man's fall did not take God by surprise. Before He said, "Let there be light," He basically said, "Let there be a plan. And there was. A Lamb slain from the creation of the world."

Genesis 1:24–25 tells of the creation of animal life. In the midst of countless creatures, hoofed and not, God created the lamb. I happen to think God is the sentimental type. It shows throughout Scripture, and we, as sentimental people, were created in His image. I don't think He created the lamb with little notice. He knew the profound significance He would cause the small, helpless creature to have. Adam wasn't created until after the animals. God saved what He considered His best for last. I think the fact that a lamb was created before a man is quite fitting. Throughout the Old Testament, man would require a heap of them.

After sin cost Adam and Eve paradise, "the LORD God made garments of skin for Adam and his wife and clothed them" (Gen. 3:21). This is the first reference to a sacrificial death. Since God dressed them with a skin, we know an animal perished for them to be covered. We have no way of knowing whether the animal was a lamb, but I can hardly picture it any other way.

Genesis 4:4 records the first sacrificial offering. "Abel brought fat portions from some of the firstborn of his flock." Cain brought an offering of fruit, but the Lord looked with favor on Abel's offering.

Not coincidentally, from the moment in Scripture that life appears outside the garden, we see sacrificial offerings. God wasn't partial to Abel.

He was partial to Abel's offering. When not distinguished otherwise, a flock almost always refers to sheep in Scripture. From the Old Testament to the New, the Lord looks with favor upon those symbolically covered by the blood of the Lamb. Verse 7 hints that Cain knew the right thing to do and had the same chance to bring a sacrificial offering. The basic tenet of all biblical rebellion is refusing the blood of the lamb.

Genesis 22 contains the account of Abraham's willingness to sacrifice his son Isaac in obedience to God. Far from coincidence, the first time in Scripture the word *lamb* is used is in Genesis 22. Fittingly, the words *sacrifice* and *worship* are introduced in the same chapter, and the word *love* appears for only the second time.

Just before Abraham actually killed his son as an offering to God, the angel of the Lord intervened. God provided a substitute sacrifice in the form of a ram caught in the thicket. I was thrilled when I read the following definition of the word for "ram" is *ayil*: "a male sheep generally more aggressive and protective of the flock." Jesus our Lamb is indeed aggressively protective of the flock—even to the spilling of His blood. Galatians calls this drama the gospel preached in advance to Abraham (Gal. 3:8; Rom. 9:7). Glory!

The ram was secured for Abraham's use by horns caught in the thicket. Horns remained very significant throughout the Old Testament and were positioned on the corners of the altar of sacrifice so that a lamb could be secured to them with ties. Revelation 5:6 says the Lamb had "seven horns and seven eyes, which are the seven spirits of God sent out into all the earth."

We don't have to fear that Christ is going to look like some frightening monstrosity. John's language is figurative. In the prophesies of both Daniel and Revelation, horns represent authority and power. The Lamb's power and authority to redeem on earth came through His willingness to be slain.

We cannot find a more perfect Old Testament picture of the blood of the sacrificial lamb than the one recorded in Exodus 12. The final plague against Egypt came in the form of the death of the firstborn. Every Hebrew family found protection through the Passover lamb's blood on the doorpost.

The concept of substitutionary atonement that unfolded immediately outside the garden echoed like a sermon from Isaac's Mt. Moriah, dripped from the doorposts of captive Israel, and remained constant throughout the Old Testament. Innumerable animals were sacrificed throughout the centuries at the altars of the tabernacle and the temple. So many were sacrificed at the dedication of Solomon's temple that they couldn't be counted.

God's wonders on behalf of Israel were astounding; as long as they followed Him, He fought for them. Then they repeatedly fell into idolatry. After sending the prophets with warnings, Old Testament Scripture comes to an abrupt halt—but not without a promise: "See, I will send you the prophet Elijah before that great and dreadful day of the LORD comes" (Mal. 4:5).

As in many other prophecies, God spoke symbolically. According to Matthew 11:12–14 John the Baptist fulfilled this prophecy. Look at the first words from John the Baptist's mouth when he saw Jesus: "Look, the Lamb of God, who takes away the sin of the world!" (John 1:29).

Luke 22 records the last supper Christ shared with His disciples. Because a Jewish day begins just after sundown and lasts until the next, Christ was actually crucified on the very same "day" they ate their final meal together. According to Luke 22:14 that day was when Jesus' hour had come.

Oh, do you realize we've only seen a glimpse, yet look at the consistency! A lamb, the lamb, the Lamb! So we wouldn't miss the woolen thread, Revelation, the book of the Bible that brings all things to completion, shouts this title like triumphant bursts from a ram's horn. Not once. Not twice. But twenty-eight times! The Lamb slain from the foundation of the world for the salvation of the world.

Man can shake his arrogant fist all he wants, but he will never shake God. The plan is firm. No plan B exists. All things are going just as He knew they would. We look around us and hang our heads over the miserable estate of this lost, depraved world. And all the while God sits upon His throne saying, As long as man has breath, I have a Lamb. "Then I looked and heard the voice of many angels, numbering thousands upon

thousands, and ten thousand times ten thousand. They encircled the
throne and the living creatures and the elders. In a loud voice they sang:

> 'Worthy is the Lamb, who was slain,
> to receive power and wealth and wisdom and strength
> and honor and glory and praise!'" (Rev. 5:11–12)

Part 10

BLESSED
BENEDICTION

Though we've reached our final chapters, don't wind down too quickly. Many sights await us on the final miles of our journey together. Some will thrill us. Others may horrify us. All of them were meant to change us . . . and prepare us for the future. No book of the Bible will make us more thankful to belong to Jesus Christ than the Book of Revelation. Never lose sight of the fact that "there is now no condemnation for those who are in Christ Jesus" (Rom. 8:1). Though we have walked side by side with many lost, our futures will literally be worlds apart. May God increase our desire to pray for unbelievers and to more willingly share— not our fears—but our faith. In the meantime, we can trust the wisdom and eternal plan of the One "who is, and who was, and who is to come, the Almighty."

Chapter 46

A SONG NO ONE ELSE CAN SING

No one could learn the song except the 144,000 who had
been redeemed from the earth. (Revelation 14:3)

We've come to such an exciting part of our study that it hardly seems to be narrowing down. In only a few chapters, though, we will embrace and say farewell, at least for a season. You have been the perfect traveling companion, and I am grateful for the privilege to walk these last few miles with you. For now our thoughts will center on Revelation 14.

You can certainly tell from the tone of this chapter that the pulse of the book just escalated. If you listen closely, you can almost hear the hiss of the sickle cutting through air thick with looming judgment. The long-prophesied Day of the Lord, when He will settle all accounts, draws nearer and nearer. The mere thought leaves me with a strange mingling of anticipation and dread. I desperately desire the coming of His kingdom, yet I yearn for all to confess Christ before judgment comes. Our next chapter will be difficult because we are going to discuss God's wrath. These Scriptures provide a prelude to prepare us for that lesson and also remind us of the perfect plan and provision of our faithful God.

The vision of the 144,000 victors with the Lamb purposely follows the harrowing prophesies concerning the two beasts described in Revelation 13. One of the first principles I learned in Bible study concerning the kingdom of darkness is that anything God does, Satan attempts to counterfeit. We shouldn't be surprised.

I'm convinced the words of Isaiah can apply only to Satan, the morning star "fallen from heaven" (14:12). In Isaiah 14:14 Satan states his blasphemous goal: "I will ascend above the tops of the clouds; / I will make myself like the Most High." All through Revelation 13 the kingdom of darkness seeks to imitate the works of God but with a twisted, evil intent.

We can hardly comprehend why God's plan for the ages makes room for the full expression of such evil, but let's try to understand that Revelation records future events that bring both light and darkness earthward. Never lose sight of the fact that the light of God is incomparably brighter than the depth of Satan's darkness.

God and Satan are not equal-though-opposite powers. God allows Satan to exist and act only in ways that ultimately satisfy certain critical elements of God's kingdom agenda for earth. Before Satan meets his inevitable doom, God will allow him to drop many of his ancient masquerades and reveal himself in some respects. Revelation centers on the ultimate unveiling of Jesus Christ, but the Bible's benediction also appropriately intimates that all things will be revealed—whether good or evil, pure or defiled, heaven or hell.

In the wake of the inconceivable massacre of Revelation 13, God refreshed the searing soul of the beloved disciple with the vision of a remnant marked for survival and the sounds of rushing waters, thunder, and harps. Capture the emotions of Revelation 14:1–5 and sip its healing tonic after the bitterness of the preceding chapter.

> Then I looked, and there before me was the Lamb, standing on Mount Zion, and with him 144,000 who had his name and his Father's name written on their foreheads. And I heard a sound from heaven like the roar of rushing waters and like a loud peal of thunder. The sound I heard was like that of harpists playing their harps. And they sang a new song before the throne and before the four living creatures and the elders. No one could learn the song except the 144,000 who had been redeemed from the earth. These are those who did not defile themselves with women, for they kept themselves pure. They follow the Lamb wherever he goes. They were purchased from among men and

offered as firstfruits to God and the Lamb. No lie was found in their mouths; they are blameless.

Scholars disagree about whether these are the same 144,000 mentioned in Revelation 7:1–8. I believe the third and fourth verses suggest that they are. The 144,000 mentioned in chapter 7 were sealed with the seal of the living God. The 144,000 of Revelation 14 bear a mark—the name of the Lamb and the Father! On their foreheads! I don't think we should automatically assume that these names were visible to earthly eyes. Remember, John was seeing a vision far exceeding the natural realm. I believe John more likely saw the marks on the 144,000 as they were visible to the hosts of heaven and the demons of hell. Why do I make this point? Because I believe we share some similarities with these 144,000. They won't be the only ones who were "sealed." Ephesians 1:13 says, "Having believed, you were marked in him with a seal, the promised Holy Spirit."

The concepts in the Word of God are very consistent from the Old Testament to the New. Under the order of the original priesthood during the time of the tabernacle, God instructed the priests to wear a turban described in Exodus 28:36–38. That headgear bore a plate inscribed "HOLY TO THE LORD" (v. 36).

Notice the parallel of the inscriptions on the "foreheads." According to 1 Peter 2:9, we are a royal priesthood. Ephesians 1:13 tells us we also bear a seal. If we are the New Testament priesthood and we also have a seal, could it possibly be on our foreheads as well? We can only imagine. I believe one thing is certain: we are marked, and in all probability this seal is visible in the supernatural realm.

Beloved, you may struggle with doubts over whether you are saved, but I don't believe a single angel or demon in the unseen world has any doubt. We who are saved bear the seal of our Father. As 2 Timothy 2:19 says, "Nevertheless, God's solid foundation stands firm, sealed with this inscription: 'The Lord knows those who are his.'" Hallelujah!

Scholars are very divided as to whether 144,000 is a literal or representative number and whether the Mount Zion in this vision is on earth or in heaven. Where the latter is concerned, the Bible clearly refers to both.

The tragedy for any student of this chapter would be arguing over the symbolism and missing the song.

What song? Take another look at verse 3. The song no one could learn . . . except the 144,000 who had been redeemed from the earth. Please don't miss that John heard the song, but he could not learn the song. Notice it was a "new song."

I am not a singer, but I dearly love to sing praise songs to my God. We have a wonderful praise team at our church. I enjoy learning a new song every week or two, but I must admit that I get frustrated on occasion when most of what we sing is unfamiliar. I often think how silly I am because every song I love was once unknown to me.

My favorite songs are the ones that become "mine" over time as I sing them to God through the filter of my own experience and affection. Though such preferences may seem self-centered and absorbed, praise and worship are very personal to me. In fact, as long as our feet are planted on the soil of earth, I know of few more intimate encounters than raising our voices in worship to the God of heaven. When I am most involved in worship, I may as well be completely alone in the sanctuary with Him.

Nothing provokes a new song in my heart like a fresh surge of hope in a wilderness season. The song "Shout to the Lord" will forever be special to me because I first heard it at a time of deep personal suffering. The words came to my soul from God as hope that I would survive . . . and even thrive once again. Allow me to use this song as an illustration for Revelation 14:3. First I "heard" the "new" song then I "learned" it. My motivation to "learn" it came through its voice to my experience in that difficult but strangely beautiful season with my God.

John "heard" the "new song," but "no one could learn the song" except the 144,000 that had been redeemed from the earth. The Greek word for "new" in reference to the new song in Revelation 14:3 implies new in quality as opposed to number. In other words, the song wasn't new like a new release in Christian contemporary music. The song of the 144,000 was new because it had an entirely different quality from anything they'd sung before. In other words, it meant something to them no other song had ever meant. Why couldn't anyone else learn it? Because no one else had ever lived it. Out of their unique experience, God gave them a song that only they could learn.

Psalm 40 tells us God gave David a new song when He lifted him out of the slimy pit. I'd like to suggest that each of us who is willing can also receive a new song from God that arises in our souls out of hardship's victories . . . not necessarily in musical notes but in fresh truths engraved on the heart. These are precious gifts that eventually come to those who keep the faith and wait to see God redeem great difficulty. These songs can be "heard" by others, but they cannot be "learned" secondhand.

This concept is both the life and near-death of me at times. I love the gift of new songs that finally emerge like frolicking whales from the deep waters of trial or suffering. At the same time, I am inexpressibly frustrated that I cannot talk someone into loving and trusting God and finding His Son to be the greatest adventure in life. I want so badly for each member of the body of Christ to love Jesus passionately and live the excitement of His abundant life that I could sob. I practically jump up and down in ministry insisting, "If He'll do this for me, He'll do this for anyone!" Until individuals let Jesus redeem their own personal lives, hurts, losses, and failures, they can hear the song, but they cannot learn it. Songs of the heart are only learned through personal faith experience. Once we learn the songs, however, no one can take them from us.

Do you have a testimony about a time when God gave you a new song or a new hope in a virtually hopeless situation? Don't forget to thank Him for it.

Chapter 47

THE WRATH OF GOD

I saw in heaven another great and marvelous sign: seven angels
with the seven last plagues—last, because with them God's
wrath is completed. (Revelation 15:1)

I deeply hope that our previous lesson prepared us to some extent for our next focus. Unfortunately, we cannot be serious students about what John seemed to want us to know most and avoid the subject of God's wrath. If Revelation were a movie, the following images would undoubtedly send me out for another refill of popcorn. However, Revelation is no movie. It's also nonfiction.

Perhaps the truest words that ever fall from tainted human lips are these: God is faithful. Indeed He is. What may trouble us is that He is always faithful. In other words, God always does what He insists He will whether we like it or not. The idealist in me wishes the wrath of God didn't even exist and would never be unleashed.

Then the realist in me
- reads accounts of unspeakable cruelties and abuses to children;
- reviews a human history blighted by war crimes and bloody crusades spearheaded by those claiming to act in God's name;
- hears the name of God mocked, profaned, and derided publicly through various forms of media;
- listens to the arrogant who have convinced themselves they are gods;
- sees the violence bred by hatred, ignorance, and prejudice; and
- stands by while princes of the earth lay their bricks on an unseen but very present Tower of Babel.

298

I look around me and shudder with horror over and over again, asking, "Where is the fear of God?" Then I shake my head and wonder what kind of inconceivable power God must use to restrain Himself.

I don't even have to look as far as the world. At times in my life I've looked no further than my own mirror or my own church and wondered the words of Lamentations 3:22, "Because of the LORD's great love we are not consumed." I have said to Him more times than I can count, "Lord, why You do not rend this earth and swallow up Your own people, not to mention this godless world, is beyond me." Of course, I know He spares believers because He did not spare His own Son (Rom. 8:32).

Why does God continue to put up with a world that increasingly mocks Him? Why does He wait? For all of time, the most succinct answer to those questions can be found in 2 Peter 3:9: "The Lord is not slow in keeping his promise, as some understand slowness. He is patient with you, not wanting anyone to perish, but everyone to come to repentance."

In some ways the wrath of God will simply finish off what man started. I am convinced that mankind will do a proficient job of nearly destroying himself and his own planet based on the wars and conflicts prophesied in Scripture. God's Word promises a new heaven and a new earth but not until this one is destroyed. Matthew 24 prophesies increasing wickedness and destruction with a mounting strength and frequency of birth pains. Toward the very end of this age, God will allow the full measure of all permissible wrath to be poured out upon this earth: the wrath of man (never underestimate it), the unholy wrath of Satan, and the holy wrath of God. No wonder this time of great tribulation will be like no other.

The wrath described in the Book of Revelation unfolds in a somewhat mysterious sequence: seals, trumpets, and bowls. The seals introduce the trumpets, and the trumpets usher in the bowls. You can read the account in the following sections of Scripture:

- The seals: Revelation 6; 8:1–5
- The trumpets: Revelation 8:6–13; 9
- The bowls: Revelation 16

Unsettling is an understatement. My horror is primarily for those who refuse to believe. In 1 Thessalonians 1:10 Paul called Jesus the one "who rescues us from the coming wrath."

I am not implying that believers won't go through terrible times. The Word clearly states we will (2 Tim. 3:1), and many Christians already are. My point is that the wrath of God described in the Book of Revelation is not toward the redeemed. They will either be delivered from it or through it. I believe the greatest evangelism explosion of all times will occur during the end of times. The inoculation against the coming wrath of God is confessing His Son as Savior and repenting of sin. No one who comes to Him with a sincere heart of reception and repentance will be refused . . . unless they wait too late. I so badly did not want to write that last phrase.

God will reveal Himself in countless ways toward the end of times, pouring out His Spirit, His wonders, and His mercies. Those mercies, however, are dealt according to demand. In other words, some people respond to tender mercies. Others don't respond until God shows severe mercies. Others don't respond at all. Never forget that God wants to save people and not destroy them. During the last days the heavens will show so many signs, and evangelists will preach so powerfully that I am convinced people will practically have to work at refusing Him. Yet many tragically will.

The apostle Paul warned that "because of your stubbornness and your unrepentant heart, you are storing up wrath against yourself for the day of God's wrath, when his righteous judgment will be revealed" (Rom. 2:5). People will not refuse Him because God didn't love them or make provision for them. Beloved, please hear my heart. The wrath of God cannot be separated from His character and person. In other words, even in His unleashed wrath, God cannot be less than who He is. God is holy. He is good. He is love. God is righteous, and God is right. The Judge will judge, but, unlike ours, His judgments are always based on truth (Rom. 2:2).

Ours is also a God of inconceivable compassion, forgiveness, and mercy. I need look no further than the hands on this keyboard for proof. How He has forgiven me! When others might have left me for dead and said I got what I deserved, He tended my filthy, self-inflicted wounds and pulled me from the ditch.

God's heart is neither mean nor unjust. He is holy. And beloved, the holy God will judge this world. The day of the Lord will come, and none will doubt He is God. He will not be mocked. He'd have to be untrue to His own character to do otherwise.

Between and woven within the sets of seals, trumpets, and bowls, God placed other messages that accompany His judgment. I love the words found in Revelation 15. John saw what looked like a sea of glass mixed with fire. The victorious believers stood beside the sea holding harps. "They . . . sang the song of Moses the servant of God and the song of the Lamb" (v. 3).

I love the reference to the song of Moses and the song of the Lamb. You see, God will bring perfect order and completion out of a season that will seem the ultimate chaos and destruction. The end of times will culminate in the brilliant plan of God rising from the smoldering tomb of earth. From the back this resurrected life looks like the old covenant. From the front it looks like the new covenant. But when all is said and done, the two will be seen as they were always intended: as one perfect whole. As one perfect life: Christ's. All will make sense.

"Great and marvelous are your deeds,
    Lord God Almighty.
Just and true are your ways,
    King of the ages.
Who will not fear you, O Lord,
    and bring glory to your name?
For you alone are holy.
All nations will come
    and worship before you,
for your righteous acts have been revealed." (Rev. 15:3–4)

Chapter 48

THE WEDDING FEAST

Let us rejoice and be glad
and give him glory!
For the wedding of the Lamb has come,
and his bride has made herself ready. (Revelation 19:7)

We've traced the footsteps of the apostle John from the Galilean shore all over Israel. Sometimes John's were the only apostle prints we found, like in the High Priest's courtyard and then nearby the cross. We followed him to Patmos and Ephesus. But one day we'll follow him home. I have loved our journey together, but it's not over yet. We'll pick up the trail together again one day when all roads for believers lead to heaven. On that great and glorious day may each of our footprints be found in the banquet hall where we'll celebrate the marriage supper of the Lamb. Until then let's anticipate.

The beauty of being in a women's Bible study is that every now and then we get the opportunity to look at a particular section of Scripture just from a woman's point of view. And I'm going to tell you something: this lesson is a woman thing. To any men reading along, I'll just have to ask for your patience.

Let's capture Revelation 19:7–9 in our imagination today. I believe I want to begin reading at verse 4:

> The twenty-four elders and the four living creatures fell down and worshiped God, who was seated on the throne. And they cried:
> "Amen and hallelujah!"

Then a voice came from the throne, saying:
"Praise our God,
   all you his servants,
you who fear him,
   both small and great!"
Then I heard what sounded like a great multitude, like the roar
of rushing waters and like loud peals of thunder, shouting:
"Hallelujah!
   For our Lord God Almighty reigns.
Let us rejoice and be glad
   and give him glory!
For the wedding of the Lamb has come,
   and his bride"
(Stop a moment and capture that, *His bride*)
"has made herself ready.
Fine linen, bright and clean,
   was given her to wear."
(Fine linen stands for the righteous acts of the saints.)
Then the angel said to me, "Write: 'Blessed are those who are
invited to the wedding supper of the Lamb!'" And he added,
"These are the true words of God."
At this I fell at his feet to worship him. But he said to me, "Do
not do it! I am a fellow servant with you and with your brothers
who hold to the testimony of Jesus. Worship God! For the testimony of Jesus is the spirit of prophecy."
I saw heaven standing open. . . . (Rev. 19:4–11)

Cinderella, here is your Prince Charming:

"And there before me was a white horse, whose rider is called
Faithful and True. With justice he judges and makes war. His eyes
are like blazing fire, and on his head are many crowns. He has a
name written on him that no one knows but he himself."
(Rev. 19:11–12)

There is a name that has been withheld from human knowledge. Never
profaned. Celebrate with me today, this name has never even touched

human lips. A name that He alone knows. "He is dressed in a robe dipped in blood, and his name is the Word of God. The armies of heaven were following Him, riding on white horses and dressed in fine linen, white and clean" (vv. 13–14).

Now who have we seen, in this context, dressed in fine linen, white and clean? That's the bride. "Out of his mouth comes a sharp sword with which to strike down the nations. 'He will rule them with an iron scepter.' He treads the winepress of the fury of the wrath of God Almighty. On his robe and on his thigh he has this name written: KING OF KINGS AND LORD OF LORDS" (vv. 15–16). For the wedding supper of the Lamb has come.

We have no idea what this wedding ceremony is going to be like. No matter what we could conjure up in our imagination, it will be far from it. But wouldn't it be fun, just you and me, if we tried to picture it based on some suggestions that we might find in Scripture? And if we could in some way prepare in such a way to build with anticipation toward that day? Would that be part of the bride making herself ready?

I can tell you that that's all we're about at my house right now. By the time you are reading this, our daughter Amanda will be a bride. We are in the throes of planning. The only part that makes the rest of the work and planning worth it is building the anticipation about what it will be like. What makes all of the details worth it is that we are anticipating a grand celebration. Now as that is true of the Moore household planning for an earthly wedding, imagine how much greater the truth applies to our upcoming wedding to Christ. I want to just look at these verses and a number of others to see some scriptural hints about what our wedding might be like.

Notice that the call to the wedding begins with a very important word: *Hallelujah.* This significant call to worship may suggest that though every single nation, tribe, and tongue will be part of this glorious wedding, God reserves the right to make sure that this wedding is decidedly Jewish. The call to worship is, "Hallelujah!" That is a very Jewish word.

So based on that little suggestion, I just want to say I have an idea. I'm not sure if I'm right about this. But I just have an idea that what we have in front of us—after all, we do have a Jewish bridegroom—is a grand Jewish wedding. And I have been to Jewish weddings. We have the wonderful blessing in Houston of being friends with some people who are Orthodox Jews. As long as I will keep my mouth shut, they invite me over. We've been able to have Passover several times, and we've been able to go to weddings.

I've been to all sorts of denominational weddings. May I just say, ain't nothin' like the Jewish version. This is the kind I want. I did quite a lot of research for this particular lesson about ancient Hebrew weddings. We're just going to consider some suggestions of what our wedding might be like based on Jewish customs through the centuries. So first of all, we've already intimated that perhaps it's going to be of a Jewish flavor.

2. In ancient Hebrew tradition, the actual wedding arrangements were the responsibility of the groom and his father. I love it that the bride is even given her dress. "Fine linen . . . was given her to wear" (v. 8). I have to tell you, never in my life has anything struck me like seeing my own twenty-two-year-old daughter in that wedding dress after we bought the veil. When they put the veil on that child, this mother has never seen anything so enchanting in my life. Thinking of that scene, I'm just trying to imagine the bride of Christ dressed in fine linen.

From among many I want to show you one particular Scripture reference to back up the point that the father prepared for the wedding. Judges 14:10 says, "Now his father went down to see the woman." This is who Samson wants to marry. "And Samson made a feast there, as was customary for bridegrooms. When he appeared, he was given thirty companions." In their tradition the father and the son made all the arrangements.

That's wonderful news for us. The words of John 14 are echoing in my mind: "I go to prepare a place for you that where I am you may be also. And I'm going to come and get you," and I'm now paraphrasing, but I believe Jesus was saying, "When the place I'm preparing is ready, I'll come back and get you." We have the wonderful fortune of having as our bridegroom someone who happens to be a carpenter. So He's building well!

Jesus is preparing a place for us, built onto His Father's house. And when it's prepared, He is coming for us. All the arrangements will be made. We are responsible for one thing. We see that in the next point.

3. *The chief responsibility of the bride was to make herself ready.* Now before I try to explain this, I want to tell you something my Jewish guide Arie shared with me. He said, "Of course, Beth, you are bringing up the contract." Because, he said, "We're one of the only peoples of the world who have to sign a contract of this sort to get married." And he said, "It's called the *ketubbah*." What he told me fascinated me. The wife does not have to sign any part of it. This is strictly about the husband, strictly about the groom.

Guess who else has to sign it? Two witnesses sign with him. They are also obligating themselves. He said, "It's really more than simply standing there as a witness. The witnesses really obligate themselves in some ways to take on responsibility for the marriage." When my Jewish friend said two witnesses, of course I'm thinking trinity thoughts.

Arie said, "Then of course the rabbi would also sign." Well, Jesus is the Rabbi, so He is the one making that binding oath that has already been made for us. Arie went on to explain that during the ceremony the groom has to speak aloud to all the listeners his commitment to this woman and how sacred she is to him. The bride holds an important place in the wedding ceremony, but in preparation for it, she's got one thing on her mind. She's got to prepare herself for her groom.

I couldn't help but think to myself of the words in Psalm 45:10: "Listen, O daughter, consider and give ear: / Forget your people and your father's house. / The king is enthralled by your beauty; / honor him, for he is your lord."

Beloved, I want to say to you: "The king is enthralled with you." You see, as we grow in Christ, we become more and more beautiful to the One for whom we are preparing ourselves. Not only that, but the Word of God says in Ephesians 5 that He is presenting us without spot or wrinkle. The bride prepares herself.

One of the prime priorities of the bride's preparation is this. She prepares herself in purity. It is very important that we are growing in purity. We are preparing for that wedding day. I want to tell you, this is great news to me and to all who have a difficult background or track record. Do you know we are being presented to our groom as pure virgins? (2 Cor. 11:2).

I have to tell you a story I also shared in *Breaking Free.* As I was preparing for our twentieth wedding anniversary, for the life of me I could not think of what I wanted to get my husband. He's a very sentimental man. You have to get him something sentimental because if he can afford it, he already owns anything he wants. So I just said, "God, you need to tell me what I can get my man. I need a really great idea." And I really prayed and prayed over it.

God began suggesting something to my heart. He started bringing to my mind the early part of our marriage and the pain of my wedding day. It was an extremely hard day for me. I don't know how to explain it to you. I didn't understand it until many, many years later. I was feeling so much shame on my wedding day because it was a day I was supposed to feel beautiful. And I did not feel beautiful.

I had even gone to a lot of trouble to make absolutely sure that I had an off-white dress instead of a white dress because I did not want to be a lie. Now some of you are already hurting because you know what I'm talking about. It's a horrible feeling. Nothing about that day seemed beautiful to me.

When I was a little girl, I had pictured that when I got married I would have a huge wedding portrait, and it would hang over our blazing fireplace. The nearest to a fireplace we had was a heater in the bathroom. And I didn't even have money enough for a photographer. I just spent the bare minimum. I didn't even buy my dress; I just rented it. You know, it just was not the kind of day you picture.

So as I contemplated our twentieth anniversary, the Lord began scratching that a little bit. He said, "You know, Beth," and of course He was speaking to my heart, "you never did get that picture made."

"What picture?"

"That wedding portrait."

"Well, it is a little too late!"

"Who said?"

And the Lord put it on my heart that it was time. He said, "My darlin' we have done so much work. And I have restored you. And it is time for you to put on a white wedding gown and get your picture taken for your husband."

I called a friend of mine who's a makeup artist in Houston, a godly, godly young woman. And I knew she would have a fit. She squealed on the phone and jumped up and down. I said, "You can't tell anyone Shannon. You cannot tell anyone. This is our secret." She said, "I'll set up everything." She said, "You show up and I'll have everything ready." And that's exactly what I did. And I'm going to tell you something. She hid me in a room and would not let me see a mirror. She had my dress sparkling white from head to toe. Zipped that thing up nice and tight. Did my makeup. Did my hair. Put on my veil. Then she pulled me out and brought me in front of the mirror. And I nearly died.

I couldn't even recognize myself. The photographer was so tender that his eyes were continually filled with tears. He said, "I've just got to be honest with you. I've never taken a picture of a bride this old." He said, "Now, that's not what I mean." He said, "I mean one that's been married for so long." Because this was a forty-one-year-old bride who had been married for twenty years.

I had it framed in the most ornate gold frame, 20 x 24. Have you got the picture? Had one made for each of my daughters. I wrote the same letter to all three of them, explaining what the portrait meant to me.

The night of our anniversary I had the girls stay with us, and I presented Keith with that picture and then their pictures to them. And they all read their letters at the same time. My husband is a tall man, very handsome, and he began to weep. He stood up with that picture, and he began walking all over the house, holding it up to places on the wall.

He would stop at one place and shake his head no, then stop at another and shake his head no. Finally he walked right over to a particular part of the wall. The girls and I went, "uhh," and caught our breath because we knew what he was looking at. He set the picture down. He took a deep breath to gather the courage, and then he pulled his trophy deer off the wall.

As I live and breathe, he had tears streaming down his cheeks, and I thought, "He's crying over the deer." He hung that picture up right there, and it still hangs there today. He stepped back, and he said, "That is the trophy of my life." That is a restored bride. And that is what every single one of us can be, fully restored, fully prepared. Are we going to believe God or not? I chose to believe Him because I was going to self-destruct if I did not.

Another part of the Jewish bride's preparation in purity involved a special bath of clean water and fragrant oil. Arie tells me that it's called the *mikveh*, the ritual bath. I was reading him all my notes, and he said, "Actually, Beth, it's not just clean water. It's living water." I went, "Ah-ha! Do tell."

I also found out that the bride chose fine jewelry to wear on her wedding day. It was a very important part of the process. The *Dictionary of Biblical Imagery* says, "A bride's jewelry represents her readiness for the groom. And often this jewelry was given by the groom and his family."[1]

I want you to see the scriptural references so that you know we're not just making this up out of customs. Their ancient customs came from the Word. Jeremiah 2:32 says, "Does a maiden forget her jewelry, / a bride her wedding ornaments?" You see, it's telling us she wore her best jewelry as part of her wedding attire.

I want to suggest what that jewelry may represent in the fulfillment of our particular new covenant. The apostle Paul wrote about the judgment seat of Christ. You and I are not going to have any kind of condemnation at our judgment. We will not stand at the great white throne pictured in Revelation. Believers will stand at the judgment seat of Christ where we will either receive reward or loss of reward. But there will be no condemnation. Nobody showing a videotape of your worst moments. That's not going to happen.

I want you to hear something from 1 Corinthians 3:12–16: "If any man builds on this foundation"—talking about the foundation of Jesus Christ—"using gold, silver, costly stones, wood, hay, or straw, his work will be shown for what it is, because the Day will bring it to light. It will be revealed with fire, and the fire will test the quality of each man's work. If what he has built survives, he will receive his reward. If it is burned up, he will suffer loss; he himself will be saved, but only as one escaping through the flames."

In other words, we'll stand before the judgment seat of Christ. And everything that we did in this lifetime that was building on the foundation of Jesus Christ—out of pure motive, out of attitude to glorify Him and not self—will become as gold, silver, and costly stones. The rest of the things that we do—all the effort, all the energy that we might pour out, that does not build on the foundation of Christ—will just burn up like wood, hay, and stubble.

So, when judgment comes after that fire of judgment has come, not to burn us up, but to decide which works stand the test of judgment, what will be left? The gold, the silver, and the precious stones. Now I believe those are the jewels that we will be wearing when we come to our wedding.

So we've seen the various parts of the preparation for the Jewish wedding. Now we turn to the ceremony itself. During the ceremony held under the wedding canopy, or *huppah,* the Jewish bride traditionally circled the groom, which according to some traditionalists, originated with Jeremiah 31:22: "A woman will surround a man."

When I asked Arie about this, he said, "You may not like this one."

I responded, "Well, try me on it."

He explained, "Well, there are differing views about it, but the chauvinist view is that she is circling around him because she will be serving him."

I said, "In other words, she'll be running circles around him."

He smiled, "Now I didn't say that; you said that."

But I said, "You know, Arie, really that won't matter to us." Because in Revelation 7 it said that we will serve Him before His throne, day and night. In serving Christ we have dignity. He gives us joy, energized by the Holy Spirit. That'll be fine with me.

Seven blessings were pronounced during the ceremony. That may be a little bit familiar to you. Now these seven blessings, I learned from Arie, would come from the dignitaries at the wedding. Usually the rabbi would begin it. And then maybe a father-in-law, maybe an uncle, maybe an older brother. But there would be seven blessings spoken. Now the seventh blessing is always the blessing over Jerusalem. I found this to be very intriguing. It's always about Jerusalem. The blessing would go something like this: "Bless You, Lord, the Builder of Jerusalem, who will rebuild the temple one day."

Then what do you suppose they do? What is the part you and I probably know the best? They break the glass. Now he said, "There are some who think that the broken glass just begins the great ceremony, but that is not what it's about." He said, "The breaking of the glass is to bring them to a very sober time of thinking that in the midst of great celebration we must remember"—and I'm quoting his exact words—"that our joy is incomplete."

I said, "OK, Arie. What makes our joy incomplete?" (Remember all the times that Christ said, "Make My joy complete"?) "What makes our joy incomplete, Arie?"

He said, "Two things. The first thing is that we have loved ones missing from the wedding that have already died. The second one is because there is no temple for now in Jerusalem."

For us as New Testament believers, both of those things have been satisfied. Regarding our loved ones: those in Christ will be present at the wedding supper of the Lamb.

In reference to the temple we read in Revelation 21:1–3, "Then I saw a new heaven and a new earth, for the first heaven and the first earth had passed away, and there was no longer any sea. I saw the Holy City, the new Jerusalem, coming down out of heaven from God, prepared as a bride beautifully dressed for her husband. And I heard a loud voice from the throne saying, 'Now the dwelling of God is with men, and he will live with them.'" Verse 22–23 of the same chapter says, "I did not see a temple in the city, because the Lord God Almighty and the Lamb are its temple. The city does not need the sun or the moon to shine on it, for the glory of God gives it light."

Is that enormous? Do you understand that our joy gets to be complete? Our loved ones will be present, and God and Christ are the temple.

This joy is pictured in the Jewish wedding. Although deep repentance and personal cleansing took place in preparation, the actual wedding day was marked by great gladness of heart. In fact, no mourning was allowed. If you were in mourning, you just couldn't come to a wedding.

Revelation 19:7 says, "Let us rejoice and be glad / and give him glory! / For the wedding of the Lamb has come." Let us rejoice! *Rejoice* means about what you think it does. But *glad* takes it a step further. It is the word, *agalliao,* in the original Greek language, which means "to exult." Rejoice with exuberance. Often to leap for joy. Show one's joy by leaping, skipping, or dancing. Denoting excessive joy.

Do you just love that idea? Excessive or ecstatic joy and delight. This is going to be some kind of wedding. We're talking leaping, skipping, exuberant joy, dancing.

I want you to also picture with me the chairs lifted up. Because that's also a picture we might have of a Jewish wedding. The Lord brought two verses to my mind. Ephesians 1:20: God has raised Christ "from the dead and seated"—there's our key word—"him at his right hand in the heavenly realms, far above all rule and authority, power and dominion." Then guess what Ephesians 2:6 says? "And God raised us up with Christ and seated us with him in the heavenly realms." I want to tell you, if that's not two chairs lifted up, I don't know what it is!

We've seen so much in Scripture about the wedding, but I want you to see Isaiah 62:5. It says, "As a bridegroom rejoices over his bride, / so will your God rejoice over you." Do you understand that your God is going to rejoice over you, and your King is going to be enthralled by your beauty? Isaiah described the event:

> On this mountain the LORD Almighty will prepare
> a feast of rich food for all peoples,
> a banquet of aged wine—
> the best of meats and the finest of wines.
> On this mountain he will destroy
> the shroud that enfolds all peoples,
> the sheet that covers all nations;
> he will swallow up death forever.
> The Sovereign LORD will wipe away the tears
> from all faces;
> he will remove the disgrace of his people
> from all the earth.
> The LORD has spoken.
> In that day they will say,

"Surely this is our God;
    we trusted in him, and he saved us.
This is the LORD, we trusted in him;
    let us rejoice and be glad in his salvation." (Isa. 25:6–9)

Do you see what those verses say? After all that's been so challenging and so difficult for us on this earth, do you realize that when everything is said and done, all that will matter is that we trusted in Him? That we'd be able to say, when we see Him face-to-face, "There is my God, and I trusted in Him."

I want to conclude our chapter with another creative writing, just to get your mind going. When I first wrote this a couple of years ago, I really thought I understood from Revelation 19 that the wedding supper would precede Jesus' second coming. But now that I look at the text, I'm not sure of that. It could be that it comes after the second coming. I don't know for sure, but I wrote this with the first understanding. But it's just a fictional writing anyway. And I pray that it blesses you as we try to picture it to the best of our imagination.

Never in the history of heaven or earth had there been such festivities. Unimaginable flowers of textures and colors no human eye has ever seen crowned each table. The smell of food permeated the banquet hall. Bread of heaven, freshly baked. Ladles of honey, creamery butter. Fruits and vegetables unique to the menus of heaven. Goblets of silver and gold filled with the fruit of the vine. The Groom had not lifted His cup since He gathered with His beloved twelve in the upper room. A dozen-less-one who had gathered around His table that fateful night had, brief centuries later, turned into ten thousand upon ten thousand.

John the Baptizer stood to his feet as the friend of the bridegroom, and offered the toast: "To the Lamb of God, who took away the sins of the world, and to His beautiful virgin bride."

"Hallelujah, our Lord reigns!" the crowd responded, as all held up the cup of gathering and drank. Laugher and joyous fellowship filled the hall, new saints celebrated with the old. Peter and John, inseparable as usual, laughed with Spurgeon, Tozer, and

Chambers. Paul sat back and smiled like a father as Timothy captivated all of his table with the old, old stories. Corrie was there. Close by were those who had met the Savior in her prison camp. They were now covered with garments of salvation and ate to their fill. Amy Carmichael broke bread and passed generous portions around her table as beautiful brown, Indian hands reached out to receive. Zacchaeus, who had only seen slices of life from the branch of a tree, asked endless questions of a man named Graham, who had traveled the seven seas.

Instruments played the songs of the ages with glorious fanfare. Many danced with tambourines. Voices sang in seven-part harmony. The Groom sat at the head of the table captivated by His bride. To everyone He talked, He touched and gave them His utmost attention. Intently listening to a story passionately told, His concentration was broken by the overwhelming sense that His Father's eyes were on Him. He squeezed the hand of the one testifying as if to explain His change in focus. Then He turned His face toward His Father's throne. No words were necessary. He knew what His expression meant. The Groom nodded and gazed upon His bride.

The sound of His chair sliding back on the floor silenced every voice in heaven. The angels froze. The guests shuddered. The bride's eyes grew wide. Nobody moved but the Groom. He rose to His feet. As if suddenly awakened from a trance, an order of angels disappeared from sight, returning seconds later with countless crowns. No one moved, yet all could see. The royal vestiges were visible from every angle of the hall. Yet when the order of angels had placed the final crown upon His head, they stepped back while saints caught their breath. Though the crowns were many, they wrapped around His head as one diadem. All dominion belonged unto the Lamb upon His throne.

A faint sound was heard in the distance. Difficult at first to distinguish, finally it neared until the sound of rhythmic hoofbeats became evident. Only the Groom was standing, but each saint sat tall and strained to see. Gabriel led the most magnificent beast ever created to His rider. His coat was white with a luster like pearls. His mane was strands of gold. His eyes were like wine. His muscles ridged under his coat, displaying his impeccable condition. The Groom stared at him with approval, then smiled with familiarity as His hand stroked his mighty neck. Two cherubim brought forth a wooden chest laden with gold and brilliant jewels. Saints covered their eyes from the blinding light as they lifted the lid. The dazzling radiance was veiled as they brought forth a crimson robe from within and placed it upon the Groom's shoulders. Gold tassels were tied around His neck, and the seraph spread forth His train. The words were embroidered in deep purple, "King of Kings and Lord of Lords." His foot went in the stirrup, and the Faithful and True mounted His horse. The beast dipped his head as if to bow then lifted it with an inexpressible assumption of responsibility. The Groom gently tugged the reigns to the right and the animal turned with exemplary obedience. No one moved. No one spoke. No one took their eyes off the Rider on the white horse. They stood ready, backs to their audience, waiting.

Suddenly, a sound erupted like rolling thunder. The earth rumbled beneath their feet. Every saint could feel the echo in his heart of the pounding like a thousand timpani. The Groom released their gaze as the walls of the banquet hall gave way with a stunning thud. And encircling them were horses no man could count, winged and ready for flight. The four creatures—one with a face like a lion, one with a face like an ox, one with a face of a man, and one with the face like a flying eagle—flew over the heads of the saints and sang the anthem, "All rise!" Each saint, dressed in white linen, rose from his chair and mounted his horse. The attentions of every saint were quickened by the Groom. His back still turned. His horse made ready. Suddenly, a vapor seeped from the ground and covered the hooves of the horse of Faithful and True. As the vapor rose to His thighs, the fog became a cloud enveloping the Rider inch by inch. Brilliance overtook Him, and He became as radiant as the sun. So great was His glory, the cloud rose to His shoulders and covered His head to shield the eyes of the saints.

The familiar surroundings of heaven were suddenly transformed, and the sky appeared under His feet. A deafening sound
emitted from the middle of heaven like the slow rending of a
heavy veil. The sky beneath their feet rolled by like a scroll, and the
inhabitants of heaven were suspended in the earth's atmosphere.
The planet was their destiny. The Groom was their cue. The
cloudy pillar that enveloped Him would plot their course. With
swiftness the cloud descended toward the Earth. The horses
behind Him kept perfect cadence. The Earth grew larger as they
made their final approach, and oceans could be distinguished
from the nations. The Earth turned until Jerusalem faced upward.
The cloudy pillar circled widely to the right for the Rider's east-
ward arrival.

The sun interrupted the night as it rose upon the city of Zion
and awakened every inhabitant in the land. The rays that poured
through their windows were unlike those of any other morning.
All who saw it sensed the imposing arrival of the supernatural. The
wicked inhabitants of Jerusalem's houses, those who had forced the
people of God from their homes, shielded their eyes as they filled
the city streets. All of Israel was awakened, and the valleys were
filled with people gazing upward as much as their vision would
permit to something awesomely beyond terrestrial. Emaciated
humans filtered one by one from every cave and crevice—those
who had not taken the mark of the beast. Their eyes tried to adjust
to such sudden and abnormal gusts of light after hiding in the
darkness for so long. Every eye looked upon the amazing cloudy
pillar as it made its approach just east of the city of Zion. The
cloud stopped midair.

Suddenly the divine veil begin to roll upward inch by inch,
exposing first only the hooves of the great white horse then the feet
of the Rider. They looked like burning brass in the stirrups. His
crimson robe was exposed little by little until it seemed to blanket
the sky. His name ascended above all names. The cloud lifted
above His shoulder and the knowledge of God was unveiled in the
face of Jesus Christ. His eyes burned like fire into every heart.
Those who had taken the mark of the beast ran for their lives,

shoving the people of God out of the way, as they took cover in the caves. The people of God's covenant and those who had come to their aid remained in the light entranced by the glorious sight. Moaning filled the air. The Rider on the white horse dismounted His beast and His feet touched down on the Mount of Olives. And the earth quaked with indescribable force. And all who were hiding lost their cover.

The large brown eyes of one small boy remained fixed upon the sight. The whiteness of his teeth contrasted with the filth covering his face as he broke into an inexperienced smile. He reached over and took his mother's bony hands from her face and held them gently. With the innocence only one sight could possibly restore, he spoke: "Look, Mom, no more crying. Surely that is our God. We trusted in Him and He saved us." Even so, Lord Jesus come quickly.

Chapter 49

THE DEVIL'S DOOM

The devil, who deceived them, was thrown in the lake of burning sulfur,
where the beast and the false prophet had been thrown. They will be
tormented day and night for ever and ever. (Revelation 20:10)

$\mathcal{F}$ew words characterize the end of times more than *intense*. As we established earlier, all things—both good and evil—will intensify like the crescendo of a shofar (ram's-horn trumpet) hailing the King of kings and a government with no end. We cannot comprehend the ways God will work out "everything in conformity with the purpose of his will" (Eph. 1:11), but we can trust an all-wise sovereign and supreme God who can do no wrong. One of the Scriptures on my personal set of index cards right now is Daniel 4:37. I insert my name rather than Nebuchadnezzar's when I read it aloud over my own life. Why don't you read this Scripture aloud and insert your own name?

> Now I, _____, praise and exalt and glorify the King of heaven, because everything He does is right and all his ways are just. And those who walk in pride He is able to humble. (Dan. 4:37)

I want to look at these related Scriptures in four parts.

Part 1: Revelation 19:11–21 gives an awesome picture of Christ at the head of His army as He comes to do battle with the beast and his followers. The result becomes the "great supper of God" (v. 17). While I look forward with more anticipation than you can imagine to the wedding supper of the Lamb, believe me, you want nothing to do with the great supper. Christ slaughters his enemies, and an angel of God summons the birds of the air to a banquet. The fowls of the air form the guest list for this feast, and all those who reject Christ form the menu.

To the astonishment of all that is reasonable, masses of people will still gather with the beast to make war against the Rider on the horse and His army. After unprecedented signs and wonders and mercies of God ranging from tender to severe, many will refuse to repent. They will exercise the foolish audacity to stand as a foe against the blazing Son of God. Why? One reason probably exceeds all others when people reject God in the face of overwhelming evidence in His favor: unwillingness to bow to authority.

Based on glorious Scriptures like Revelation 7:9, I believe great numbers of people will turn to Christ and be saved in the last days. Revelation 19 and 20 also tell us that many will perish in their arrogant refusal to turn to Truth. I can't help but focus on the reference to the "kings of the earth." The Word intimates that some of those who refuse to bow will be the reputed power brokers of the earth. Their lust for dominance will literally be the death of them. How foolish! In their refusal to bow to a righteous God, they will bow instead to the prince of hell.

Satan's scheme is as old as his first appearance in the garden. He tries to convince humans that they can be their own bosses, their own gods. It's a sham. We were created to worship and bow down. (Perhaps that's the very reason God created our legs with knees.) We were fashioned to serve under a greater rule. Man has no sovereign authority. We cannot be our own bosses no matter how we deny our purpose. Yes, God ordains human government and places people in high positions—but always under His divine dominion. Nebuchadnezzar could teach us the life principle in Daniel 4:37 like few others. He learned the hard way that those who take credit for the kingdoms of the earth pay a hefty price.

Revelation 19:15, 21 make it clear exactly how Christ will strike down His foes—with the sword of His mouth. I believe a sword symbolizes Christ's tongue because He will strike down His foes by the words of His mouth. His is the same mouth that spoke the universe into existence and whirled the earth into orbit. Unlike me Christ doesn't have to use His hands to speak or to strike His foe. He speaks, and His will is accomplished.

How fitting that God assigned John the Revelator the privilege of announcing Christ's returning title as stated in Revelation 19:13: "He is dressed in a robe dipped in blood, and his name is the Word of God." No other inspired writer was given the insight into the *Logos*. The same Word made flesh to dwell among us will also return with the shout of victory as His foes fall at His feet. Every knee will bow . . . one way or the other.

Now look with me to the next portion of the text.

Part 2: In Revelation 20:1–6 John saw an angel come down from heaven, holding two things. The angel had the key to the abyss and a great chain. "He seized the dragon, that ancient serpent, who is the devil, or Satan, and bound him for a thousand years" (v. 2).

What irony that references to a "great chain" and being "set free" are right here in passages prophesying the devil's future. Scripture tells us that Satan will be bound for a thousand years before he is thrown into the lake of burning sulfur (Rev. 20:10). Scholars are very divided over the meaning of the time reference. I have no trouble picturing an actual thousand-year reign of Christ on the earth. At the same time, I also recognize 2 Peter 3:8 that says a thousand years is as a day to the Lord. This verse discourages us from dogmatism about dating the thousand years.

I see one fact as undeniable in Revelation 20:2. No matter the time frame, Satan will be bound. I couldn't be happier that the means is a great chain. How appropriate! Some may wonder why God will bother chaining him for a time rather than simply casting him immediately into the lake of fire. Beloved, as far as I'm concerned, the last days will be high time for Satan to be bound in chains! Perhaps for all of us who have cried, "How long, O Sovereign Lord, until You avenge our bondage?" I can't wait for him to know how chains feel. In fact, I hope the "great chain" is made from all the ones that have fallen off our ankles!

I want Satan to experience the same sense of powerlessness with which he deceived many of us, seeing others who are free yet not knowing for the life of us how to become one of them. Praise God for truth that sets us free! Satan tried his hardest to keep me bound and to destroy my life, my family, my testimony, and my ministry, but God defeated him by the power of His outstretched arm. The future will show Satan not only defeated but his wickedness toward us avenged. I suspect you feel the same way.

A serious set of chains will avenge the wrongs Satan dealt us quite sufficiently. What will the world be like while Satan is in chains? Based on my own personal study of last things, I tend to think the period of Satan's bondage in the abyss coincides with the kingdom of Christ on earth, a kingdom characterized by peace, righteousness, and security. Keep in mind, however, that faithful students of God's Word see a variety of ways to understand the passage. God will accomplish His will in His own way regardless of opinion. When all is done, we will probably all stand with our mouths open in wonder.

Revelation 20:3 offers what may be the ultimate irony. After a season of bondage, Satan will be "set free" by God for "a short time." May I say somewhat tongue in cheek that this example could suggest that God can set anyone free! Of course, this "freedom" will not be liberty from sin and rebellion but freedom to rise up once again in rebellion against God. Our next passage tells us what will happen.

Part 3: Revelation 20:7–10 tells us the devil will again gather forces to fight against God. He and his army will surround "the camp of God's people, the city he loves." But fire will come down from heaven and devour them (v. 9). I suppose we need not worry whether Satan will learn his lesson while chained in the abyss. He is the embodiment of evil. He will return to his old tricks the moment he is released, exceedingly empowered by ever-increasing rage.

John 8:44 provides one of Scripture's most succinct synopses of Satan. Jesus said he "was a murderer from the beginning, not holding to the truth, for there is no truth in him. When he lies, he speaks his native language, for he is a liar and the father of lies."

When Satan is released upon the masses once more, he will come speaking his native language. His is so effectively deceptive that, if undefended, he can delude the brightest human and then use that person to lie to others. Make no mistake about it: deceived people deceive people. If you have ever dealt with a deeply deceived and deceiving person, you know that the only defense is prayer. Rationalizing is useless. Only the wonder-working power of God Himself can break the cycle of deception.

At the end of time, Satan will know he only has one last shot at us. You can see from Scripture that he will obviously shoot his best shot. In the final rebellion, masses of people will choose to stand in defiance against the holy Son of God. Mind you, by this time Christ will be fully revealed. We can only imagine what schemes of deception the evil one will use to convince them that he can promise them more than God their Maker. My guess is that they will be deluded into thinking that they are choosing their own lusts and greeds rather than an eternity of holiness in the presence of God. They will know the truth, yet they will choose a lie. Thinking they are choosing themselves, they will choose the devil.

Unlike the boastful and crude philosophies of modern man, hell will not be one big party. Hell will be eternal bondage to torment. I cannot bear the thought of it and want no one to go there. Let's take a look at the last segment of Scripture in our lesson.

Part 4: Revelation 20:11–15 tells us of the "great white throne judgment." Based on my understanding of Scripture and the final judgments, only the lost will stand at the great white throne. This seat of judgment seems to differ from the one described in both 1 Corinthians 3:10–15 and 2 Corinthians 5:1–10. Those who know Christ will stand before the judgment seat of Christ where those who have served Him lovingly and obediently will receive rewards. The judgment seat for the saved will not be a place of condemnation (Rom. 8:1).

Our passages in Revelation describe a very different scene. As you can see, the great white throne appears to be a seat upon which only condemnation takes place. Every person who has refused God will stand before Him on this dreadful day. Though the earth and sky will try to flee from His awesome presence, those who have refused God will have no place to run.

Revelation 20:13 states how each person who stands before the great white throne will be judged: "Each person was judged according to what he had done." One similarity will exist between our judgments. Reward will be given according to the deeds of those saved by the blood of the

Lamb. Likewise, punishment will be given according to the deeds of those who refused Jesus' work on their behalf.

I am convinced Revelation 20:13 suggests differing levels of punishment according to the depths and lengths of the evil accomplished by each person. Why would I have ever thought otherwise? Is our God not just? Does He not look upon the individual hearts and deeds of every responsible man and woman? The lake of fire will be a place of torment for every inhabitant, but I believe Scripture clearly teaches that punishment will vary according to each person's deeds. The Righteous Judge knows every thought and rightly discerns every motive of our hearts. As we learned in Romans 2:2, His judgments are based on truth.

God began His magnificent creation of humankind with one man. Though the plains of planet Earth now bulge with six billion people, God still breathes life into each being, one at a time. We were fashioned for God and designed to seek Him. He created a universe and an order with the divine purpose of bearing constant witness to His existence. Heaven unceasingly declares His glory, and all who truly seek Him find Him.

Not one person's absence from heaven will go unnoticed by God. Not one will get past God haphazardly. Not one will accidentally get swept away in a sea of nameless souls. God is not careless. He intimately knows every soul that will refuse to know Him. Because He created us for fellowship, God's judgments cannot be rendered with cold, sterile detachment. For God so loved the world that He sent His Son to seek and to save the lost. Though none can refuse to be seen, many will incomprehensibly refuse to be "found."

The passionate plea of Ezekiel 33:11 rises in volume as the day draws nearer: "As surely as I live, declares the Sovereign LORD, I take no pleasure in the death of the wicked, but rather that they turn from their ways and live. Turn! Turn from your evil ways! Why will you die, O house of Israel?"

Chapter 50

THE NEW JERUSALEM

I saw the Holy City, the new Jerusalem, coming down out of heaven from
God, prepared as a bride beautifully dressed for her husband. (Revelation 21:2)

*T*hroughout our overview of Revelation we have preoccupied ourselves with what John saw. As our next segment unfolds, I'd like us to recapture who was appointed to behold such sights. I have grown to love John through this study. I enjoy imagining him as nothing more than a teenager when Christ bade him follow. Did the others pick on him unmercifully yet favor him? These men shared deep interpersonal relationships. They worked together, traveled together, ate together, slept under the stars together. They saw wonders and horrors together. They grieved and hoped together. I'm not sure many of us could boast the kinds of relationships these men shared.

Years passed, and that small band of apostles scattered like seed cast from the hand of the Gardener. His sovereign fingers cast some of the seed into soil not far from their homeland, but at the flick of His wrist others sailed seas. John was one of those. His exile to Patmos invited many unwelcome opportunities, but one of the bittersweet gifts of the desolate island surely was remembrance. Like the sun reflecting off the briny waters, John must have reflected on all the twists and turns of divine destiny that had brought him to the mounds of rock rising from the sea.

Then came a loud voice behind him like a trumpet that said, "Write on a scroll what you see." So he wrote, in human vocabulary that could do little more than suggest the profundity of an indescribable reality. Imagine having been the one to see what John described! Do you realize that John "saw" Satan? Like us, he had seen his activity in thousands of ways, but he had never seen his visible and unholy essence. In the Revelation 20 vision, John saw him bound, loosed, then doomed. Keep in mind that John probably survived his stay on Patmos. Writings of the early church fathers indicate he returned to Ephesus after his exile.

We have no idea how long John lived, but imagine how his vision of Satan affected how he thought and taught from that time forward. Then imagine John seeing the final judgment of the lost at the great white throne. Don't separate his sights from his personality and emotional makeup through which they were processed. Think about the tender heart of this disciple. John had more to say about the love of God and love for one another than any other New Testament writer. Perhaps no one wanted less than John to see people shun the love of God and perish. Before his very eyes the sea, death, and Hades gave up their unbelieving dead, and they were judged for their deeds. After death and Hades were thrown in the lake of fire, the unbelieving were cast there as well. John saw this! Such sights must have affected his ministry from that time forward.

Now look at the first word of Revelation 21:1: "Then." Oh, Beloved, how I thank God for "then." Your life may be excruciating right now. Your challenges may be more than you can stand. Your strength may be sapped. Your health may be terrible. No matter how difficult this present season, dear one, God has a "then" on your time line of faith. Every believer has a new chapter ahead filled with dreams come true. Whatever you are facing is not the end of the story.

I want to encourage you to read all of Revelation 21, continually contrasting its hopes with the horrors of the chapter preceding it. No two chapters of New Testament Scripture provide a more profound side-by-side contrast of eternal destiny for the lost and the saved.

I want to look at the elements in Revelation 21 that may have meant the most to the apostle John. According to Revelation 21:1, the first obvious difference between the new heavens and the new earth is "no more sea." The coast just a few miles from Ephesus could be seen from the tip of Patmos on a clear day. Imagine how John longed for those he served, aching to see them and with tears fully plead that they return to their first love. Imagine what the sea between them might have represented to John.

I long for the day when seas will no longer separate brothers and sisters in the family of God. I want to know my faithful brothers and sisters in Sudan, Iran, and all over the world.

My dear coworker, Sabrina, loves the ocean like I love the mountains. She would hardly be able to imagine heaven with no sea. We know that the new earth will have at least two bodies of water because Revelation records rivers and a crystal sea. Remember, much of the terminology in the final book of the Bible is figurative. I believe the reference in Revelation 21:1 to "no longer any sea" means that nothing else will ever separate us. We will be one just as Christ asked the Father. We will have all the beauty of the oceans without the obstacles they pose here.

After telling us the new heavens and earth will not be disjointed by seas, John described the new Jerusalem. Meditate on his words: "I saw the Holy City." I am confident that most of us Gentiles cannot relate to the attachment many Jews through the centuries have felt toward their homeland. Even those whose feet never touched the Holy Land yearned for it like a lost child longs for its mother.

I saw this peculiar bond just weeks ago in the face of my Hebrew friend and ancient lands guide, Arie. He and his family are now residents of Tel Aviv, but his heart never departs Jerusalem. The turmoil erupting within and around Jerusalem doesn't just concern or upset him. It brings him pain. I asked him how he felt about the ongoing crises in the Holy Land. As I witnessed the agony in his face, I sorrowed that I had asked something so obviously intimate. I consider myself very patriotic, yet I had to acknowledge that I knew nothing of his attachment to his own homeland.

Remember that Arie told me that the deeply heartfelt commitment to keep Jerusalem ever before them is restated at every orthodox Jewish wedding? In the midst of joy, they always "remember" Jerusalem and the tragic loss of the temple.

If Arie and other Jews through the ages have experienced an indescribable attachment to the Holy City and a sense of grief concerning the temple, try to imagine the strength of John's ties. He grew up on the shores of Galilee at the peak of Jerusalem's splendor since the days of Solomon. Herod's temple was one of the greatest wonders of John's world. No Jew could behold her splendor without marveling. Even weeping.

John knew every wall and gate of the Holy City. He walked the lengths and breadths with the Savior Himself. He sat near Him on the Mount of Olives, overlooking its beauty. John was also part of the generation who witnessed the total destruction in A.D. 70. By the time Jerusalem fell, John probably was already stationed in Ephesus, but the news traveled fast, and the sobs echoed louder with every mile. The grief of the diaspora mixed with the unreasonable guilt of not having died with the city surely shook their homesick souls.

Then John "saw the Holy city, the new Jerusalem, coming down out of heaven from God, prepared as a bride beautifully dressed for her husband" (Rev. 21:2). How his heart must have leapt with unspeakable joy! There it was! Not just restored but created anew with splendor beyond compare. "God will wipe away every tear from their eyes" (Rev. 7:17). I wonder if John was weeping at the sight.

Some people say that we won't be able to cry in the new heavens and earth. Clearly we get at least one last good cry since God will wipe away every tear! I cannot imagine that I will see my Christ, my God, and His heavenly kingdom with dry eyes. Our last tears, however, will no longer be those shed in mourning for "there will be no more death or mourning or crying or pain, for the old order of things has passed away" (Rev. 21:4).

Meditate on the words "old order of things." Since Adam and Eve grieved the loss of intimate fellowship with God and the agony of one son murdered by the other, this present Earth has been characterized by the "old order." We are shocked by pain again and again, yet this present world order is literally characterized by it. None of us will avoid it. We can anesthetize it, but without it we will never fully experience the old order or celebrate the new.

The new order will bring all things to completion and prepare the heavens and the earth for eternal bliss. "Now the dwelling of God is with men" (v. 3). Hallelujah! The sorrow of man's expulsion from the garden will only be exceeded by the unquenchable joy of God dwelling with men. Take note of the fact that John did not see a temple, sun, or moon in this new Jerusalem. These elements will be absent in the new Holy City "because the Lord God Almighty and the Lamb are its temple. The city does not need the sun or the moon to shine on it, for the glory of God gives it light, and the Lamb is its lamp" (Rev. 21:22–23).

Perhaps you also noticed another reference to "the kings of the earth" (v. 24). These kings stand in stark contrast to the kings of the earth in Revelation 19:19 who will rise against the Rider called Faithful and True. I believe the "kings of the earth" who will bring splendor into the new Holy City may be the redeemed described in Revelation 20:4 and others like them. "I saw the souls of those who had been beheaded because of their testimony for Jesus and because of the word of God. They had not worshiped the beast or his image and had not received his mark on their foreheads or their hands. They came to life and reigned with Christ a thousand years."

When God creates the new heaven and the new earth, I think quite possibly those who reign with Him in the kingdom—not as equals but as those ruling under His authority—will be among those bringing "their splendor into" the new Holy City. I also believe that prior to the end of times, kings of many nations will bow their knees in adoration and confession of Jesus Christ, the Son of God. Indeed, "the glory and honor of the nations will be brought into it" (Rev. 21:26). Our future is beyond the words and imaginations of scholars, poets, and movie producers. We will bask in the brilliance of our God when He proclaims a new beginning and creates a heaven and an earth out of the ideal of His imagination.

As we conclude this chapter, let's take one last glimpse at a detail in the new Jerusalem that might have had a fairly profound impact on John. "The wall of the city had twelve foundations, and on them were the names of the twelve apostles of the Lamb" (Rev. 21:14).

Beloved, do you realize that among them John saw his own name? In the days he remained on this earth, can you imagine what kinds of thoughts he had as he recaptured that sight in his memory? I have no idea what being one of Jesus' apostles was like, but I don't think that they felt superhuman or vaguely worthy of their calling. I'm not even sure those original disciples ever grasped that what they were doing would make a world-changing impact. I can't picture them thinking, *What I'm doing this moment will go down in history and be recorded in the eternal annals of glory.* I think they probably got down on themselves just like you and I do. I also think they were terribly overwhelmed at the prospect of reaching their world with the gospel of Christ and seeing only handfuls of converts most of the time.

Days and months later when John stared at that wall and its foundations again in his memory, can't you imagine he was nearly overcome that God esteemed them? Don't you think he marveled that the plan had worked . . . considering the mortal agents Christ had chosen to use?

Every day I deal with a measure of low self-esteem in ministry. I never feel up to the task. Never smart enough. Never strong enough. Never prayed up enough. Never prepared enough. Do you feel the same way? Then perhaps you also feel the same flood of emotions when this truth washes over you: God loves us. He prepares an inconceivable place for those who receive His love. He highly esteems those who choose to believe His call over the paralyzing screams of their own insecurities. No, our names won't be written on the foundations of the new Jerusalem, but they are engraved in the palms of His hands.

Chapter 51

SEEING HIS FACE

They will see his face, and his name will be on their foreheads.
(Revelation 22:4)

I can't believe my eyes. How could this journey have passed so quickly? The last chapter of study is always the most difficult for me to write, primarily because I hate good-byes. Years ago in my broken estate, I begged God to completely consume my imagination because I knew I would never be free until He transformed my thinking. In answer to that prayer, God has granted me an imagination to picture spiritual realities almost as vividly as physical realities. The journey you and I have taken on these pages is as real to me as anything we could have experienced face-to-face.

Even though I may never have seen your face, I have "pictured" you hundreds of times, esteemed your place in the body of Christ, and grown very fond of your company. We have walked side by side. I do not want to be someone others follow. My deepest desire has been to journey beside you, opening God's Word together and conversing over its truths.

Another reason the last chapter of study is difficult to write is that I want to say so much before we part. I felt the same way when I left Amanda at college for the first time. As the tears welled in our eyes, I said, "Baby, I had so much I wanted to say, and right now I am so overcome, I'm at a loss for words." I'll never forget her response. "Mom, you said it all yesterday . . . and the day before that." We both laughed. That's what I get for talking so much.

I've already used up all my good words by the time a really profound moment rolls around. You've heard far too many words from me as it is.

I grin as I remember a letter I received from a woman who tried to do one of my Bible studies. She described my approach like this: "So many words. So little said." I laughed my head off and added a hearty "Amen!" I say too much. Talk too long. Get too involved. I'm passionate to the point of looking foolish to my critics. I am over my head and underqualified, but this I can assure you: I love. It's real. And I have loved you.

Before we say good-bye, let's sit down for a little while and open our Bibles together. A river happens to be in our reading. Why don't we go sit on a rock on its shore, take off our sandals, and put our feet in? If you have your Bible, please read the last chapter in the entire inspired Word of God, Revelation 22.

Note the additional details concerning the new heaven and earth:

- the river of the water of life flowing from the throne
- the tree of life, bearing twelve crops of fruit, yielding its fruit every month
- the leaves of the tree for the healing of the nations
- no more curse
- no more night because the Lamb is the light
- the presence of the Lamb in the city

Twice toward the end of the Revelation, John became so overwhelmed at the sight of such glorious visions, he fell at the feet of the angel (Rev. 19:10; 22:9). Both times John received a swift rebuke and a reminder that the angel was nothing more than a "fellow servant." Amazing, isn't it? Those who serve God work side by side with the angels from glory. They are our fellow servants! Remember that next time you feel alone in your task.

I'd also like to draw another application from John's untimely buckling of the knees. John did not make the mistake of falling down at the feet of the angel when the visions were difficult and frightening to behold. He fell over the good news. God has performed the phenomenal over the last several years of Bible studies. We have increasingly heard from members of every conceivable denomination and segment in the body of Christ. Nothing could be more thrilling to me since my call to interdenominationalism is deep. At the same time, please let me issue a warning. Satan's primary objective is to entice us to bow to anything and anyone other than God. I believe Christians will be most tempted to fall down and worship spokespersons who tell us what we want to hear. In the words of the angel, "Do not do it!" Worship God alone. Now let's camp on Revelation 22:2 for a moment. You can compare this heavenly reality with an earthly allegory in Psalm 1:1–3.

During our stay on this earth, we are meant to be like trees of life bringing forth fruit in our seasons so others can "taste and see that the LORD is good" (Ps. 34:8). In order to bear much fruit, we've got to stay by the river. Perhaps even in it!

Ezekiel told of a related vision in Ezekiel 47:1–12. In Ezekiel's vision the river flowed from the temple in Jerusalem. The river in both visions seems to represent the outpouring of God's power and anointing. He not only cares for us with an incredible love; He makes absolute and complete provision for us.

I pray we've progressed in our walk with God, taken off our rationalizing seat belts, and thrown ourselves into His Great Adventure. How deeply do you see yourself in the figurative river of Christ's power and activity? Reflect on where you were when we began this journey. Beloved, I don't want you to be discouraged if you're not waist deep or swimming. I am only asking if we are more deeply immersed in Christ than when we began. Are we progressing? That's one of the most important questions of all. Mind you, we can swim one season and crawl our way right back to the bank and even into the desert the next. We will not be completely healed of our inconsistencies, infirmities, and weaknesses until we see Christ face-to-face.

Face-to-face. I can't think of a more fitting focus for our last few moments together. I don't want you to miss the most beautiful statement in the final chapter of Scripture: "They will see his face" (Rev. 22:4). For many of us, the very sight of Christ's face will be heaven enough. Everything else is the river overflowing its banks.

Until then we who are redeemed are like spirit-people wrapped in prison walls of flesh. Our view is impaired by the steel bars of mortal vision. We are not unlike Moses who experienced God's presence but could not see His face. To him and to all confined momentarily by mortality, God has said, "You cannot see my face, for no one may see me and live" (Exod. 33:20).

When all is said and done, we who are alive in Christ will indeed see His face and live. Happily ever after. I can hardly wait—yet right this moment I am absorbed by the thought of someone else seeing that face. Someone I've grown to love and appreciate so deeply through the months of study for this book. Several of the early church fathers plant the apostle John back in the soil of Ephesus again after the conclusion of his exile on the Island of Patmos. I wonder what kinds of thoughts swirled through his mind as the boat returned him to the shores of Asia Minor. I've made this trip by sea, and though it is beautiful, it is not brief. As his thinning gray hair blew across his face, he had time to experience a host of emotions. We have gotten to know him well. What kinds of things do you imagine he thought and felt on the ride back to Ephesus?

John lived to be a very old man. We have no idea how many years he lived beyond his exile. The earliest historians indicate, however, that the vitality of his spirit far exceeded the strength of his frame. His passionate heart continued to beat wildly for the Savior he loved so long. John took personally the words God poured through him. They did not simply run through the human quill and spill on the page. John's entire inner man was indelibly stained by *rhema* ink. In closing, read some of the words obviously inscribed on his heart from that last earthly night with Jesus:

My command is this: Love each other as I have loved you. Greater love has no one than this, that he lay down his life for his friends. You are my friends if you do what I command. I no longer call you servants, because a servant does not know his master's business. Instead, I have called you friends, for everything that I learned from my Father I have made known to you. You did not choose me, but I chose you and appointed you to go and bear fruit—fruit that will last. Then the Father will give you whatever you ask in my name. This is my command: Love each other. (John 15:12–17)

John lived the essence of John 15:12–17. He ended his life a true "friend" of Christ, for he took on His interests as surely as Elisha took on the cloak of Elijah. Early church fathers reported that long after John lacked the strength to walk, younger believers carried the beloved disciple in a chair through crowds gathered for worship. His final sermons were short and sweet: "My little children, love one another!" He poured his life into love. Christ's love. The focus of his final days captures the two concepts I've learned above all others in this journey:

- Christ calls His beloved disciples to forsake ambition for affection. John moved from his "pillar" position in the Jerusalem church to relative obscurity. Better to pour out our lives in places unknown than to become dry bones in the places we've always been.

- Only disciples who are convinced they are beloved will in turn love beyond themselves. Actively embracing the lavish love of God is our only means of extending divine love to injured hearts. We simply cannot give what we do not have.

Our Abba seems to have made a practice of telling us almost nothing about the actual deaths of His saints. According to Psalm 116:15, we know that their deaths were precious to Him. In fact, we might surmise that the exclusion of details is precisely because they were so precious to Him. Intimate. And none of our business. But don't think for a moment the Savior wasn't nearby when the sounds of an old Son of Thunder grew faint and then silent. After all, John was among the very few who stood nearby when the Incarnate Word fell silent.

John's death marked the close of the most critical era of human history. He was the solitary remaining apostle who could make the claims of his own pen: "That which was from the beginning, which we have heard, which we have seen with our eyes, which we have looked at and our hands have touched—this we proclaim concerning the Word of life" (1 John 1:1). "We" had turned to "I," and soon "I" would turn to "they."

At his age John's fragile body probably showed symptoms of failing some hours or even days before he breathed his last. If loved ones gathered around him, they likely did what most of us would do. They tried to make him as comfortable as possible. They may have gently slipped a pillow under his head to help support him as his lungs heaved for air. That's what we did when my mother's fragile frame could no longer sustain the strength to house her soul.

I'm not sure John needed a pillow, however. Somehow I picture him in his death much like he had been in his life. To me, the scene that captures the beloved disciple most is recorded in John 13:23. The event occurred at a certain table decades earlier. The Amplified Bible says it best. "One of His disciples, whom Jesus loved [whom He esteemed and delighted in] was reclining [next to Him] on Jesus' bosom" (John 13:23). Yes, I like to think that John died just as he lived. Nestled close. Reclining on the breast of an unseen but very present Savior, John's weary head in His tender arms.

The Spirit and the bride said, "Come!"

And in the distance could be heard a gentle thunder.

Notes

Chapter 2

1. R. Alan Culpepper, *John, Son of Zebedee* (Minneapolis: First Fortress Press, 2000), 7.
2. Ibid., 9.

Chapter 3

1. Ronald F. Youngblood and F. F. Bruce, eds. *Nelson's New Illustrated Bible Dictionary* (Nashville: Thomas Nelson, 1999), 473.
2. Ibid., 182.
3. Culpepper, *John,* 11.
4. James Strong, *New Strong's Exhaustive Concordance* (Nashville: Thomas Nelson, 1995), #1689, 30.

Chapter 5

1. Matthew Henry, *Matthew to John: Matthew Henry's Commentary on the Whole Bible,* vol. 5 (Grand Rapids: Fleming H. Revell Company, 1985), 456.

Chapter 6

1. Frederick William Danker, ed., *Greek-English Lexicon of the New Testament,* 3^d. ed. (Chicago: The University of Chicago Press, 2000), 391.
2. Frank Gaebelein and J. D. Douglas, *The Expositor's Bible Commentary,* vol. 8 (Grand Rapids: Zondervan Publishing, 1984), 629.

Chapter 8

1. A. W. Tozer, *The Pursuit of God* (Camp Hill, Penn.: Christian Publications, 1993), 64.

Chapter 10

1. Ronald F. Youngblood and F. F. Bruce, eds., *Nelson's New Illustrated Bible Dictionary* (Nashville: Thomas Nelson, 1999), 473.

Chapter 14

1. Frank Gaebelein and J. D. Douglas, *The Expositor's Bible Commentary* (Grand Rapids: Zondervan Publishing, 1984), 260.

Chapter 15

1. Spiros Zodhiates, "Lexical Aids to the Old Testament," #344 in Spiros Zodhiates, Warren Baker, and David Kemp, *Hebrew-Greek Key Study Bible* (Chattanooga, Tenn.: AMG Publishers, 1996), 1503.

Chapter 16

1. James Stalker, *The Two St. Johns of the New Testament* (New York: American Tract Society, 1895), 148.

Chapter 18

1. R. D. H. Lenski, *Commentary on the New Testament* (Columbus, Ohio: Wartburg Press, 1942), 89.

Chapter 19

1. R. Alan Culpepper, "John and Ephesus," *Biblical Illustrator*, Fall 1977, 3.
2. Stalker, *Two St. Johns,* 156.
3. Ibid., 157–58.

Chapter 20

1. Lynn M. Poland, "The New Criticism, Neoorthodoxy, and the New Testament," quoted in Culpepper, *John,* 139.
2. Lawrence O. Richards, ed., *The Revell Bible Dictionary* (Grand Rapids: Fleming H. Revell, 1990), 775.

Chapter 21

1. Spiros Zodhiates, *The Complete Word Study Dictionary; New Testament* (Chattanooga, Tenn.: AMG Publishers, 1994), #5485, 1469.
2. Augustine, *Confessions,* trans. R. S. Pine-Coffin (New York: Penguin Books, 1961).
3. Jonathan Edwards "The End for Which God Created the World," *The Works of Jonathan Edwards* (New York: Yale University Press), 495.
4. C. S. Lewis, *The Weight of His Glory and Other Addresses* (Grand Rapids: Eerdmans, 1965).
5. John Piper, *The Dangerous Duty of Delight* (Sisters, Ore.: Multnomah Publishers, 2001), 21.

6. Spiros Zodhiates, *The Complete Word Study Dictionary; New Testament* (Chattanooga, Tenn.: AMG Publishers, 1994), #4053, 1151.

Chapter 22

1. Eusebius, quoted in Andreas J. Kostenberger, *Encountering John* (Grand Rapids: Baker Books, 1999), 35.

2. Augustine, quoted in Kostenberger, *Encountering John,* 19.

3. Kostenberger, *Encountering John,* 56.

Chapter 24

1. Spiros Zodhiates, *The Complete Word Study Dictionary; New Testament* (Chattanooga, Tenn.: AMG Publishers, 1994), #2889, 880.

2. *The Worldbook Encyclopedia 2001,* vol. 8 (Chicago: World Book Inc., 2001), 8–8a.

Chapter 28

1. Spiros Zodhiates, *The Complete Word Study Dictionary; New Testament* (Chattanooga, Tenn.: AMG Publishers, 1994), #1718, 578.

2. R. D. H. Lenski, *Commentary on the New Testament* (Columbus, Ohio: Wartburg Press, 1942), 1008.

Chapter 29

1. Carolyn Curtis James, *When Life and Beliefs Collide* (Grand Rapids: Mich.: Zondervan, 2001), 18.

Chapter 31

1. Spiros Zodhiates, "Lexical Aids to the Old Testament," #344 in Spiros Zodhiates, Warren Baker, and David Kemp, *Hebrew-Greek Key Study Bible,* 1437.

2. Spiros Zodhiates, *The Complete Word Study Dictionary; New Testament* (Chattanooga, TN: AMG Publishers, 1994), #3674, 1046.

3. Ibid., #3670, 1045.

Chapter 32

1. Spiros Zodhiates, *The Complete Word Study Dictionary; New Testament* (Chattanooga, Tenn.: AMG Publishers, 1994), #4217, 1204.

Chapter 33

1. "John, A Last Word on Love" *Biblical Illustrator,* Summer 1976, 26.

2. Culpepper, *John,* 142–43.

Chapter 36

1. Tertullian, *On Prescription Against Heretics,* as quoted in Culpepper, *John,* 140.

2. Oswald Chambers, *My Utmost for His Highest* (New York: Dodd Mead & Company, 1963), 211.

Chapter 37

1. Spiros Zodhiates, "Lexical Aids to the New Testament" #918 in Spiros Zodhiates, Warren Baker, and David Kemp, *Hebrew-Greek Key Study Bible,* 1596.

Chapter 38

1. Timothy Trammell, "Smyrna," *Biblical Illustrator,* Spring 1992, 3.

2. Ronald F. Youngblood and F. F. Bruce, eds., *Nelson's New Illustrated Bible Dictionary* (Nashville: Thomas Nelson, 1999), 1187.

3. W. Grinton Berry, ed., *Foxe's Book of Martyrs* (Grand Rapids: Baker Book House, 1992), 21–24.

4. E. Glen Hinson, "Smyrna," *Biblical Illustrator,* Winter 1980, 72, 86.

5. Youngblood and Bruce, *Nelson's New Illustrated Bible Dictionary,* 1187.

6. Taken from *Foxe's Book of Martyrs* by John Foxe, chapter 2, www.biblenet.net/library/foxesMartyrs.

Chapter 39

1. Frank Gaebelein and J. D. Douglas, *Expositor's Bible Commentary* (Grand Rapids: Zondervan Publishing, 1984), 440.

2. Ibid.

3. A. T. Robertson, *Word Pictures in the New Testament,* vol. 5 (Nashville: Broadman Press, 1960), 307.

Chapter 40

1. Larry E. McKinney, "Thyatira," *Biblical Illustrator,* Spring 1992, 70, 107.

2. Ronald F. Youngblood and F. F. Bruce, eds., *Nelson's New Illustrated Bible Dictionary* (Nashville: Thomas Nelson, 1999), 679.

Chapter 41

1. William M. Ramsay, *The Letters to the Seven Churches of Asia* (London: Hodder & Stoughton, 1904), 375, quoted in Frank Gaebelein and J. D. Douglas *Expositor's Bible Commentary,* 447.

2. William Barclay, *Letters to the Seven Churches* (New York: Abingdon, 1957), quoted in *Expositor's Commentary,* 71.

Chapter 42

1. Joseph Green, "The Seven Churches of Revelation," *Biblical Illustrator,* Spring 1980, 49.

Chapter 43

1. Henry L. Peterson, "The Church at Laodicea," *Biblical Illustrator,* Spring 1982, 74–75.

Chapter 44

1. Spiros Zodhiates, "Lexical Aids to the New Testament," #2525 in Spiros Zodhiates, Warren Baker, and David Kemp, *Hebrew-Greek Key Study Bible,* 1631.

Chapter 48

1. Leland Ryken, James C. Wilhoit, and Tremper Longman III., eds., *Dictionary of Biblical Imagery* (Downers Grove, Ill.: InterVarsity Press, 1998), 938.

Moore on the life of John!

**Beloved
Disciple:
*The Life and
Ministry of John***
is the latest Bible
study from renowned
Christian author
and speaker
Beth Moore.

This new, in-depth, video-
based interactive study, filmed
on location in Greece and Turkey,
explores the life of the apostle
John—the one often referred to
as the "beloved disciple." Learn
how John's deep love relationship
with Christ influenced his own
thoughts and actions—and how
Christ desires the same kind of
trusting relationship with His disciples today.

(10 sessions, plus introduction)